Beyond Humanism

About the Editor

Dr. Saji Varghese, is presently an Associate Professor at Lady Keane College, Shillong. He has done Master's Degree in Philosophy from North Eastern Hill University, Shillong and also completed his Doctoral Degree from NEHU, Shillong in 2003. He is the author of three books, *Political Philosophy of Antonio Gramsci (2008), An Introduction to Social and Political Philosophy (2007), A Guide to Philosophy (2005).* Besides publishing papers in journals of national and international repute, he has presented papers in a number of National and International seminars.

Beyond Humanism

Philosophical Essays on Environmental Ethics

Edited by
Saji Varghese

Published for

Department of Philosophy,
Lady Keane College, Shillong
by
CONCEPT PUBLISHING COMPANY PVT. LTD.
NEW DELHI-110059

ISBN-13: 978-93-5125-106-4

First Published 2014

Published and Printed by

Concept Since 1974

Concept Publishing Company Pvt. Ltd.
A/15-16, Commercial Block, Mohan Garden
New Delhi-110059 (India)
T : 25351460, 25351794, *F* : 091-11-25357109
E: publishing@conceptpub.com, W: www.conceptpub.com
Editorial Office: H-13, Bali Nagar, New Delhi-110 015, India.

Cataloging in Publication Data--*Courtesy:* D.K. Agencies (P) Ltd. <docinfo@dkagencies.com>

'Environmental Ethics in Tribal Societies: with special reference to North East India' (Seminar) (2012 : Lady Keane College)

Beyond humanism : philosophical essays on environmental ethics / edited by Saji Varghese.

p. cm.
Includes bibliographical references and index.
ISBN 9789351251064

1. Environmental ethics--India, Northeastern--Congresses. 2. Indigenous peoples--Ecology--India, Northeastern--Congresses. 3. Tribes--India, Northeastern--Social life and customs--Congresses. I. Varghese, Saji (Associate professor of philosophy) II. Lady Keane College (Shillong, India). Philosophy Department. III. Title.

DDC 179.109541 23

Preface

Environmental Ethics as a field of enquiry is a rational response to man's relation to nature. Traditional ethics is predominantly man centred as human beings only are treated as moral agents. It denies or ignores the values of nature. The objective of environmental ethics, on the other hand is contrary to traditional ethics. It tries to annihilate the view that only humans are the legitimate moral agents and apart from human, no other sentient being has that right. Environmental ethics tries to resist the materialistic trend of environmental dualism and thereby conceives all biotic community as the members of a single, unified whole. It is concerned with the intimate relationship between man and nature. It tries to restore the moral dignity of all sentient beings by admitting the intrinsic or non-instrumental value of nature. It is needless to mention here the concerns shown, in the recent past, by the scientists and leaders of the different countries to protect the environment and making the world realize the danger involved in ignoring it. The need for such urgency is because of the extent of damage which has already been caused to the environment. Till the recent past, we, the human species, viewed ourselves as the most important component of the earth, believing that the resources were inexhaustible and felt God made everything for the use of man. We could exploit anything, to any limit that we needed or desired to. The degradation of the environment has assumed a global dimension in the present scenario and at the threshold of the twenty-first century, man has learnt to realise the ill consequences of his conscious and unconscious activities for the fulfilment of his never ending desires.

The present volume, a conglomerate of a number of historical and Philosophical essays from scholars of different regions of India, do present varieties of perspectives on environment. It is a comprehensive attempt to understand the ethical response humans ought to have towards the nature. The pernicious degradation on the environment results in a threat to the existence of life itself on the earth. The 'wakeup call', though late, is an effort to let the world know about the need to create an awareness among the so called 'rationales' of the moral values attached to various ingredients of the nature of which he is a part. There are also attempts to remind ourselves of the traditional arguments presented by thinkers on the moral concerns of the environment. The book is an outcome of the National Seminar on the theme 'Environmental Ethics in Tribal Societies: With Special Reference to North-East India' organized by the Department of Philosophy, Lady Keane College, Shillong on 21st and 22nd of November, 2012.

Saji Varghese

Acknowledgements

The chapters in this book are mostly the papers contributed by different scholars to the National Seminar conducted by the Department of Philosophy, Lady Keane College on the theme 'Environmental Ethics in Tribal Societies: With Special Reference to North-East India' on 21st and 22nd of November, 2012. The seminar was sponsored by the Indian Council of Philosophical Research, New Delhi and co-sponsored by Indian Council of Social Science Research, NERC, Shillong. The Department of Philosophy, Lady Keane College, Shillong expresses its gratitude to the generous sponsors of the seminar, and also the contributors to this book. It also conveys its gratitude to the editor Dr Saji Varghese of this volume for his sincere and hard work. Its gratitude also goes to the Concept Publishing Company Pvt. Ltd. for publishing this volume.

Dr. Sabita Das
Head, Department of Philosophy,
Lady Keane College
Shillong

Contents

The Contributors

B.K. Agarwala, a scholar in the field of culture and phenomenology, is a professor in the Department of Philosophy, North Eastern Hill University, Shillong.

Dr. C.P. Alexander, Pro-Vice Chancellor ICFAI University, Dimapur, Nagaland is a scholar in the field of Psychoanalysis, Clinical Philosophy, and Philosophy for Management.

Rev. Fr. (Dr.) K.J. Joy is a Gandhian Scholar, at present is attached to the administration of Don Bosco College, Tura, Meghalaya.

Xavier Mao is a Professor in the Department of Philosophy, North Eastern Hill University, Shillong.

A. Raghuramaraju, a well known contemporary Indian Philosopher, is a professor in the Department of Philosophy Hyderabad University, Hyderabad.

Sebastian Velassery, is a Professor in the Department of Philosophy in Panjab University, Chandigarh.

Karilemla, is a Ph.D. Research Scholar in the Department of Humanities and Social Sciences, IIT-Bombay, Mumbai.

Dr. Siby. K. George, is an Associate Professor in the Department of Humanities and Social Sciences, IIT-Bombay, Mumbai.

Dr. R.K. Behera is an Associate Professor in the Deptt. of Philosophy, at Patkai Christian College, Dimapur, Nagaland.

Dr. Shephali Vidyanta is an Associate Professor in the Department of Philosophy, at Mahadevananda Mahavidyalaya, Barrackpore, under Jadavpur University, Kolkatta.

Dr. Wojanbeni Shitiri Yanthan, is an Assistant Professor in the Department of Philosophy, Patkai Christian College, Dimapur, Nagaland.

Vanlalghak, a scholar in the field of Applied Ethical Philosophy, is a

Professor in the Department of Philosophy in North Eastern Hill University, Shillong.

Amiya Dey, is an Associate Professor in the Department of Philosophy, Raid Laban College, Shillong.

Rev. Fr. (Dr.) Jacob Aluckal, is the Chief Editor of *Echoes from the North East*, a regional Catholic Publication, Arch Bishop's House, Shillong.

Introduction

Environmental ethics has captured an increasing amount of interdisciplinary interest over the past fifty years, largely attributed to the emergence of the environmental movement and the widespread concerns brought about by the industrial impact of Western Civilization. It is needless to mention here the concerns shown, in the recent past, by the scientists and leaders of the different countries to protect the environment and making the world realize the danger involved in ignoring it. The need for such urgency is because of the extent of damage which has already been caused to the environment. Till the recent past, we, the human species, viewed ourselves as the most important component of the earth, believing that the resources were inexhaustible and felt God made everything for the use of man. We could exploit anything, to any limit that we needed or desired to. An eminent authority on high energy physics, Fritj of Capra says "Even discounting the threat of a nuclear catastrophe, the global ecosystem and the further evolution of life on earth are seriously endangered and may well end in a large-scale ecological disaster. Overpopulation and industrial technology have contributed in various ways to a severe degradation of the natural environment upon which we are completely dependent for life". The practical purpose of environmental ethics is to provide moral grounds for social policies aimed at protecting the earth's environment and remedying environmental degradation. While predictions concerning the scale and extent of humanity's environmental impact are often scientifically and politically controversial, ethicists have sought to construe theoretical frameworks that could adequately characterize the morality of human interaction with the non-human aspects of the ecosphere. The development of environmental ethics has been one of the most exciting developments in contemporary philosophy, second only, perhaps, to the development of feminist philosophy. Along with feminism, environmentalism addresses real problems in contemporary society that demand the development of wise discussions and dispositions. In all, both have produced some excellent and challenging insights. These are timely issues that have attracted the attention of people in many fields; the discussions are not limited merely among philosophers. In fact, if we count nature writing, such as Thoreau's Walden, as the beginning, environmentalism arrived substantially earlier in literature, than in philosophy. Meanwhile, it has attracted the interest of historians, economists, public policy specialists, and others.

In all religious and philosophical traditions, one's sense of moral obligation—be it to other human beings, to animals, or to nature always involves a specific understanding of both the moral self and the other to whom the self relates in moral action. All the major ethical theories in the Western philosophical tradition—from Socrates and Plato, through Aristotelian virtue ethics and Kantian deontology, to utilitarianism—have disagreed about two related ideas: what it means to be human and what it means to relate morally to an 'other'.

However, all of these traditions have shared the basic assumption that the morally significant other is human: family, friends, fellow citizens, or fellow human beings. This is true even when these moral relationships are established or supported by God. Given this tradition, any deep shift in our relationship to nature will require a new understanding of what it means for human beings to relate to the natural world and to live a moral life as part of that world.

In most of the Western religious and philosophical tradition, the nonhuman world is thought to exist for the sake of human beings. This metaphysical and ethical position has come to be known as anthropocentrism.

There seems to be 'divine sanction' for the supremacy of the humans over the other aspects of nature. The assumed superiority of human beings over the rest of the world has religious expression in the first account of creation in *Genesis.* God commands human beings, who have the unique status of being created in the image of God, to "be masters of. all the wild beasts" (*Genesis* 1 : 26) and to "fill the earth and conquer it" (*Genesis* 1 : 28). There are statements of anthropocentrism in the Western philosophical tradition beginning with the ancient Greeks. Xenophon formulated the classic position in his dialogue, *Memorabilia,* in which his "Socrates" says, *Tell me, Euthydemus, has it ever occurred to you to reflect on the care the gods have taken to furnish man with what he needs? Now, seeing that we need food, think how they make the earth to yield it, and provide to that end appropriate seasons which furnish in abundance the diverse things that minister not only to our wants but to our enjoyment..... and is it not evident that they [the lower animals] too receive life and food for the sake of man?* (*Xenophon,* Book IV, Chapter III, 3, 5, 10).

The general point is that the structure of the cosmos shows that it is the result of a design, and more specifically that it is designed for the sake of human beings. Human beings have needs and the nonhuman world exists to satisfy these needs. There are classic statements of anthropocentrism in Aristotle, in Aquinas—who with typical exhaustiveness offers some seven arguments in the *Summa Contra Gentiles* (Aquinas, 115-119) Immanuel Kant's position is typical: "Animals are not self-conscious and are there merely as a means to an end. That end is man. We can ask, 'Why do animals exist?' But to ask, 'Why does man exist?' is a meaningless question" (Kant, 1775-1780, 239). The otherness of animals, their very existence and their difference from human beings, is explained and understood in terms of this relation to human needs.

In the light of the history of environmental destruction and the heedless treatment of animals that is the Western legacy, especially since the advent of scientifically-based technology and industry; it is hardly surprising to see the appearance of fundamental critiques of the entire anthropocentric tradition. 'The root of the problem is not a doctrine at all, but an actual process: anthropocentrization, the narrowing and relentless humanizing of the actual world, a world that we make and that pervasively remakes itself both experientially and conceptually'. Some forms of this critique are focused on sentient animals, and these theories typically involve *extending* to animals the moral consideration that has traditionally been restricted to human beings.

Ethics began by stretching the circle of the self first to include some other humans (family, community, etc.) and then, eventually, to a "universal" view on which all humans count. The familiar extensionist argument insists that we cannot justly draw the line at the boundary of the human species either. Why should the species border be any more impenetrable, truly any more natural, than the boundaries of human clan or nation? Other animals present themselves—first only some, then arguably all. The "expanding circle," as Peter Singer famously called it, keeps pushing outward: to all living things next, including plants and trees, which may not be conscious subjects but are surely self-organized and responsive systems. Then to the land—the community of life. Farther still and we have to consider the rivers, mountains, the air as well, and perhaps even the Earth as a whole. In Indian traditions there is reverence shown to the land and other natural phenomena. Alley (2000) writes, "Symbolic representations of space in Hindu sacred texts and ancient concepts associated with them call for an approach to ecological understanding that moves beyond the secular notions of the environment". (Alley, Kelley D., 2000. *Idioms of Degeneracy*. In Nelson, 2000.)

The unicentricism leading its way to multi centricism where the focal point lies in embodiment of certain values in each and every element, living and the non-living. Nature is a composite whole, the ingredients of which are transitory. Humans are an important part of the nature. On the dualistic conception, human beings are thought to be partly natural (on account of their having bodies) and partly non-natural (on account of their having souls or minds). So although a man has a certain size, shape and mass, he is thought also to possess a radically non-natural part, a soul or a mind. However, environmentalists like me do consider humans as a part of nature.

Another aspect which is internal and reflects immensely in the external is one's response or I relation with the 'world' which is outside. To take an extreme step is to hold such a position that to describe how I am, is to describe a world I inhabit. What is more, it is a world I find myself always already inhabiting; interacting with things (for instance) even before I step back to reflect on that interaction. So to specify how I am at this precise moment, I find that I must refer, not just to the various things with which I am pre-reflectively interacting (the chair, the pen, etc.) but also to the general situation in which I find myself (sitting in a restaurant) and the various possibilities that the particular situation affords (primarily, the possibility of dinner). And in all this, I find that I must refer to *others*—the waiters chatting by the stairs, for instance, or the potential presence of other diners. True, I can conceive of myself as an isolated subject confronted by an objective order of things. But that is not what presents itself to me prior to reflection. Pre-reflectively, I am presented with what Heidegger calls a unitary complex of being-in-the-world. However, the primary question remains, how I ought to respond to what is outside of me? To answer such a question one must know the kind of 'engagement' one has with nature/world.

There are two interrelated senses in which we are in-the-world. First, we are *involved* with it, which is to say that whatever shows up in our experience does so because it connects with our lived concerns in some way, because it matters to us. Second, we *inhere* in it, which (very roughly) is to say that we are made of the same stuff as the worldly things we encounter. Thus, involvement and inherence are the two ways by which we relate ourselves with the world. To be in-the-world is, we have seen, to be practically involved with some sort of world or environment. In natural contexts, it is to be so involved with a natural environment to be at home in it. But to be in-the-world is not just to be with the world in this way but also to *inhere* in it, to be a part of it in a compositional sense. Merleau-Ponty, for instance, maintains that we are 'of the same stuff' as the world, 'caught' in its 'fabric', our 'cohesion that of a thing', albeit one that 'holds things in a circle around itself'. In this sense what affects the other also oneself both in mind and body. In this respect, and as the following passage from David Abram nicely shows, the narrow between the world and the subject: My life and the world's life are deeply intertwined; 'when I wake up one morning to find that a week-long illness has subsided and that my strength has returned, the world, when I step outside, fairly sparkles with energy and activity: swallows are swooping by in vivid flight; waves of heat rise from the newly paved road smelling strongly of tar; the old red barn across the field juts into the sky at an intense angle. Likewise, when a haze descends upon the valley in which I dwell, it descends upon my awareness as well, muddling my thoughts, making my muscles yearn for sleep.' [Abram, D. (1996) *The Spell of the Sensuous: Perception and Language in a More-Than-Human World* (New York: Vintage Books].

Our outlook on the world is not ours alone, but is to some extent shared by our non-human 'ingredients'. For another, although we necessarily perceive a world lit up in terms of our concerns, we, fragile corporeal beings that we are, are only able to do this because we inhere in a world with which we are involved, because we are of the same 'flesh' as the things we perceive. Indeed, this perceiving is in a certain sense not *our* doing at all. It is the manifestation of nature working in us and through us—*natura naturans*, as Spinoza might have said, rather than *natura naturata*; nature as an active presence working behind the scenes, rather than the nature one finds represented in works of science or metaphysics.

Nature, in this sense, is not something that we perceive; it is at work in our perception. It is not something we can capture in understanding, but something into which we are always already, and for the most part unknowingly, taken up. Therefore the 'care' must be of the kind that we make towards the ligaments or organs of our body.

Saji Varghese

1

Environmental Ethics of Three Old Words from the Hills

Binod Kumar Agarwala

I am asked to present a paper on environmental ethics of tribes of North Eastern India. It occurred to me to write on the environmental ethics of tribes of Hills of head hunters, the Khasi Hills, and the Lusai Hills. This leads me to the question: where does one look for the environmental ethics of the tribes when they have not explicitly discussed the issue? None of the tribes had ever risen to the level of philosophical discussion to think of an environmental ethics. Here memory of the book of *Genesis* especially the myth of creation where the environmental ethics was encapsuled without discussing it explicitly came to me as I had studied (not merely read) Holy *Bible* from cover to cover nearly twenty years back. God created the entire world which was good by distinctions in words. This world became the environment for mankind. The image of God that has emerged up to *Genesis* 1.25 is that he created the world and everything in it created so far is by making distinctions through his word and by seeing that the distinctions he has created in words is well harmonized as good (1.4, 1.10, 1.12, 1.18, 1.21, 1.25) six times. In 1.26: "Then God said, 'Let us make humankind in our image, according to our likeness; and let them have dominion over the fish of the sea, and over the birds of the air, and over the cattle, and over all the wild animals of the earth, and over every creeping thing that creeps upon the earth'." In 1:27 "So God created humankind in his image, in the image of God he created them; male and female he created them." The mankind was created in the image of God, hence he also has the further creative power by use of words to make distinctions and harmonizing the distinguished things in such a way that it is "good. So, in *Genesis* 1:28 when he speaks for the first time to mankind "God blessed them, and God said to them, 'Be fruitful and multiply, and fill the earth and subdue it; and have dominion over the fish of the sea and over the birds of the air and over every living thing that moves upon the earth' ". The two words 'dominion' (1.26 and 1.28) and 'subdue' (1.28) are translation of the Hebrew terms '*rada*' and '*kabas*' respectively. Hebrew term '*rada*' means to '*cut*' like cutting meat or cutting into pieces, here to cut is used in the sense of to distinguish to separate, like the catagorein of the Greeks. So when dominion was given to man it was in the sense of distinguishing and separating the created things further by naming and use of words. When the Hebrew term '*kabas*' is used it is meant to subdue things in friction, conflict. Hence when mankind was given the task of subduing further it was part of the creator image, as he has to harmonize the distinguished things when they are in conflict and friction that too by seeing that the harmony is good. But it is a different thing that Official Christianity turned these '*rada*' and '*kabas*' into political power of man and not part of the God's image in which mankind was made and created a situation that would ultimately lead to environmental disaster.

The God had created the physical environment and left the creation of cultural environment to mankind by creating them in his own image. This is testified by what God says to mankind further in 1.29 and 1.30 as He started speaking to them in *Genesis* for the first time in 1.28. In 1.29 and 1.30 of *Genesis* it is stated: [1 : 29] "God said, 'See, I have given you every plant yielding seed that is upon the face of all the earth, and every tree with seed in its fruit; you shall have them for food.' [1:30] 'And to every beast of the earth, and to every bird of the air, and to everything that creeps on the earth, everything that has the breath of life, I have given every green plant for food.' And it was so." After speaking to mankind the truth, he finally evaluated his creation, one last time in the creation myth, the creation of the world as environment for mankind, together with mankind in it with the creative word to create culture: [1:31] "God saw everything that he had made, and indeed, it was very good. And there was evening and there was morning, the sixth day." The entire environmental ethics of harmony of nature, harmony of mankind with nature and harmony of mankind's culture creating word with nature was encapsuled in the creation myth in the book of *Genesis.*

So, it occurred to me to throw some light on the three old words: the word of the Hills of head hunters, the word of the Khasi Hills, and the word of the Lusai Hills if I want to look for environmental ethics of the tribes. The entire ethics, including the environmental ethics, and the entire reason of the people who reside in the three hills is present in these three old words from these Hills. What light can I throw on these three words?

I am a Christian by conviction if not by baptism. So I shall throw the light that is spoken of in John 1:1-5: "**In the beginning was the Word, and the Word was with God, and the Word was God. He was in the beginning with God. All things were made through Him, and without Him nothing was made that was made. In Him was life, and the life was the light of men. And the light shines in the darkness, and the darkness did not comprehend it.**" John 1:14 "**And the Word became flesh and dwelt among us, and we beheld His glory, the glory as of the only begotten of the Father, full of grace and truth**".

Do men really know what that word is, which is in the beginning, the word that was with the God, the word that was God, the word in which there was life, the life that was the light of men, the word that became flesh and dwelt among us? I am afraid even though "the light shines in the darkness", "the darkness did not comprehend it", that's why in Luke 23:34 Jesus said, "**Father, forgive them, for they do not know what they are doing.** And they divided up his clothes by casting lots." We are not merely dividing the clothes but also dividing the shroud without comprehending the light of life of word of God. Even the Official Christianity recovered neither the knowledge Jesus spoke of, nor the light of life that was in the word. Why? Because the

Word which was with the God (*John* 1.1) was turned into the multiple finite words of proclamation which the missionaries carried, while the Word of God is the infinite unspoken one creative word behind every finite word that human beings speak. Who can really utter that One infinite word of God, as the Word is God (John 1.1)? The One Infinite Word always remains in the beginning (John 1.1) as unuttered in every uttering of the word as uttered word is always next and is never at the beginning. When the Word became flesh (John 1.14), it was an unequal relation, as flesh did not become Word. Uttered words are a total transformation of the One Word, where the infinite becomes finite, the one becomes many, and the unuttered becomes uttered, the unmanifest becomes manifest. But the uttered many finite words are not the One Infinite Word in the Beginning. The many finite uttered words are only human words which have become the home of His (John 1.14). He, the One Infinite Unuttered Word of the Beginning is always at the beginning as unuttered in every finite human speaking. That is how He dwells among us (John 1.14). This is the structure of intensionality of human speaking. Unless Christianity recovers the One Infinite Unspoken Word at the Beginning behind every finite word that is spoken by any man, and unless they cease to think that the missionaries carry the word of God as proclamation, they will remain ignorant of the knowledge that Christ spoke of. It is only when the One infinite unspoken word is in the beginning that the speaking becomes alive with light (the emanation of the Holy Son from the Holy Father, the Word becoming flesh) and the spoken finite word being the flesh and blood (which Jesus sacrificed for redemption of mankind) of Holy spirit to be distributed (the way Jesus distributed the bread and wine in the last supper) over mankind to suffuse them with Holy Spirit to bring them in One Church that is the body of the Christ.

So how can I throw light on the three old words I have picked up for enlightening? We can do so by recovering One Infinite Unspoken Word at the beginning of every finite word that is spoken. How do we recover it? We recover it not by focusing on it, not by making it a theme of any finite discourse in words, but by feeling it unconsciously as being present unspoken behind every finite word spoken. When we feel it, there is life in it and this life becomes the light that enlightens everything. You may think that I am either ludicrous or indulging in mysticism. But it is neither. Let me draw your attention to Kant's ***Critique of Judgment.*** "To apprehend a regular and appropriate building with one's cognitive faculties, be the mode of representation clear or confused, is quite different thing from being conscious of this representation with an accompanying sensation of delight. Here the representation is referred wholly to the subject, and what is more to its feeling of life—under the name of the feeling of pleasure or displeasure—and this forms the basis of a quite separate faculty of discriminating and estimating, that contributes nothing to knowledge. All it does is to compare the given representation in the subject with the entire faculty of representations of which the mind (Gemüt) is conscious in the feeling of its state." [*Critique of Judgment.* §1] Kant recognized two capacities of discrimination: one faculty of conscious discrimination by articulation but another faculty of discrimination by feeling of life whose functioning was obscure to him. So there is always accompanying any conscious articulation an unconscious feeling of life which is the feeling of one infinite word behind every word that is spoken.

Here there is a need to undertake a digressive excursus to anticipate a few objections before I take up the thread of discussion further. Some readers of the Holy *Bible* may object to my relating the word of the book of John with the saying of the word by God in *Genesis* as I have done above. The objection can be on the ground that the context of the word of the book of John is different from the saying of the word by God in the first book of Genesis and hence should not be related. My reply is as follows: listen to the John 1.3 carefully. It says: *All things were made through Him, and without Him nothing was made that was made.* The pronoun 'he' refers to the one word in the beginning that was with God. So, the one word of the book of John is what is uttered by God in the book of *Genesis.* Apart from the above textual evidence, one can also reply that vivisection of what tradition has presented as one Holly *Bible* merely indicates a poor biblical hermeneutics. Vivisection of text by an hermeneutist is nothing but hermeneutic inability dressed up as a thesis of hermeneutics. As far as I am concerned it makes perfect hermeneutic sense why *Old Testament* from Genesis to Maccabees and the *New Testament* word of Jesus and word revolving round Jesus form a unified one text of Holy *Bible*.

Some other readers of *Bible* will object to my mirroring of mystery of the Trinity in the miracle of speaking of language with true intensionality and correct intentionality. My reply is as follows: The word is true, because it says what the thing is as intension/intention, but by itself it is nothing and does not seek to be anything. The word has its being in its revealing of intension/intention. Exactly the same thing is true of the mystery of the Trinity. Here too the important thing is not the earthly appearance of the Redeemer as such, but rather his complete divinity, his consubstantiality with God. To grasp the independent personal existence of Christ within this sameness of being is the task of theology. Here a human analogue—the mental word, the verbum intellectus with intension/intention—is helpful. This is more than a mere metaphor, for the human relationship between thought with intension/intention and speech corresponds, despite its imperfections, to the divine relationship of the Trinity. The inner mental word with intension/intention is just as consubstantial with thought as is God the Son with God the Father. And also inner mental word with intension/intention transforms into the external word, to be studied by linguists, completing the analogy with the trinity. Here I call two witnesses from the Christian tradition: A Doctor of the Church, St. Augustine and the Scholastics. When Augustine and the Scholastics consider the problem of the verbum in order to attain the conceptual means to elucidate the mystery of the Trinity, they are concerned exclusively with this inner word, the word of the heart, and its relation to the "intelligentia" (Latin, and not the modern).

Let us come back from this little digressive excursus to pick up the thread of discussion again. So, let me throw light on the three words by, comparing them with the one infinite unspoken but felt word that is behind every finite spoken word. First we need to recover the three old words from the Hills. Let us make a beginning with the word of the Hills of head hunters.

For the tribe of the Head Hunters red hornbill earrings are a visible sign that a man has taken a head. Glittering, red, dangling from the upper earlobes, the earrings are a badge indicating, for all to see, that the wearer has decapitated a fellow human being. Men take heads to show their manhood and to acquire *amet*, and they acquire *amet* in order to wear red hornbill earrings. An earring represents an *amet* and an *amet* is a personal adornment. Similarly, men acquire *amet* because they take heads and men take heads in order to acquire *amet*.

The first step in acquiring red hornbill earrings is to court the heart of the victim. The heart is the life-force of a person and the spirit that survives after death. Ritually, raiders prepare themselves by having a person of knowledge call the hearts of potential victims toward the men who hope to take heads. The heart, understood in this context as life force or spirit, flies toward the raiders and alights on the upper earlobes where it perches, birdlike being that it is, precisely where the red hornbill earrings of the successful headhunter will be worn.

The night after the hearts of the victims have been called the raiders go into the forest and listen for the calls of omen-birds, one among which is the red hornbill whose scarlet beak is used in making the earrings. A bird call from in front, in the planned direction of the raid, is a favourable omen which indicates that the victim's heart and the raider are still in accord. The earrings, the beheading, and the heart are all present, as conceptually linked, from the very inception of the raid. The logic here is one of mutual connections and resemblances. The heart, that is, the mobile life-force of the victim is like a bird in that it flies and perches, and the omen-bird is like the heart of the victim to which it gives audible voice. The birdlike heart of the victim itself comes to perch on the upper earlobes of the raider, and thus in its location it is like a red hornbill earring. And the red hornbill earring, of course, being made from the beak of one, is like a bird as well as like the heart of the victim. Thus, in an unbroken chain of resemblances, a heart is like a bird and a bird is like a heart, and both are like red hornbill earrings which in turn are like hearts and birds.

Red hornbill earrings differ from most other red ornaments

for the body both because they may be worn only after a man has taken a head and because they are made from the beak of the red hornbill bird. **The connection between headhunting and the red hornbill is that, the cry of the hornbill is like the scream of a victim in pain as it is being struck its deathblows.**

It surely is no accident that the cowry shell may be worn only after the pig has been sacrificed and the beheader's body has hardened enough to bear the graphic recollection of the victim. The less graphic red hornbill earrings, in contrast, are the first crafted ornaments that may be worn after taking a head. Red hornbill earrings are not lesser because less graphic, but instead are first among equals because they are the first among the headhunting ornaments that may adorn the human body

The earrings could be compared with the youthful beheader himself. Ideally, he is unmarried and by taking a head he has embarked on the longer course courtship, marriage, and having children—that will project him into the world of adult men as an equal among peers. **Though the red hornbill earrings can confer the admiration of young women, they enable youths to reply to the boasts of their fellow men, and in this sense they give them a voice they never had before. The red hornbill earrings give youths an emergent voice in the world of adult men in the tribe of head hunters.** Like youth itself, red hornbill earrings are alert, taut, poised, and about to make a beginning. They are on the edge, in transition, but moving more toward manhood than away from boyhood. It would never do, however, to say that the significance of red hornbill earrings has come to rest in youth, a passing phase of the life cycle. Instead youth is but one more exemplification of the conceptions embodied in the earrings.

Let us ask why the initial ritual courting of the victims heart makes it alight as hornbill on the upper portion of earlobe and what the ritual courting is really courting for? The real courting in the ritual courting is the courting of the cry of the hornbill which is really the scream of a victim in pain as it is being struck its deathblows. That's why the courted victim's heart alights on the upper portion of the earlobe as hornbill to cry and scream in the raider's ears. The hornbill in front crying as omen for raiding party leads the raider to the victim so that the raider can hear the real scream of a victim in pain as it is being struck its deathblows. Without hearing this scream the raider is without voice in the world of adult head hunters. The raider wrests the scream of the victim to make it his voice. The scream of the victim enters the raider as his voice in the adult world of the head hunters. The scream deducted from the victim to use Foucauldian vocabulary is the voice added to the raider. The minus and plus being equal the total voice, or the total word, the total amount of the word of the head hunters remains the same, a constant finite amount. The head hunters word is a constant finite word which neither increases nor decreases and hence needing wresting of the scream of other by decapitating him to get voice oneself. The word of the head hunters is constant at every level: at the level of the individual adult head hunter, at the level of his family and the level of the clan and even at the level of all the clans of headhunters constituting their world.

Not having a voice is the heaviness of the heart of the child, the heart is heavy because it has not yet acquired the lightness of the voice to make the heart light. But the moment a growing adult has gained voice by wresting it from some other clan of tribe making their word less than the constant amount that it is the concentrated anger erupts in real anger to wrest back the word taken. The constant conserved word is in equilibrium. The deducted word is in disequilibrium leading to conflict in the head hunters' clan. The raider who is an "other" has literally "belittled" the tribe which is the same thing as having "shamed" the tribe. So, they have to wrest back the voice lost, by taking a head from the raiders side so that they get back the original amount of word they had. It will once again restore the word to its original amount, restore the equilibrium, and still the live anger to make it once again concentrated anger of the new raiders, the counter raiders. For the headhunters the death, deduction of word, shame and anger and dissension are different aspect of one and same phenomenon. It explains why a child who has no voice if answers back an adult headhunter it is the latter's shame as his word has been deducted by the child and it invites wrath or anger of the adult as it is as good as death for him. The child learns it; he remains silent and obedient to the adult headhunter. Similarly a dissension in the family is as good as deduction of word and as good as death, as dissension marks the imbalance of word caused by deduction of word. So the headhunters word is a constant finite amount easily deductible easily imbalanced creating a moral economy of constant finite word revolving round shame, and overcoming shame, anger and overcoming anger in concentrated anger, death and decapitating, loss of voice and regaining of voice all being part of the zero sum game of the constant finite word. A moral economy of constant finite word revolving round shame, and overcoming shame, anger and overcoming anger in concentrated anger, death and decapitating, loss of voice and regaining of voice all being part of the zero sum game is still going on in the hills of head hunters, only the weapons have been modernized. Only the early spear, bow and arrow and poisoned darts have been replaced by modern pistols, guns and rifles.

What kind of environmental ethics is there in the finite constant word of the Hill of head hunters? This word is not a creative word as no finite word is a creative word. It merely enlists the support or hostility of the finite creation already existent. When the finite nature (world) comes to assist as omen to the raider, at the same time the same nature (world) is hostile and bad omen to the victim. The spirit of the forest, who desires to eat a sacrificial pig, leads the heart of the victim to the raider as shrieking hornbill the good omen for the raider. After the successful raid, the raider sacrifices a pig to the spirits of the forest and only then he gets to wear the hornbill ear ring. Can we really talk of harmony of man with nature here?

That, my friends, is the word of the hills of head hunters exactly the opposite of the one infinite unspoken word that is God of Christianity which has made home in our finite many spoken words. I can only pray that the constant finite word of the hills of head hunters is replaced by the one infinite word of God so that they can keep it in the beginning as the unspoken of the word they speak rather than merely carrying it in their hands only on Sundays.

Let me now come to the word of the Khasi Hills. I shall simply give you the conclusion for if I discuss the fables the talk will become too long. The old word of Khasi hills was without a script. This shows absence of word of philosophy in the Khasi Hills. It is only with the introduction of script and the subsequent advent of literacy according to the great classicist Havelock's *Preface to Plato* that the Greek ego frees itself from the word of tradition and begins the word of philosophy independently of it.[1] "The doctrine of the autonomous psyche is the counterpart of the rejection of the oral culture".[2] Only with introduction of script and literacy that autonomous psyche and word of philosophy emerged in Greek civilization. According to Havelock, "...philosophy as an intellectual discipline is a post-alphabetic invention."[3] This is how the transition from mythos to logos took place in classical Greece. But this never happened in the Khasi Hills. It is only the colonial Christian missionaries who gave the gift of script and Christian religion to the Khasis. The word of the Khasi Hills never turned to word of philosophy.

The absence of word of philosophy has impact on the psyche exhibited and hence the word exhibited in the Khasi Hills. The psyche exhibited is a conglomerate of multiple psyhe. First, there is mention of so-called soul (*Ka mynsiem*) which after death goes to distant place (*Khyndai Trep*, the Nine Huts). But this so-called soul is only life force that flees at death. So far no scholar of philosophy of tribal culture has ever demonstrated with philological analysis that this so called soul is the locus where all the different thoughts and feelings occur. There is also another soul *Ka Rngiew* which remains on earth to look after his kith and kin. *Ka Rngiew* is also another kind of life force that is also capable of moving to *ramia* the world of illusions or dreams and in case of tiger man to the world of tigers. There is also no philological study to show that this is a site of thinking and feeling. Man's body is referred to as *Ka Met* when alive, *rub pyut* (rotted cage) after death, which when purified by fire, returns to mother earth. *Ka Met* appears to refer to the skin, not understood in modern anatomical sense of that part of body that can be peeled up but skin in the sense of surface, as the outer border of the figure of man, as the foundation of colour. That's why

Met-sawdoh is an adjective meaning 'of a brown complexion' which is applicable to persons only. *Met-iaw* is also an adjective meaning 'of mature age' as it shows on the skin. Expression *ka met-ka-phat* means 'feels good' as one feels with skin. What this composition of man shows is that Khasis had no conception of single autonomous inner soul or mind in its standard post-Platonic sense, which is the independent locus of thinking and feeling, which is consistent with absence of script. Breakdown of the psyche into a conglomerate of different souls is nothing but indicative of the word of Khasi Hills as a broken or cracked word, broken or cracked like the cracked mirror.

The word of Khasi Hills is a cracked word, cracked along multiple fault lines, temporal, spatial, traditions and clan-lines etc. One hears the Khasi word: implement the law, but after some time again one hears the Khasi word: don't implement the law. The Khasi word is broken along the temporal dimension. You cannot expect it to be consistent across time like the One Word of God as it is a broken word. You hear the word of Khasi Hills: it appears to be that of khasi-panar, suddenly, you hear it only as word of Khasi minus panar, the next moment you hear it only the word of Khasi of Shillong it is no more the word of all Khasis, next you hear the word of the Khasi of Mawlai and for all you know it suddenly is a word only of Khasi of only Mawkynrho. This word of Khasi Hills is like shifting images of a cracked mirror. One has no clue as to the identity of the word. So, Word of the Khasi Hills is not one word like the Word of God, it is a cracked word. Like anything cracked it is only a finite word if not a constant word like that of the Hills of head hunters.

A finite cracked word because of multiple fault-lines is always seeking identity but not knowing what identity it is seeking, the identity of the whole mirror, or the identity of a piece of mirror across time or across space, or across traditions or across clans. The Khasi word, like the image in a cracked mirror is an agitated word, agitated to move and moving, yet not knowing where to move. The entire moral economy of the Khasi hills is a play of movement, play of directionless movement: movement against foreigners but remaining indecisive about who are foreigners; movement against aliens but remaining indecisive about who are aliens; movement for sons of soil yet remaining indecisive about who are the sons of soil, khasi panar Garo together, or only Khasi panar, or Khasi minus panar; movement for identity yet remaining indecisive about what identity to seek, Khasi identity, or Church Going Khasi identity, or Seng Khasi identity, or traditional Khasi of pre- British Khasi tribal religion.

What kind of environmental ethics one can find encapsuled in the cracked finite word of the Khasi Hills? Not an environmental ethics of harmony of man with infinite nature living peacefully with others one can find in such a cracked and agitated word. One can find only an environmental ethics of dividing and exploiting finite nature in a hurry with word agitated to prevent others from sharing in the same finite nature, of course without any clarity as to who the others are. Here it is pertinent to remember once again the finite word is not a creative productive word, as to be creative and productive it has to be one infinite word. So, a finite cracked word merely can use finite nature already existent getting involved only in distributional issues regarding the finite bounties of nature and the finite nature itself. One is not surprised at the stories in Khasi Hills regarding falling of man against nature and not in harmony with nature especially in the story of the cutting of the *Iei* (Or Diengiei) Tree.

That my friends is the word of Khasi Hills with its unstated environmental ethics. We must keep in mind that the One word of God which is infinite can never be cracked, even if you speak many finite words the word of God in the beginning remains the same one infinite word. I can only pray that the finite cracked word of the Khasi hills is replaced by the one infinite word of God so that they can keep it in the beginning as the unspoken of the word they speak rather than merely carrying it in their hands in many pieces only on Sundays.

Let me come at last to the old word of Lusai Hills. Let me approach it through the figure of Chhurbura. Chhurbura also called Chhura is one of the most popular characters of folktales from Lusai Hills. He is portrayed as a simpleton yet full of tricks. Chhura is cunning and at the same time foolish. Many of the folktales woven around this character show him playing his cunning tricks to emerge successful out of difficult situation. Also this trickster from the Lusai Hills emerges as a "selfish-fool"—"selfish" because much of the trickster's activity is oriented toward the gratification of his enormous appetites for food, wealth and sex, and "fool" because the tricks sometimes backfire, leaving the trickster looking incredibly foolish. We can say that Chhura is an unabashed glutton and sex mongering cunning knave, he is—as one may say—so natural that people in Lusai Hills have laughed at him and enjoyed a pleasant sense of superiority. But the paradox of the figure of Chhura is that at the same time he is perceived by the audience in the Lusai Hills as their alter ego as if he winks at them and they are delighted at the discovery that they are also like him only. R. Thangvunga, a scholar from Lusai Hills writes regarding Chhura comparing him with Machiavelli, "He is with us, in all of us. Let us admit it and make a virtue of our imperfections by being honest with ourselves."[4]

But from the foolish trickster Chhura let us move to the legendary heroine of the Mizos named Mauruangi. What lessons are implicit in her story? From the first to last the story is full of cunning reason. The story opens with Mauruangi's father preparing the ground to kill his wife cunningly taking advantage of her expression of fear of crossing the old bridge. Next important character to appear is Bingtaii's mother, a widow, who when Mauruangi goes to her to seek some fire, taking advantage of the dire need of fire for the hearth of family of Mauruangi, agrees to give fire on the condition that Mauruangi's father marries her. Of course she succeeds through her cunning reason.

Even Mauruangi uses her cunning reason time and again to survive and have an upper hand in the situation. By cunning reason Mauruangi manages to 'marry'. When the servants of *vai lalpa* (lord of plains men) said, "We are in search of a wife for our master. Would you be willing to marry him?" she realizes the impossibility of her marriage before Bingtaii gets married unless she uses her cunning reason. "My step-mother will not allow me, as she has her own daughter Bingtaii to marry off. So the only way out is, come to our house and ask for Bingtaii's hand. I will follow to see her off, and after passing the village you can leave her and take me along instead." Here Mauruangi's cunning intelligence is in full play to devise a stratagem to reach the man's house as his 'bride'. She follows her cunning plan to a fault and succeeded in reaching the grooms home as his 'bride' even though it was Bingtaii's hand that was asked for and given for marriage. One last time the cunning deception was used in the tale by *vai lalpa* to get rid of Bingtaii declared by the story teller as 'imposter' who had come to his home in place of Mauruangi. He wanted to get rid of Bingtaii, and decided to let the two women fight a duel. He covered Mauruangi with a thick new blanket and gave her a sharp sword. But he wrapped Bingtaii in thin clothes and gave her a blunt sword. When they were ready, Mauruangi said to her step-sister, as she was part of the deception, "Cut me first." Bingtaii hit her with the sword but could not hurt her at all. Then Mauruangi attacked and killed her with the sharp sword. Mauruangi, possesses all the cunning reason to triumph over all odds, is not only a legendary heroine of Lusai Hills, but also the epitome of ideal womanhood in tradition of Lusai Hills. In spite of all imaginable suffering under a callous father and true-to-tradition wicked step-mother, she survives by her cunning word to grow up into a lovely woman. This appears to be the real import of the tale that permeates the word of Lusai Hills immanently, i.e., without being explicit. The word of Lusai Hills is a cunning word, a deceptive word.

The figures human or animal one and all are externally focused, i.e., concerned with the external world. Each is responding to the changing circumstances as if by necessity to overcome the challenge of circumstances. Even desires, passions, love, etc., are not internal to the person, i.e., under his volitional control, rather they are like part of the situation they are into which they respond by necessity. The story teller did not conceive of these matters as actions of the intellect or the soul. Figures like Mauruangi, Zwalpala, Tualvungi and others are no doubt described, but the reactions of these figures, however, significant, are not explicitly presented in their volitional or intellectual form as exhibiting 'character', i.e. as arising from individual intellect and individual soul. The human figures of the fables of Lusai Hills do not regard themselves as the source of their decisions. These actions are set only as response of necessity to the situation to overcome it. The 'character' of an individual is not yet recognized in these stories. None of the story ever indicates any self-reflection or self-awareness. Therefore, it is not the inner 'character' of the individual that determines the response but the elusive cunning reason of the figures out of necessity of the changing situations responds appropriately by a lie, or deception, or a stratagem, a ruse, i.e., whatever the circumstance requires to overcome it. What one finds in the fables from Lusai Hills is the figure of man, emerging out of nature, with his natural powers fighting against the fateful forces of the same nature. He has to survive in this natural world which is either indifferent or hostile to him. In such situation natural power of man has to be united with cunning calculative reason, for each situation of fate requires an appropriate response suited for dealing with it. These Fables from Lusai Hills are attempts to solve this problem of man. The stories show power as well as limitations of cunning reason, i.e., show the success as well as failure of cunning reason. In none of the stories any protagonist is ever clothed in any transcendent good quality like the Christian virtues. These figures in the stories are alone with their natural powers to face the hostile forces of nature. The fables of Lusai Hills, therefore, allow the protagonist to take up any measure, a lie, a deceit, or anything for the purposes of subduing the hostile powers of nature. In these stories the powers of nature have advanced to the level of forces of life, but they are yet to be tempered with transcendent good qualities or absolute values. The fables of Lusai Hills are the implicit recognition, acceptance and justification of the necessity of cunning reason to take up appropriate measure to meet the exigencies of the situation to overcome the adversity, without stating it explicitly as the word of Lusai Hills lacked concepts to express it. And yet, when listeners of these tales recognized this lesson their recognition came to them as a discovery rather than as a didactic lesson imposed externally and the lesson was as convincing as a revelation. These folktales of exercise of cunning reason were very effective in imparting their cunning word to the listener.

Native scholars from Lusai Hills accept the view that myths express the ethics of a people as these are means of passing on value systems from generation to generation. The story of Mauruangi, the legendary heroine of Lusai Hills, is supposed to articulate the human qualities that people of Lusai Hills, both ancient and modern, regard highly. Let me repeat according to a scholar from Lusai Hills Malsawmi Jacob, "In spite of all imaginable suffering under a callous father and true-to-tradition wicked step mother, she grows up into a lovely woman. She possesses all the virtues, triumphs over all odds and has a happy ending."[5] When scholars utter such words what is the sense of 'morality' espoused by them? These scholars understand by 'morality' any standard for word of praise and blame, intended to influence human conduct and ways of life that prevail in a society at a given time. In this sense every society has morality for the simple reason that the word of praising and blaming one another and of trying to influence each other's behaviour and life style is an inescapable part of a society. But these scholars forget that not all word of praising and blaming is *moral* praising and blaming. A person may be praised in words for his professional accomplishments without calling him a good person, for he may be ambitious who has achieved much professionally by always putting his own interest before the interest of others. When a person is praised in words morally there is evaluation of volition and the source of volition, especially the volition is not supposed to be based on self-interest. The folktales from Lusai Hills carry word of morality only in the first sense and do not utter word of morality in the second sense. No doubt native scholars of Lusai Hills understand word of morality in the first sense only. The people of Lusai Hills give word of praise and blame to one another for things that they do and do not do, but the issue of withholding word of moral judgment until a proper assessment of agent's motives could be made is not a part of their scheme of use of word. The latter sense of morality is not possible for the people of Lusai Hills for the simple reason that there is no word of inwardness of self in folktales of Lusai Hills. The stories from the Lusai Hills espouse an ethics of success and of self-interest individual or collective, which is a value scheme of agon (competition, war, fight). And in such ethics results are clearly what count most. Success is so imperative that only results have any value. Intentions are unimportant and, therefore, there is no effort either to develop an evaluative word for intentions by native scholars when they unfold the word of 'morality' embodied in the myths. So the only morality and the only rationality is that of cunning reason in the stories from Lusai Hills.

So, the study of Mizo folklore clearly demonstrates the word of Lusai Hills to be a cunning word a deceptive word. In words of R. Thangvunga, a scholar from Lusai Hills, "Then, as now, life was hard, unfeeling, cruel, hopeless and morally unrewarding. The world then, as now, had no soft corner for people with soft constitutions and impractical ideals. Machiavelli in Mizo folklores is only the tip of his cold nose. He is with us, in all of us. Let us admit it and make a virtue of our imperfections by being honest with ourselves."[6] Thangvunga is referring to the character called Chhura as Machiavelli in Mizo folklore.[7] What can be a better confirmation of the fact that the word of Lusai Hills is a cunning deceptive Machiavellian word.

Here we must remember that the word in the hills is generally interpreted in terms of either the initial situation or in terms of the final result. But this is not the correct principle of hermeneutics of the folktales of Hills, the word of Hills. In the trickster stories, stories involving cunning reason, the aesthetic quality does not depend on its protagonist's victories and achievements. What interests the listener and holds him in thrall, is the mechanism and modality of the trick and stratagem, the inventive and imaginative combination of its elements in the spectrum of the trickster's ruses put in the word. So the word the listener learns implicitly from such stories is the word that reveals the pattern or model of activity, a pattern that can be introduced into new situations of his own, providing a model to follow in his own new circumstances. These implicit patterns, implicit in the word of the folk tales, provide building blocks for new constructions in his life situations. This is the educative value of the folktales and the word from the hills.

A society learns effectively neither because some specific means of instruction are employed nor because some explicit didactic principles are imparted in the classrooms. It is the unwritten laws, the ethos prevailing in the societies as embodied in the word of folktales and folklores that secretly moulds human beings. The pedagogical efficacy of the word of folktales and folklore is due to the fact that in it something is expressed which reflects the spirit prevailing in the community. The folktales of the Lusai hills present the cunning deceptive word. The virtue of the trickster tales and episodes of trickery lies in the obliqueness of its message: it never counsels the folk overtly, never tells the people who they are or how they should behave. Thus, when a people recognize the word that is at the beginning they see their selves mirrored in it. So, in the trickster, their recognition comes to them as a discovery rather than as a lesson imposed from outside and carries with it the conviction characteristic of revelation. There lies the effectiveness of the word of trickster folktales, the effectiveness of the cunning and deceptive word of the Lusai Hills.

Here we must not forget that early man in Hills, especially in the forest of hills found himself surrounded with hostile forces. The trickster is the man fighting against a universe of hostile, spiritual and natural powers—and winning—by virtue of his cleverness, his cunning reason. The trickster is the man, according to the early hillman, struggling by himself to become what he feels he must become—master of his universe. Trickster tales and tales of cunning are significant because of the function it performs in the life of hills. The moral ambiguity of the trick, its negative evaluation as violating expected behaviour, yet acceptance for success, reminds that cultural constructs and systems of expected behaviour are neither firm nor fixed. In fact one of the social consequences of the trickster may be to prepare the way for adaptation and change in an unstable ethos. But problem with the cunning word is that it engenders instability and instability in its turn engenders cunning word forming a vicious circle. The calm of Lusai Hills is deceptive. One can feel the currents of agitation and how deceptive the peace is, if he is a Bru, Chakma, Pawis, Lais, Reangs or any other tribe that finds itself in the Lusai Hills among the majority tribe that claims the Lusai Hills to be their home.

May be this circle is the reason why the one infinite unspoken but transparent word of God has not yet found a foothold in the beginning of the finite unstable word of culture of the Lusai hills and they continue to carry the word of God in their hands on Sundays.

What kind of environmental ethics one can find encapsuled in such finite deceptive word of the Lusai Hills. Once again not an environmental ethics of harmony of man with infinite nature living peacefully with others one can find in the finite deceptive word of Lusai Hills. A finite deceptive word is not a creative word capable of creating infinite world to make room for everybody in harmony. In a finite deceptive word, one can find only an environmental ethics of fierce possession of finite nature, already existent as created, with much word spent on creating a web of deception to prevent others from possessing the same nature. This finite nature is their mother. By deception others are either step-children or children of step-mother. How can the finite deceptive word of Lusai hills allow the step-children or the children of step-mother to play in the bosom of their mother nature and suckle the breast of their mother nature? No doubt the story of Tualbhungi and Zwalpala highlights the falling apart of man and woman from their own culture does not highlight the harmony of the protagonists with their culture, and also it highlights that because of their deceptive false word to cover of their fear failed to be together in their nature, and yet longing to possess each other in their nature so fiercely and to the extent of being consumed by death.

That my friend is the word of Lusai Hills with its environmental ethics. I can only pray that the deceptive cunning word of the Lusai hills is replaced by the one infinite transparent stable word of God, like the life of Jesus, so that they can keep it in the beginning as the unspoken of the word they speak rather than merely carrying it in their hands deceptively only on Sundays. AMEN.

NOTES

1. Eric A. Havelock, *Preface to Plato*, Cambridge, Mass.: Belknap Press of Harvard University Press; Toronto: S. J. Reginald Saunders. 1963, p. 200.

2. *Preface to Plato*, p. 200.
3. Eric A. Havelock, *The Literate Revolution in Greece and its Cultural Consequences*, Princeton, NJ: Princeton University Press, 1982, p. 8.
4. "Machiavelli in Mizo Folk Tales," *Indian Folklife*, A quarterly Newsletter from National Folklore Support Center, Serial No. 34, November 2009, p. 10.
5. http://mizowritinginenglish.com/2008/08/mauruangi-malsawmi-jacob.html, accessed on June 04, 2011, at 7 pm.
6. "Machiavelli in Mizo Folk Tales," *Indian Folklife*, A quarterly Newsletter from National Folklore Support Center, Serial No. 34, November 2009, p. 10.
7. "Machiavelli in Mizo Folk Tales," *Indian Folklife*, A quarterly Newsletter from National Folklore Support Center, Serial No. 34, November 2009, pp. 8-10.

2

Environmental Ethics

A Study with Clinical Philosophy

C.P. Alexander

Ethics, as such has been a subject that looms at large in all sorts of human endeavour, ranging from Academic discourse to Business Operations to Resource Allocations to Medical Research. This seminar being in the area of applied philosophy; it is deemed to be concerned with the practical issues of life-situations—specifically with judicious usage of resources for durable and sustainable outcome. Thus, any discourse on environmental ethics has to be under a tripartite schema of (1) the necessity, (2) the luxury, and (3) the welfare of all. The *necessity* is the amount of resources that a living organism needs for its survival; nothing more nothing less! It is species specific. The quantitative requirement of the humans will be relatively different than that of other species. However, the quantitative requirement of resources for the survival of all members of the same species will be the same. Thus, for example the nutritional requirements of all the human beings will be same, for a healthy living.

When there is an imbalance in this, it becomes a matter of concern; and if this imbalance is due to improper distribution of resources then it, certainly, becomes an ethical issue. This is so, because as Plato says *justice lies in giving everyone what is due!* The crux of the matter here is that all the living creatures need to be treated on an equal pedestal; because all the living beings need resources for its survival—recourses are its survival necessity. It is obvious from the genealogy and archeology of the cosmic economy that the quanta of the resources neither increases nor diminish; but that the quality of the resources is such flexible that it could be transformed into something else, as envisaged by nuclear physics and molecular biology. One may not be taken wrong for the statement that given the original state-of-affairs of our planet, all the species on earth were to live together, sharing the resources for survival. This in other words, means that as the necessity of each species is different, there would not be shortage of resources; rather the consumption pattern of one species will lead to the production of the requirement of some other species—like the carbon dioxide consumption by plants tend to release oxygen for animals.

Yet another primordial order of ecological balance was that of the shared aptitude of all species to decode the meaning of natural forces, prior to the development of modern languages; a characteristic still observable in lower animals—the lower animals could easily read-in and predict natural calamities such as earth quack, tornado and so on. It could, then speculatively, thought that all the species had the same (primordial) language; all the species could understand each other and communicate with each other, because meaning as such was just the deciphering of the patterns of events and forces. The organic species had a common enemy—the inorganic world and the associated natural forces. This organic-inorganic dichotomy led to the development of survival strategies and devices; although the survival strategy had to do a lot with the terrain and geography of inhabitation.

However, though, this had its advantage in maintaining the organic solidarity, had more of disadvantages for Homo sapiens; because as Homo sapiens being physiologically the weakest of all animals had to face the devastating torture in the hands of both nature and other animals—and that had been the turning point in evolutionary process. The Homo sapiens not only began to develop separate language and devices, but also began to explore the potentialities for using the natural forces for their own advantage. The initial venture into developing devices for sustaining and perpetuating the human existence on earth intrigued the inquisitive nature of man to delve into many more physical and metaphysical realms. So, the trend in human enquiry began to shift from *what should I do to sustain my existence on earth?* to *what is it all about?* This has also brought forth some subsequent questions such *what more can I know?* and *How can I know more than what I know through my senses?* Man realized that knowing the world around him and above him is more important for sustaining one's mundane existence in the phase of entropy and chaos, rather than merely depending on one's natural instincts. Hence, the urge for sustenance through knowledge has become prime focus of the evolving Homo sapiens; this urge has led to many remarkable feats, from discovery of metals for creating weapons to landing in other planets to the modern gadget-oriented living.

One remarkable existential factor that has been motivating every activity of man, as Adler would put it, the *will to power*: to be more powerful than the fellow animals, and plants; to be more powerful than other races; to be more powerful than other tribes; to be more powerful than even one's own kith and kin! Incidentally, the factor that precipitates the *will to power* is the developmental-fear of annihilation of one's genealogy from the face of the earth. Thus, although the initial intent and purport of the human enquiry tradition has been that of the discovery of weaponry for the defence of oneself and that of one's dependence or kinsmen, man has never retreated from his efforts in perfecting and amassing the weaponry. Indubitably, the modern defence surveillance system has advanced from simple archery to missile technology; where missile is an advanced form of archery!

The drive for accruing the necessities for sustaining the human existence, coupled with the *will to power*, further intrigued the inquisitive drive in man. This inquisitive drive further ignited a sense of *the other is the hell* (an existentialists expression), and the *will to superpower*. One may not be wrong in saying that there are three layers of this power game—the individual, the racial, and the global. Over the years, the *power* game had developed several concurrent dimensions to it: such as the *will to be affluent*; *the will to less manual work and more comfort*; *the will to occupy other planets and the outer space; to conquer death and illness; the will to be a creator and so on.* This proclivity of human species, directly or indirectly, inspired what

I would call the hegemony through the *luxurious* way of living. Thus, power is not only measured by the ability to combat the enemy but also by the standard of living; which had enthused the competitive spirit in knowledge acquisition.

It is a fact that the greed for supremacy had enabled man in exploring many areas of life, and the globe, for knowledge acquisition; making knowledge an added dimension of power. Additionally, in this new mode of the human endeavours the right is not only the might of the majority, but also the might of the informed. The continued knowledge expansion has not only led to several unprecedented events and order of things but also a different order of thought processes and practices. This happened to be the turning point in human civilization; a turning point where the traditional mode of respecting the nature preserving the natural recourses was brushed aside as unfounded superstition. In the new order of things the *nature* has become an *object* of enquiry for revenue generation rather than a source of sustenance—the excavations, deforestation, genetic engineering, outer-space stations, cloud-net activities, and so on are the result of new mode of thinking and practices. It is the outcome of an ongoing species-specific perspective to reign over others as the most powerful global-being. This tendency in human efforts has led to several devastating Frankenstein effects, such as draught, ozone layer, black hole, global warming, earthquakes, tsunami, species annihilation, accidental creation of new species of microorganisms and diseases, genetic deformities in new born, and many more.

It may not be out of context to say that man is the most selfish of all the species on earth, and that the entire enquiry tradition has been driven in a linear manner to derive some form of benefits to human race; and now it has become almost impossible for him to turn away from his too familiar ways of acquiring knowledge for manipulating the world for his benefits. Nonetheless, this, in some way, turns out to be detrimental for global sustenance in general and human sustenance in particular, as an uncompromising ecological balance is required for global equanimity. An uncompromising ecological balance is what I would reckon as the *welfare of all*—the fellow humans, fellow animals, and plants. The environmental ethics being a topic concerned with the human actions towards the nature and other species, these actions needs to be evaluated on the basis of the intention behind them; and obviously the intention is loud and clear—the supremacy. Thus, the core issue in environmental ethics is that of changing man's attitude towards existence, and the perspective towards supremacy. This becomes possible only when man *intents* to shed *fear of the other,* and *stop instigating fear in others* at all levels. This would, perhaps, ignite an enlightened mode of thinking and practices, which would cater to the need of all species across the globe. The ethical evaluation of an action is determined by the intention of the actor, and the intention of the actor is always motivated by the perspective she/he holds.

3

Debate on Traditional Ethical Theories and Contemporary Environment Ethics

Amiya Dey

The word "environment" is derived from French *viren* to turn, and *in/viron* meaning to encircle. To encircle implies a centre, suggesting that other things of greater interest lie within. All living organisms live in some sort of environment. Their physiological processes, which are essential for the maintenance of life, are dependent upon environmental conditions and substances. Each component of the environment or the environmental factors affects the life of organisms, human and non-human. Environment consists of abiotic (physical) and biotic (living entities). The abiotic entities include air, light, temperature, water and soil. The biotic entities include all organisms of the habitat. The term "environment" means surroundings, in which the organisms live and interact. The environment and the organisms undergo continuous change from the time of their origin. But human beings are the only species among the biotic entities that can change the environment and manipulate it according to their requirements. This is because of their high degree of intelligence, memory, skilled hands and power or reasoning. However, the increasing human activities, especially during the last millennium, have adversely affected our environment at all levels. Therefore, preservation of environment has assumed a great significance in the context of survival of human race. Human activities like industrialization, power generation, urbanization, etc., are strongly polluting our life support system, i.e., air, water and soil. Such activities are also leading to an increase in green-house gases in the atmosphere causing the recently recognized phenomena of global warming and ozone hole. Human beings have the ability to tamper with the environment and modify it for their own benefits. But they cannot change the natural laws of life and basic requirements of life at their will. Wherever human beings may go, whether in space or on another planet, they always require an imitation of earthly environment, providing the same basic nature. If human beings have to live a better life on earth, they have to protect environment for their own survival and the survival of other biotic entities that they need. They cannot exploit the resources without bothering their future generation to the level that degrade the global environment seriously.

Environmental ethics is the discipline in philosophy that studies the moral relationship of human beings to, and also the value and moral status of, the environment and its non-human contents. During the last four or five decades moral philosophers have started playing a lot of attention to environmental ethics which was not there in the traditional, human-centric, approach to ethics. The entire field of moral relation was restricted to human beings only. The eco-centric approach to ethics extends the field of moral relation to the whole eco-systems. The human-centric and the eco-centric ethicists' responses to the environmental questions have been varying according to their own conception of morality and the views which they entertain about the nature of biotic and abiotic entities. A distinction is generally made between instrumental value and intrinsic value. The former is said to be the value of things as means to further some other ends, whereas the latter is said to be the value of things as ends in themselves regardless of whether or not they are useful as means to some other ends. For instance, certain fruits are said to have instrumental value for bats who feed on them, since feeding on the fruits is a means to survival for the bats. However, it is not widely agreed that fruits have value as ends in themselves. We can likewise think of a person who teaches others as having instrumental value for those who want to acquire knowledge. Yet, in addition to any such value, it is normally said that a person, as a person, has intrinsic value, i.e., value in his or her own right independently of his or her prospects for serving the ends of others. A certain wild plant may have value because it provides the ingredients for some medicine or as an aesthetic object for human observers. But if the plant also has some value in itself independently of its prospects for furthering some other ends such as human health, or the pleasure from aesthetic experience, then the plant also has intrinsic value. Because the intrinsically valuable is that which is good as an end in itself; it is commonly agreed that something's possession of intrinsic value generates a *prima facie* direct moral duty on the part of moral agents to protect it or at least refrain from damaging it.

The traditional western approaches to ethics, teleological or deontological, were anthropocentric or human-centred. They either assign intrinsic value to human beings alone (i.e., what we might call anthropocentric in a strong sense) or they assign a significantly greater amount of intrinsic value to human beings than to any non-human things such that the protection or promotion of human interests or well-being at the expense of non-human things turns out to be nearly always justified (i.e., what we might call anthropocentric in a weak sense). For example, Aristotle maintains that "nature has made all things specifically for the sake of man" and that the value of non-human things in nature is merely instrumental. Generally, anthropocentric positions find it problematic to articulate what is wrong with the cruel treatment of non-human animals, except to the extent that such treatment may lead to bad consequences for human beings. Immanuel Kant, for instance, suggests that cruelty towards a dog might encourage a person to develop a character which would be desensitized to cruelty towards humans. From this standpoint, cruelty towards non-human animals would be instrumentally, rather than intrinsically, wrong. Likewise, anthropocentrism often recognizes some non-intrinsic wrongness of anthropogenic (i.e., human-caused) environmental devastation. Such destruction might damage the well-being of human beings now and in the future since our well-being is essentially dependent on a sustainable environment. Contemporary anthropocentric ethicists extend the human-centric model to deal with the issues relating to environment. In their view, human beings can have moral relation to their environment, to the plants, animals, rivers, air, water, soil, hills, etc., which occupy a large part of the world and which are useful in so many ways to human beings. Our obligation to non-human entities arises from the fact that the non-human entities serve some of our interests or needs or useful as means or sources deriving some benefits. For example, Baxter argues that our obligations regarding the environment are to be determined solely on the basis of human interests. Our welfare depends on breathable air, drinkable water and edible food. Thus polluting the environment to the extent that damages the air, water and land is unacceptable because it damages public welfare. Animals and plants are considered non-rational beings and are, therefore, not considered in the same moral category as humans. However, Baxter does not approve of man destruction of these objects because people do depend on them in many ways and they should be preserved to the degree that humans depend on them. Clean air and water are good for plants and animals too, but their preservation will in no way take precedence over any human interests. These moral philosophers consider human well-being as an adequate basis for moral relationships that holds between human and non-human. Michael Allen Fox, Mary Anne Warren, Taylor, H.J. MacCloskey also holds the similar view.

They have argued variously on the different grounds that animals have no moral status. In their view, only human beings have the moral status, and hence deserve moral consideration simply because it is they who are rational, capable of having interests, possess self-awareness, have linguistic abilities and can represent the future.

Non-anthropocentric ethicists reject the human-centric model of environmental ethics. They argue variously on the different grounds, but maintain the view that all human and non-human entities have moral status. The humane moralists like Tom, Regan, Peter Singer, Frey R.G., Clark S. Eugene C Hargrove and John Passmore argue extensively on the different grounds to show that animals do have moral standing at par with humans because they have the capacity of suffering even though they are deprived of reason, speech forethought, moral agency, autonomy and self-awareness, and hence ought to be treated equally without any bias. These moral philosophers, however, did not extend the domain of moral community beyond humans and animals. But those who subscribe to the holistic view of morality extend the domain of moral community to both biotic and abiotic entities. In their view, the class of morally considerable entities is co-extensive with the class of eco-systems and their biotic and abiotic elements. Aldo Leopold, the father of the modern environmental movement, claims that we must abandon the old anthropocentric (human-centric) conception of ethics and replace it with a non-anthropocentric (environment-centred) ethics. Historically, people thought ethics was concerned only about the needs and interests of humans. Most people never questioned whether using the environment for our purposes were morally acceptable. Those few who worried about the environment were worried only because they feared that by damaging the environment we would ultimately harm ourselves (polluted water, radioactive waste, deforestation, etc.). In short, if the environment had any value, its value was entirely instrumental. Most people at that time thought the environment was nothing more than an economic resource. Sterba James P. claims that anthropocentric and non-anthropocentric ethics actually share a similar practical outlook. Specifically, although these competing views lead us to think about the environment differently, they typically give us the same practical guidance on particular environmental questions. Sterba's implicit suggestion is that ethical theory, though important, is not as important as many philosophers have thought, what ultimately matters are one's theoretical commitments, but rather the practical advice that those commitments entail. Starba's analysis of these competing views of ethics also reintroduces two theoretical friends: the act/omission distinction, and debate about the nature and importance of equality. Devall and Sessions argue that the well-being and flourishing of human and non-human life have value in themselves.

Although environmental ethicists often try to distance themselves from the anthropocentrism embedded in traditional ethical views (Passmore 1974, Norton 1991 are exceptions), they also quite often draw their theoretical resources from traditional ethical systems and theories. Consider the following two basic moral questions: (1) What kinds of thing are intrinsically valuable, good or bad? (2) What makes an action right or wrong?

Consequentialist ethical theories consider intrinsic "value"/"disvalue" or "goodness"/"badness" to be more fundamental moral notions than "rightness"/"wrongness", and maintain that whether an action is right/wrong is determined by whether its consequences are good/bad. From this perspective, answers to question (2) are informed by answers to question (1). For instance, utilitarianism, a paradigm case of consequentialism, regards pleasure (or, more broadly construed, the satisfaction of interest, desire, and/or preference) as the only intrinsic value in the world, whereas pain (or the frustration of desire, interest, and/or preference) the only intrinsic disvalue, and maintains that right actions are those that would produce the greatest balance of pleasure over pain.

As the utilitarian focus is the balance of pleasure and pain as such, the question of to whom a pleasure or pain belongs is irrelevant to the calculation and assessment of the rightness or wrongness of actions. Hence, the eighteenth century utilitarian Jeremy Bentham (1789), and now Peter Singer (1993), have argued that the interests of all the sentient beings (i.e., beings who are capable of experiencing pleasure or pain)—including nonhuman ones—affected by an action should be taken equally into consideration in assessing the action. Furthermore, rather like Routley, Singer argues that the anthropocentric privileging of members of the species Homo sapiens is arbitrary, and that it is a kind of "speciesism" as unjustifiable as sexism and racism. Singer regards the animal liberation movement as comparable to the liberation movements of women and people of colour. Unlike the environmental philosophers who attribute intrinsic value to the natural environment and its inhabitants, Singer and utilitarians in general attribute intrinsic value to the experience of pleasure or interest satisfaction as such, not to the beings who have the experience. Similarly, for the utilitarian, non-sentient objects in the environment such as plant species, rivers, mountains, and landscapes, all of which are the objects of moral concern for environmentalists, are of no intrinsic but at most instrumental value to the satisfaction of sentient beings. Furthermore, because right actions, for the utilitarian, are those that maximize the overall balance of interest satisfaction over frustration, practices such as whale-hunting and the killing of an elephant for ivory, which cause suffering to nonhuman animals, might turn out to be right after all: such practices might produce considerable amounts of interest-satisfaction for human beings, which, on the utilitarian calculation, outweigh the nonhuman interest-frustration involved. As the result of all the above considerations, it is unclear to what extent a utilitarian ethic can also be an environmental ethic. This point may not so readily apply to a wider consequentialist approach, which attributes intrinsic value not only to pleasure or satisfaction, but also to various objects and processes in the natural environment.

Deontological ethical theories, in contrast, maintain that whether an action is right or wrong is for the most part independent of whether its consequences are good or bad. From the deontologist perspective, there are several distinct moral rules or duties (e.g., "not to kill or otherwise harm the innocent", "not to lie", "to respect the rights of others", "to keep promises"), the observance/violation of which is intrinsically right/wrong; i.e., right/wrong in itself regardless of consequences. When asked to justify an alleged moral rule, duty or its corresponding right, deontologists may appeal to the intrinsic value of those beings to whom it applies. For instance, "animal rights" advocate Tom Regan (1983) argues that those animals with intrinsic value (or what he calls "inherent value") have the moral right to respectful treatment, which then generates a general moral duty on our part not to treat them as mere means to other ends. We have, in particular, a *prima facie* moral duty not to harm them. Regan maintains that certain practices (such as sport or commercial hunting, and experimentation on animals) violate the moral right of intrinsically valuable animals to respectful treatment. Such practices, he argues, are intrinsically wrong regardless of whether or not some better consequences ever flow from them. Exactly which animals have intrinsic value and, therefore, the moral right to respectful treatment? Regan's answer is: those that meet the criterion of being the "subject-of-a-life". To be such a subject is a sufficient (though not necessary) condition for having intrinsic value, and to be a subject-of-a-life involves, among other things, having sense-perceptions, beliefs, desires, motives, memory, a sense of the future, and a psychological identity over time.

Some authors have extended concern for individual well-being further, arguing for the intrinsic value of organisms achieving their own good, whether those organisms are capable of consciousness or not. Paul Taylor's version of this view (1981 and 1986), which we might call *biocentrism*, is a deontological example. He argues that each individual living thing in nature—whether it is an animal, a plant, or a micro-organism—is a "teleological-centre-of-life" having a good or well-being of its own which can be enhanced or damaged, and that all individuals who are teleological-centres-of life have equal intrinsic value (or what he calls "inherent worth") which entitles them to moral respect. Furthermore, Taylor maintains that the intrinsic value of wild living things generates a *prima facie* moral duty on our part to preserve or promote their goods as ends in themselves, and that any practices which treat those beings as mere means and thus display a lack of respect for them are intrinsically wrong. A more recent and biologically detailed defence of the idea that living things have representations and goals and hence have moral worth is found in Agar 2001. Unlike Taylor's egalitarian and deontological biocentrism, Robin Attfield (1987) argues for a hierarchical view that while all beings having a good of their own have intrinsic value, some of them (e.g., persons) have intrinsic value to a greater extent. Attfield also endorses a form of consequentialism which takes into consideration, and attempts to balance, the many and possibly conflicting goods of different living things. However, some critics have pointed out that the notion of biological good or well-being is only descriptive not prescriptive. For instance, the fact that HIV has a good of its own does not mean that we ought to assign any positive moral weight to the realization of that good.

Note that the ethics of animal liberation or animal rights and biocentrism are both *individualistic* in that their various moral concerns are directed towards individuals only—not ecological wholes such as species, populations, biotic communities, and ecosystems. None of these is sentient, a subject-of-a-life, or a teleological-centre-of-life, but the preservation of these collective entities is a major concern for many environmentalists. Moreover, the goals of animal liberationists, such as the reduction of animal suffering and death, may conflict with the goals of environmentalists. For example, the preservation of the integrity of an ecosystem may require the culling of feral animals or of some indigenous populations that threaten to destroy fragile habitats. So there are disputes about whether the ethics of animal liberation is a proper branch of environmental ethics.

Criticizing the individualistic approach in general for failing to accommodate conservation concerns for ecological wholes, J. Baird Callicott (1980) has advocated a version of land-ethical *holism* which takes Leopold's statement "A thing is right when it tends to preserve the integrity, stability, and beauty of the biotic community. It is wrong when it tends otherwise" to be the supreme deontological principle. In this theory, the earth's biotic community *per se* is the sole locus of intrinsic value, whereas the value of its individual members is merely instrumental and dependent on their contribution to the "integrity, stability, and beauty" of the larger community. A straightforward implication of this version of the land ethics is that an individual member of the biotic community ought to be sacrificed whenever that is needed for the protection of the holistic good of the community. For instance, Callicott maintains that if culling a white-tailed deer is necessary for the protection of the holistic biotic good, then it is a land-ethical requirement to do so. But, to be consistent, the same point also applies to human individuals because they are also members of the biotic community. Not surprisingly, the misanthropy implied by Callicott's land-ethical holism has been widely criticized and regarded as a reductio of the position. Tom Regan (1983, p. 362), for example, has condemned the holistic land ethic's disregard of the rights of the individual as "environmental fascism". Under the pressure from the charge of ecofascism and misanthropy, Callicott (1989 Ch. 5, and 1999, Ch. 4) has later revised his position and now maintains that the biotic community (indeed, any community to which we belong) as well as its individual members (indeed, any individual who shares with us membership in some common community) all have intrinsic value. The controversy surrounding Callicott's original position, however, has inspired efforts in environment ethics to investigate possibilities of attributing intrinsic value to ecological wholes, not just their individual constituent. Following in Callicott's footsteps, and inspired by Næss's relational account of value, Warwick Fox in his most recent work has championed a theory of "responsive cohesion" which apparently gives supreme moral priority to the maintenance of ecosystems and the biophysical world. It remains to be seen if this position will escape the charges of misanthropy and totalitarianism laid against earlier holistic and relational theories of value.

Individual natural entities (whether sentient or not, living or not), Andrew Brennan (1984) argues, are not designed by anyone to fulfil any purpose and, therefore, lack "intrinsic function" (i.e., the function of a thing that constitutes part of its essence or identity conditions). This, he proposes, is a reason for thinking that individual natural entities should not be treated as mere instruments, and thus a reason for assigning them intrinsic value. Furthermore, he argues that the same moral point applies to the case of natural ecosystems, to the extent that they lack intrinsic function. In the light of Brennan's proposal, Eric Katz (1991 and 1997) argues that all natural entities, whether individuals or wholes, have intrinsic value in virtue of their ontological independence from human purpose, activity, and interest, and maintains the deontological principle that nature as a whole is an "autonomous subject" which deserves moral respect and must not be treated as a mere means to human ends. Carrying the project of attributing intrinsic value to nature to its ultimate form, Robert Elliot (1997) argues that naturalness itself is a property in virtue of possessing which all natural things, events, and state of affairs, attain intrinsic value. Furthermore, Elliot argues that even a consequentialist, who in principle allows the possibility of trading off intrinsic value from naturalness for intrinsic value from other sources, could no longer justify such kind of trade-off in reality. This is because the reduction of intrinsic value due to the depletion of naturalness on earth, according to him, has reached such a level that any further reduction of it could not be compensated by any amount of intrinsic value generated in other ways, no matter how great it is.

As the notion of "natural" is understood in terms of the lack of human contrivance and is often opposed to the notion of "artifactual", one much contested issue is about the value of those parts of nature that have been interfered with by human artifice—for instance, previously degraded natural environments which have been humanly restored. Based on the premise that the properties of being naturally evolved and having a natural continuity with the remote past are "value adding" (i.e., adding intrinsic value to those things which possess those two properties), Elliot argues that even a perfectly restored environment would necessarily lack those two value-adding properties and, therefore, be less valuable than the originally undegraded natural environment. Katz, on the other hand, argues that a restored nature is really just an artifact designed and created for the satisfaction of human ends, and that the value of restored environments is merely instrumental. However, some critics have pointed out that advocates of moral dualism between the natural and the artifactual run the risk of diminishing the value of human life and culture, and fail to recognize that the natural environments interfered with by humans may still have morally relevant qualities other than pure naturalness. Two other issues central to this debate are that the key concept "natural" seems ambiguous in many different ways, and that those who argue that human interference reduces the intrinsic value of nature seems to have simply assumed the crucial premise that naturalness is a source of intrinsic value. Some thinkers maintain that the natural, or the "wild" construed as that which "is not humanized" or to some degree "not under human control" is intrinsically valuable. Yet, as Bernard Williams points out, we may, paradoxically, need to use our technological powers to retain a sense of something not being in our power. The retention of wild areas may thus involve planetary and ecological management to maintain, or even "imprison" such areas, raising a question over the extent to which national parks and wilderness areas are free from our control. An important message underlying the debate, perhaps, is that even if ecological restoration is achievable, it might have been better to have left nature intact in the first place.

As an alternative to consequentialism and deontology both of which consider "thin" concepts such as "goodness" and "rightness" as essential to morality, *virtue ethics* proposes to understand morality—and assess the ethical quality of actions—in terms of "thick" concepts such as "kindness", "honesty", "sincerity" and "justice". As virtue ethics speaks quite a different language from the other two kinds of ethical theory, its theoretical focus is not so much on what kind of things are good/bad, or what makes an action right/wrong. Indeed, the richness of the language of virtues, and the emphasis on moral character, is sometimes cited as a reason for exploring a virtues-based approach to the complex and always-changing questions of sustainability and environmental care. One question central to virtue ethics is what the moral reasons are for acting one way or another. For instance, from the perspective of virtue ethics, kindness and loyalty would be moral reasons for helping a friend in hardship. These are quite different from the deontologist's reason (that the action is demanded by a moral rule) or the consequentialist reason (that the action will lead to a better overall balance of good over evil in the world). From the perspective of virtue ethics, the motivation and justification of actions are both inseparable from the character traits of the acting agent. Furthermore, unlike deontology or consequentialism the moral focus of which is other people or states of the world, one central issue for virtue ethics is how to live a flourishing human life, this being a central concern of the moral agent himself or herself. "Living virtuously" is Aristotle's recipe for flourishing. Versions of virtue ethics advocating virtues such as "benevolence", "piety", "filiality", and "courage", have also been held by thinkers in the Chinese Confucian tradition. The connection between morality and psychology is another core subject of investigation for virtue ethics. It is sometimes suggested that human virtues, which constitute an important aspect of a flourishing human life, must be compatible with human needs and desires, and perhaps also sensitive to individual affection and temperaments. As its central focus is human flourishing as such, virtue ethics may seem unavoidably anthropocentric and unable to support a genuine moral concern for the nonhuman environment. But just as Aristotle has argued that a flourishing human life requires friendships and one can have genuine friendships only if one genuinely values, loves, respects, and cares for one's friends for their own sake, not merely for the benefits that they may bring to oneself, some have argued that a flourishing human life requires the moral capacities to value, love, respect, and care for the nonhuman natural world as an end in itself.

The expression "intrinsic value" was used by Kant, for him every being whose existence in itself is an end in itself—that is humanity and more generally, rational beings—have intrinsic value. All the rest is considered as a means, as an instrumental value Environmental ethics will refer to this position as "anthropocentric". It only recognises the moral dignity of humans excluding the rest, i.e., nature, which is considered simply as a set of resources. What environmental ethics aim to reach is the opposite, i.e., to show that natural entities also have moral dignity and "intrinsic values". The idea is that where there are means, there are necessarily ends. All living things, from the simplest to the most complex, whether they are animals (even lacking sensitivity), plants or monocellular organisms, all maintain themselves within existence and reproduce. They do this by using complex adaptive strategies, which are all means to reach an end. There are, therefore, ends in nature. All living beings can be considered as the functional equivalent of a set of intentional acts, like something that is "an end in itself". The opposition between humans and things, characteristic of anthropocentrism, becomes substituted by a whole range of teleonomic individualities which can all lay claim to being ends in themselves and, therefore, to having an intrinsic value.

A different system of values living individual is, being equal to any other, worthy of moral consideration: this is what is called biocentrism, its standard-bearers are Paul Taylor and Holmes Rolston. Biocentric environmental ethics, thus recognise an ethical point of view that extends inherent value to all living things. It stands in contrast to anthropocentrism which centres on the value of humans. This justifies an attention to living things that has rapidly gained supporters. The 'intrinsic value' has become the war cry of numerous nature protection activists. The preamble to The Rio Convention on Biological Diversity (1992) stressed the "intrinsic value of biological diversity" underlining the importance given to the intrinsic value.

In conclusion, we humans act as the owners of the earth but without any collective responsibility to make it a better place for future generations. We claim rights to own and use the earth but forget about our responsibilities to take care and use it in a sustainable manner. We have disputes over land and resources but lack ways to improve them and preserve them. We create new ways of consuming resources but lack creativity to generate alternative ways of making a better use of what we have. A moral responsibility to transform in positive ways the world is needed today. The condition of the earth is not only in God's hands but also in our hands. It is explained in the Hebrew tradition by the experience of the Jewish people who were slaves in Egypt. They experienced the power of God. This experience held them responsible for their own community and for transforming their own world. God was just with them and it is their responsibility to be just and have mercy on others who could experience social injustice or inequality. Social oppression was not supported by God and if oppression existed as part of the social order, this social order has to be transformed.

References

Benson. John, *Environmental Ethics*, Routledge Publication, London and New York, 2000.

Brennan, Andrew., *Thinking About Nature: An Investigation of Nature, Value and Ecology*, London, New York Rutledge, 1988.

Brown Christopher A., "Kantianism and Mere Means", *Environmental Ethics*, A publication of the center for Environmental Philosophy and the University of North Texas, Vol. 32, No. 3, Fall, 2010.

Crawford, S.C., *The Evolution of Hindu Ethical Ideals*, Calcutta, Firma K.L. Mukhopadhyay, 1974.

Hollander M. Jack., *The Real Environmental Crisis*, University of California Press, 2004.

Holmes Rolston III., *Environmental Ethics: Duties to and Values in the Natural World,* Temple University Press, Philadelphia, 1988.

LaFollette Hugh, (ed), *Ethics in Practice: An Anthology*, Blackwell Publishing Ltd., 2003.

Passmore, John., *Man's Responsibility for Nature*, London: Duckworth, 1974, 2nd ed., 1980.

4
Christianity and Ecological Concerns

Jacob Aluckal

Christianity as a religion established by Christ in order to redeem and liberate human beings from this world and lead them to heaven, is primarily concerned with the spiritual realities, the Kingdom of God which is to be realized in its fullness in the life to come. While the environment is something related to this world, here and now, and hence, belongs primarily to the domain of the civil society, the earthly kingdom, from which man is to be liberated. What then is the relationship between Christianity and environment? Is it that of confrontation or that of co-existence and tolerance, or that of cooperation or collaboration? A glance through the history of the Church brings out the growth and development of eco-theology down through the centuries.

During the first centuries of the history of Christianity, when the Church was undergoing severe persecution from the world, we notice a strong awareness of the pilgrim nature and eschatological dimension of the Church. Denial of the world led to the possession of the Kingdom of God. In fact, Christians were called 'saints', citizens of the Kingdom to come. They were aware of the words to Jesus to Pilate that his kingdom does not belong to this world or his words: "give to Caesar what belongs to Caesar and give to God what belongs to God". The strong eschatological awareness which existed in the early Church promoted a sense of detachment of man from this world and hence, he was not concerned with building up of the earthly kingdom.

But things took a dramatic turn beginning with the fourth century, when Christianity became the state religion. There was very little distinction between the state and the religion. In fact, they functioned as one. The early general councils of the Church were all convened by the emperors. Sciences flourished under the patronage of the Church. The first universities were founded by the Church. Music, arts, literature, architecture, all flourished under the inspiration of the Church. The Church sponsored many discoveries and inventions. The Church was very much involved in building up of the earthly kingdom.

But gradually, secular sciences began to assert themselves, and acquire certain autonomy and independence from the Church, encouraged by the several scientific discoveries. Copernicus in the sixteenth century showed that the earth is no more the centre of the universe, but only a tiny planet circling around the sun. Dislodging of the earth from the centre of the universe was a severe blow to man, who considered himself to be the master of the planet earth, which in turn was the centre of the universe. It was an invitation to be humble. Charles Darwin showed that human beings gradually evolved from nature. They are not a separate category which is above nature and thus licensed to subdue and manipulate God's creation. Then there was the rise of materialism and consumerism, which deified wealth, the mammon. The culmination of such a trend was the rise of communism and the denial of God, the Creator.

The Second Vatican Council (1962-1965) acknowledges that secular sciences do enjoy certain autonomy and can flourish independently of the Church (GS 36). But it is not an absolute autonomy. The Church in the Modern World goes on to say that "However, if by the term 'the autonomy of the earthly affairs' is meant that material being does not depend on God and that man can use it as if it had no relation to its creator, then the falsity of such claim will be obvious to anyone who believes in God. Without a creator, there can be no creature" (GS 36). Church's concern for the environment is to be understood in the context of its integral or holistic approach to creation.

Christianity's concern for ecology as we understand today is rather recent. Only from 1970, Church leaders were speaking about pollution, conservation, increasing consumption of natural resources and other environmental problems. "We begin to ask" said Pope John Paul II, "How we can have destroyed so much. We also ask anxiously, if it is possible to remedy the damage which has already been done". Orthodox Patriarch Dimtrios said: "we cannot continue plundering God's creation without reaping the results of its eventual destruction".

In June 1992, the Earth Summit took place in Rio de Janeiro, (Brazil). The historical gathering brought together delegates from the nations of the world for the United Nations Conference on Environment and Development. The World Council of Churches sponsored a major Ecumenical Meeting, which was hosted by the Catholic Church, in which representatives of over 70 countries participated. The theme of that conference was: Searching for the New Heavens and the New Earth: An Ecumenical response to UNCED.

Even today, we often speak of and live as if, the earth, the planet, the animal, and all the rest of creation, were there only for our benefit. Any land not cultivated, any river not harnessed for power generation, are regarded as worthless and useless. The value of everything was measured solely in terms of its usefulness to 'man'. Since we thought that the world was something separate from us and not related to us, we felt free to dominate it and subdue it. Thanks to the greater ecological awareness, the "createdness" of creation, such an attitude is changing gradually

In the Biblical creation story, we read "God saw all he had made, and indeed it was very good" (*Genesis* 1:31). This statement is repeated several times in the same chapter, after separating the earth from the waters, after making the earth all kinds of trees, plants and vegetation, after creating all living creatures in the waters, after populating the earth with all kinds of animals and living creations, and above all after creating humans in his own image and likeness. All that God had created shared and reflected the goodness of God. The creation was good.

The creation is good in itself irrespective of its usefulness to man, who came into this world in the last moment. Human beings, with their anthropocentric way of thinking, thought foolishly that every river that is not harnessed and every land that is not cultivated is "useless". Scientists are discovering more and more the value of even the minutest being and its usefulness in sustaining the planet earth, and their marvellous interdependence. The ecological balance must be maintained at all cost.

God gave the following command to our first parents: "Be fruitful, multiply, fill the earth and subdue it. Be masters of the fish of the sea, the birds of heaven and all the living creatures that move on earth" (Genesis: 28). Humans did not always understand this command of God as he intended. The wrong interpretation of this command of God led to two disastrous consequences, namely population explosion and unchecked exploitation of natural resources.

Fortunately, there is a significant change in understanding and interpreting the command of God mentioned above. Christian thinkers are gradually moving away from the concept of "dominion" to that of "stewardship". Humans, created in the image and likeness of God and as the crown of creation, are called upon to collaborate with God in protecting, caring and make the creation fruitful in keeping with the design of God and as responsible stewards. They are called upon not to "exploit" or "manipulate" the creation to satisfy their own needs, unmindful of others, be it human beings or voiceless or powerless creatures.

Jesus said, "The time is fulfilled and the Kingdom of God is close at hand: Repent and believe the Gospel" (*Mk* 1:15). These are the words with which the Kingdom of God was ushered into this world. Fortunately, there is greater awareness today than even before about the damage we are doing to creation. Numerous species of plants and animals have disappeared from the face of the earth forever. The command of God "Thou shall not kill" is to be understood in its wider perspective so as to include the entire creation.

God completed the work of creation in six days and he rested on the seventh day and he blessed the seventh day and made it holy (confer Genesis, 2: 1-3). The Sabbatical observance is an invitation from God to rest from activity from time to time. It is an exhortation not to become 'workaholics", leaving no time to rest, reflect and think about God, our creator and to understand his designs for us and for the creation. The rest is not limited only to humans, but also to animals, plants and the land. The frequent bundhs and breakdowns are God's ways of reminding us about this precept. Along with giving praise and glory to God, Sundays can be used also to care for the marginalized, like the sick, lonely, the poor and to pay more attention to creation.

We must listen to the Good News proclaimed not only by humans, but also by the animals, plants and the most insignificant beings on earth. The whole creation is God's revelation or manifests his glory. The creation is an open book through which we can come to know God and his plans for us and for the entire creation. We have to be attentive to the voice of God speaking and revealing to us.

The tribal communities live closer to nature than other sophisticated communities of the present world and hence they can feel with the creation. They have and live by many ecologically sound values. Their sense of justice, democracy and social awareness are eco-friendly values. The Benedictine communities invite to be more self-reliant communities without exploiting the creation. The Franciscan spirituality invites us to live simpler lives. St. Francis lived so close to nature, that he was able to understand and communicate with the sun, moon, animals and plants. His oneness with nature was really admirable.

Jesus was fully aware of his environment and surroundings. His parables speak about the farms, the fishing, weeds, seeds, harvest, rivers and fruitfulness. His concern for plants is reflected in his parables of the shepherd, lilies of the field and the birds of the air. He warns against creating surplus and of accumulating riches. All these proclaim valuable ecological values.

God so loved the world that he sent his only son to redeem the world. Jesus is also the first born of all creation. The ecologically broken and wounded world has to be restored in Christ. Establishing the Kingdom of God here on earth means total transformation and all creation living in harmony and peace as it existed at the beginning of creation.

At present, the creation is in bondage and groaning for

liberation and for the arrival of the Messianic Kingdom. We await the arrival of the new heavens and the new earth as promised in the book of Revelation, when God will live among human beings, when He will make his home among them. "They will be his people, and he will be their God. He will wipe away all tears from their eyes; and he will be their God, God with them. He will wipe away all tears from their eyes; there will be no more death, or no more mourning, or sadness or pain." (*Rev.* 21:4). Then Christ will be the Alpha and the Omega, the beginning and the end.

The Christian perspective towards Ecology and environment is rather optimistic and it does not agree with the ideas of prophets of doom. When we need the signs of times, we notice that there is a greater awareness today of the ecological degradation taking place around us and the willingness to give greater attention and care to creation. Not only Christianity, but all religions are waking up and extend their cooperation and collaboration to restore creation to its pristine glory. All religions can come together in a spirit of ecumenism and dialogue and work together with the states, NGOs and all people of goodwill to protect and care for creation and the Mother Earth.

5

Environmental Ethics

A Gandhian Perspective

K.J. Joy

In the face of the constant admonitions by the environmentalists of the impending ecological disasters[1] caused by humanity's reckless exploitation of nature, every social institution and right thinking individual began to rethink their attitude and approach to the earth and its resources and to chalk out action plans on a war-footing to save the planet. It is frequently construed that the environmental concerns were neglected in the past often blinded by the industrial and technological progress of the nineteenth and twentieth centuries. However, today there is a concerted effort on the part of everyone to rediscover and continue "to rediscover the broader community of creatures which includes not only human beings, but the whole creation."[2] As a result, today we have the discipline of environmental ethics, which concerns itself with the personal conduct towards ecosystem. It looks at the moral responsibility that the humans have towards the environment. A number of thinkers and social activists too have come up in the course of history to remind people of the importance of preserving the environment. Mahatma Gandhi, the father of our nation, was not only a political giant, a revolutionary of an extraordinary type, a humanist and pacifist of international fame but also an environmentalist who was able to foresee the future and visualize the dangers inherent in the kind of development the nations chose to go in for following the Industrial Revolution in the West.[3] In this essay, I shall begin with a brief discussion on the nature of environmental ethics. The article then goes on to examine the thoughts of Gandhi on the need to conserve the environment and how he could be viewed as an environmentalist. The last part of the article proffers some of the Gandhian solutions to the environmental crisis that rattle our present-day world. All in all, the article is an attempt at unravelling the important contributions that Gandhi made for the preservation of our mother earth. It is also an invitation to emulate his teachings especially on simplicity of life-style by eschewing the unlimited wants to which people can easily fall prey to so that our environment can be safeguarded for the generations to come.

What is Environmental Ethics?

Philosophers in every age, and especially in the West, have thought about nature and philosophised about the structure and the various characteristics of environment. Although there is an ethic implicit in many of their thinking, the moral implications were not really developed. On the contrary, with the renaissance and its aftermath movements like the industrial revolution, the scientific resurgence and the Enlightenment, many philosophers began to regard nature as a valueless realm governed by mechanistic causal forces. For them values and ethical delineations arose only with the interests and preferences of humans.

However, when the environmental crisis threatened the very existence of life in the planet, a concerted effort was initiated by philosophers, scientists, social activists and practitioners of religions to avert the disaster. Even then, powerful lobbies both in the West and everywhere argued that the current crisis of the environment is exaggerated. To them growth in population is a major factor of environmental crisis. They relied on the scientific and philosophical theories enunciated during the renaissance by both philosophers as well as scientists. The empiricist thinkers like Francis Bacon and later philosophers like Descartes, Spinoza and Leibniz viewed the role of mathematics as final in the human societies.[4] The scientific temper to a large extent was linked to the capitalistic economic order. Neo-liberal thinkers argued for free economy stressing that economic life should not be trampled over. They held that capitalism itself has no ills and given full options to the individuals, they by themselves will have interest in preserving a good environment. Thus, environmental issues did not really come under their philosophical investigations.

It is against this background that the contemporary thinkers, who experienced for themselves the untold miseries of natural disasters, envisaged an ethic that will concern itself with the wellbeing of our planet. Environmental ethics can be construed as a theory and practice about appropriate concern for, values in and duties regarding the natural world. Ethics, as we understand, deals with moral choices, about the values that lie behind them, the reasons people give for them, and the language they use to describe them. It is about innocence and guilt, right and wrong, and, about good and bad. In other words, ethics is concerned about people relating to people in justice and love. Its subject matter is human conduct, those actions that a person performs consciously and wilfully and for which he/she is held accountable.

Now, environmental ethics starts with human concerns for quality surroundings, and some think this shapes the ethics from the beginning to the end. Others hold that, beyond inter-human concerns, values are at stake when humans relate to animals, plants, species and ecosystems. According to their vision, humans ought to construe nature as morally significant in itself, and this turns ethics into new directions. We can define environmental ethics as an ecological conscience or moral that reflects a commitment and responsibility towards the environment, including plants and animals as well as present and future generations of people. It is oriented towards human societies living in harmony with the natural world on which they depend for their survival and well-being.

Further, in ethics we speak of moral responsibility. The term 'moral responsibility' implies knowledge, capacity, choice and value significance. When a person is morally responsible to do something, it implies that he/she is capable of performing it, can freely choose whether or not to do it and the performance thereof affects the welfare and/or liberty of other beings. Since one's response to these requirements reflects upon his/her value as a person, we say that this response has 'moral significance.' Such an analysis of 'moral responsibility' can help us to better explain why environmental ethics has only recently attracted the attention and concern of moral philosophers. Until recently, as we have already discussed above, our interactions with the natural environment were morally neutral since nature was assumed to be both impersonal and too vast to be injured by our interventions, or else, at the very least, we were quite unable to foresee the harm resulting from our interference with nature. Now, of course, we know better about nature. Humans can cause massive and permanent damage to natural landscapes, deplete natural resources and harm ecosystems. Not only do we know that we can cause these injuries to nature, we also know how we cause them, and how we can prevent or remedy them. Having known all these facts, we have now an obligation for a moral obligation to act with care, prudence and, at times, with moderation and restraint.

Environmental ethics can also be called as eco-ethics. "Eco-ethics focuses on obligations towards wholeness of human life built on justice, freedom, participation, dignity and solidarity and its organic connectedness to nature and its eco-system"[5] Thus, it is basically an issue of justice. Often many environmentalists fail to concede the deep co-relation that exists between our approach to nature and social relationships. Commenting on this inconsistency, Felix Wilfred writes: "The destruction of the ecosystem at the same time causes wounds of injustice in the body of society.... An equitable distribution of natural resources is the best guarantee against the exploitative use of them that is causing the present environmental crisis."[6] Ecological justice covers the human society in the present and future and all living and non-living beings on the planet. "Spirit is life; its opposite is not matter but death and all that lead to death, such as oppression, injustice, and destruction of our homely habitat."[7]

The basic assumption of environmental ethics is that nature has value. When modern science and technology degraded nature to the level of mere resources to be exploited at will for self-aggrandisement, the primeval cultures had greater sensitivity towards the meaning and mystery of nature. They considered earth as a mother providing everything that they required. This understanding of the earth as mother became central to the organic cosmology of the classical period. Hence the present day ecological movements need to revisit the values of the pre-modern organic worldview.[8] According to B. Lonergan everything including nature finds its value ultimately in the final cause, which is the ground of every dependent being. "The final cause, then, is the ground of value, and it is the ultimate cause of causes for it overcomes contingence at its deepest level. Being cannot be arbitrary, and contingent being must be a reasonably realized possibility. Its possibility is grounded in the exemplary cause, its realisation in the efficient cause, but its reasonableness in the final cause."[9]

A deeper understanding of nature will reveal the fact that in nature we discern three levels of values. Freya Matthews identifies them as background value, intrinsic value and instrumental value. Matthews derives background value from the intrinsic value of the cosmos. The cosmos as a whole is considered as a self-maintaining self and as such possessing intrinsic value. The third level of instrumental value applies when something promotes the wellbeing of something else. Environmental ethics stems from such a value system that the universe possesses.[10] Ken Wilber corroborates this view when he writes: "Because human beings contain matter and life and mind, as components in their own make up, then of course we must honour all these holons,[11] not only for their own intrinsic worth, which is the most important, but also because they are components in our own being, and destroying them is literally suicidal for us."[12]

The earth with life abounding is a miraculous event and we cannot take it for granted or exploit it to satisfy our unlimited wants. Instead, as rational and spiritual beings, humans must grow in sensitivity to appreciate the value-laden character of nature with respect and learn to preserve it. We need to look for role models who lived their lives in tune with nature and promoted the need to preserve nature through their writings and actions.

Gandhi and Environmental Concerns

Mahatma Gandhi who played a stellar role in India's freedom struggle is also known for his views on the need to safeguard the environment. His main contribution lay in the fact that he bridged the gulf between the intelligentsia and the masses and widened the concept of *Swaraj*[13] to include almost every aspect of social, economic, moral, religious and environmental regeneration. When we delve deep into his thought and writings, we will immediately understand that he had insights and foresights that were quite bewildering. One is really appalled by his farsightedness so clearly and emphatically expressed in the *Hind Swaraj*[14] which was published a century ago in 1909 when few people talked of environmental problems and hazards. Similarly, one is overwhelmed by his grasp of the resultant human predicament and his ingenuity to suggest appropriate measures to root out the problem rather than search for a solution to control it. In this sense, he is prophetic.

It is true that Gandhi never explicitly spoke of environment protection. However, what he said and did make him an environmentalist. *Hind Swaraj* cautioned humankind against the unrestricted industrialisation and the resultant materialistic and consumerist worldview. He did not want India to follow the West in this regard and warned that if India, with its vast population, tried to imitate the West then the resources of the earth would not be enough. He argued that industrialisation and machines not only have an adverse effect on the health of people but also on the wellbeing of our planet.

Gandhi was of the view that humans exploited nature to the extent of disturbing its normal functioning. Dr J.C. Kumarappa, the enunciator of Gandhian economics, proffers the rationale behind it. He writes:

> Work in nature consists in the effort put forth by the various factors—insentient and sentient—which cooperate to complete this cycle of life. If this cycle is broken, at any stage, at any time, consciously or unconsciously, violence results as a consequence of such a break. When

> violence intervenes in this way, growth or progress is stopped, ending finally in destruction and waste. Nature is unforgiving and ruthless. Therefore, self-interest and self-preservation demand complete non-violence; cooperation and submission to the way of nature if we are to maintain permanency by non-interference with and by not short-circuiting the cycle of life.[15]

One of the root causes of this unchecked exploitation of nature, according to Gandhi, is consumerism and materialism. In fact, consumerism goes hand in hand with materialism. Materialism can be defined as a tendency to consider material possessions and physical comfort more important than spiritual values.[16] Consumerism, on the other hand, can be understood as a preoccupation with consumer goods and their acquisition. Thus, consumerism is concerned with the acquisition of, or the process of obtaining goods. To satiate the materialistic and consumerist urge of the modern society, nature had to be exploited to the point of its degradation.

All these result in a conflict between humans and nature. When the humans extract the resources from mother earth to meet their ever-increasing needs, the nature tries to maintain its stability. However, if the exploitation goes beyond a limit, nature is not able to maintain the balance and is unable to replenish and cure herself.[17] The notion that science and technology increase the quantity of good is a myth because the production of any good requires both natural resources and human-made factors of production. When we increase the productivity of labour, capital and organisation, we have to use more land or the available land intensively. Raw materials are also required but they come from nature. High-level technology requires more energy. Thus, nature is over-taxed.

This becomes all the more a pertinent issue in a capitalist economy, where the production is carried out purely with profit motive. The entrepreneurs go on increasing their production to maximise their profits. They utilise and exploit all the available resources both natural and human-made. But the reservoir of resources is limited.

Further, in the process of this large scale production, humans can pollute the environment unlike birds and animals, which do not degrade the environment. The wastes generated by the individuals and the industries are not properly processed and recycled; instead, they are thrown, often at random, in the open, thus, polluting the environment. We can enumerate different forms of pollution that have adverse effects not only on the humans but also on the environment: air pollution, water pollution, noise pollution, etc.

Thus the cost of modern form of development is disastrous. It disturbs and harms every form of life in the planet. It is in this context that Gandhi comes up with his model of development and a life style that can ensure the preservation of nature.

Gandhian Response to Environmental Crisis

Gandhi offers adequate responses to the environmental crisis, first in his book *Hind Swaraj* and later through his other writings, actions and of course, through his very life. *Hind Swaraj* termed modern contemporary industrial civilization as satanic. After a century of its publication, today more than ever, after experiencing the ill effects of environmental degradation, we can rightly state that Gandhi was right in his condemnation of the rapid industrialisation. At the time of its publication, many condemned the book as taking humankind to the pre-historic times. But the fact of the matter is that he was able to foresee the direction in which the industrial civilization and mechanization were moving. He held that the industrialised societies were becoming selfish, competitive and grossly destructive of nature. He held that the distinguishing characteristic of modern civilization was that it multiplied infinite number of wants in humans. Large scale industrial units had to be set up to satisfy the unlimited wants of the people. The raw materials to feed these industries have to be extracted from nature in large quantities which are non-renewable and hence depleting the resources at a pace much faster than nature can replenish. Against such a mistaken view of development Gandhi wrote: "civilization, in the real sense of the term, consists not in the multiplication but in the deliberate and voluntary reduction of wants."[18]

In the place of such large scale industrial enterprises and wanton consumerist outlook, Gandhi suggested a simple life-style based on physical labour.[19] He implored people to live in simplicity so that others as well as the future generations can also enjoy the bounty of nature. He believed that earth provides enough to satisfy every person's need but not every person's greed. The rich need to restrict their wants and consider themselves as mere trustees of their wealth and use it for the welfare of the poor. This can be done only if people can distinguish between their real needs and artificial wants and control the latter. In fact, he felt that "man falls from the pursuit of the ideal of plain living and high thinking the moment he wants to multiply his daily wants."[20]

Further, to satisfy all their wants, people have to forage far and wide for new materials and commodities. This also brings to the fore the concept of globalisation. The governments have to liberalize, privatise and effect structural adjustments in order to establish new industrial units in far away locations and transport the finished goods to satisfy the inordinate wants of the people. Against this fast globalizing world where capitalism is gradually becoming the order of the day, Gandhi proposed the concept of decentralization of means and resources. He advocated a model of economic development which talked of developing villages as an independent production and administrative unit.[21] This has become more relevant today in order to save us from the various economic, social, ethical and emotional hazards caused by the large scale industrialization and have become silent killers of the human race.

Introducing the concept of *swadeshi*, which in fact, he included as one of the eleven vows that he stipulated to his followers who lived in his *ashrams*, Gandhi attempted to counteract the harmful consequences of globalisation. The vow of *swadeshi* means the spirit, which restricts persons to the use of services available in the immediate surroundings to the exclusion of the more remote. In other words, it implies production for neighbours. However, he was quick to add: "A votary of *swadeshi* will never harbour ill-will towards the foreigner; he will not be actuated by antagonism towards anybody on earth.

Swadeshism is not a cult of hatred. It is a doctrine of selfless service that has its roots in the purest *ahimsa*, that is, love."[22] His idea of *swadeshi* if applied to the world at large with his theory of *antyodaya* (the last man) which speaks of providing every individual with the basic necessities can counteract the undesirable effects of globalization by ensuring that everyone benefits from the fruits of development.

In the place of large scale mechanisation,[23] Gandhi proposed labour intensive production. His emphasis on labour intensive production does not indicate that he was advocating obsolete machinery with less productivity. He was in favour of simple tools, which save individual labour and lighten the burden of millions of cottages.[24] While clarifying the role of machinery, he held that "mechanisation is good when the hands are few for the work intended to be accomplished. It is an evil when there are more hands than required for the works, as is the case in India. The problem is how to utilize their idle hours, which are equal to the working days of six months in the year."[25] He was against the craze for machinery in a labour-surplus economy like India and accepted the utilisation of modern tools and implements only if they help in reducing unnecessary human labour. He wanted the production by the masses and not mass production. According to Gandhi, "the saving of labour of the individual should be the object, and honest humanitarian considerations, and not greed, the motive."[26]

The World Development Report 1990 corroborated these Gandhian views on machinery. It advised the developing countries to adopt labour-intensive technique of production to create job opportunities. "Against the background of achievement, it is all the more staggering, shameful that more than one billion people in the developing world are living in poverty. Progress in raising average incomes, however welcome, must not distract attention from this massive and continuing burden of poverty."[27] For removal of poverty and unemployment, the Report was of the opinion that "rapid and politically sustainable progress on poverty has been achieved by pursuing a strategy that has two equally important elements. The first element is to promote the productive use of the poor's most abundant asset—labour. It calls for policies that harness market incentives, social and political institutions, infrastructure and technology to that end. Switching to an efficient, labour intensive pattern of development and investing more in the human capital of the poor are not only consistent with faster long-term growth; they contribute to it."[28] It was further noted "since labour is an abundant resource, encouraging its use is generally consistent with rapid and efficient growth."[29] Indian Planners are not unfamiliar with these views and suggestions as they were discussed by Gandhi over years ago, initially in *Hind Swaraj* and then in *Young India* and *Harijan* with special focus on Khadi and village industries. He stated "I have not contemplated, much less advised, the abandonment of a single, healthy, life-giving industrial activity for the sake of hand-spinning. The entire foundation of the spinning-wheel rests on the fact that there are crores of semi-unemployment people in India. The spinning wheel is destructive of no enterprise whatsoever. It is life-giving activity."[30]

The essence of the Gandhian approach to technological progress lies in the fact that we need to treat nature as a friend and benefactor. This approach is opposite to what has been practised so far in the name of technology. All decentralized technological systems which make use of nature's in-built processes demand a pattern different from the way technology is used in the present day capitalistic model of production. If we can introduce appropriate technology[31] that fits small-scale, grassroots and community-centred rural masses, then they can become the harbingers of advancement, leading development that is eco-friendly. The patterns of income distribution, inequality, poverty and unemployment still exist today as they were when Gandhi advocated the spinning wheel as a panacea for all ills. Hence, we can say that his emphasis on Khadi and village industries was not a temporary measure, but a permanent solution to overcome the root problems of poverty and unemployment in India without harming the environment.

In advocating the simplicity of life-style, Gandhi was influenced by the *Isavasya Upanishadic* dictum: renounce to enjoy. It means that in order to enjoy life, one cannot be selfishly attached to money, possessions, power or prestige, even family or friends. The moment one is selfishly attached, he/she becomes a prisoner. Hence Gandhi believed that one is allowed to enjoy the resources of nature without being attached to them. This is because the humans are not the real owners of the natural resources and hence have no right to exploit them. Instead, they can use them for their requirements leaving the rest for others.

Thus, Gandhi proposed a voluntary reduction of wants. If this mad rush for industrialization and globalisation consists in multiplication of wants, the only alternative is in reduction of wants voluntarily. People need to realise the importance of simplicity of life and the simplification of the machinery of living. Since Gandhi believed that one must be the change that one wants to see in the world, he practised simplicity in his own life. His life was his message. He opted for voluntary simplicity to end over-consumption. He held that consuming more than one's need would ultimately be at the expense of earth's resources. Thus, for example, he used scrapes of papers to write brief notes and used envelops for sending letters.[32] Even when he used to bathe in the free flowing Sabarmati river, he was conscious to use only the minimum water needed for taking bath. However, he did not equate simple living with abject poverty. In fact, he believed that to deny a person the ordinary amenities of life is far worse than starving the body. It is also starving the soul which dwells in the body. He wanted poverty to be eradicated and that can be done only when everyone uses only his/her share without grabbing what belong to others. He believed in the principle justice where everyone is entitled to his/her due. He also championed the cause of social justice wherein he believed that everyone deserves equal economic, political and social rights and opportunities.

Gandhi stressed the significance of recycling of resources. A sustainable society has to aim at working in partnership with nature and conserve resources and energy, reduce wastes and avoid degradation of renewable resources. It should produce goods that are easy to recycle, reuse and repair after use. The methods of growing food and raising livestock have to be based on the use of soil and water conservation, bio-fertilizers and biological control of pests. The society should largely be a solar/wind/bio-mass based society together with a whole range of environment friendly technologies mainly based on renewable resources. Even these resources should be utilized prudently and the basic needs of people are to be met without any serious detriment to the environment. Gandhi also believed that non-violence and compassion are not to be practised only towards living beings, but also towards inanimate materials. Overuse of the latter, motivated by greed and the desire for undue profit at the expense of biosphere, is also violence, since it deprives others of the use of such materials.

Gandhi advocated an ecology that concerns itself with the interrelationship of living organisms, plants, animals or humans and their environments. Every form of development that alleviates the poverty of the masses should be in tune with nature. Gandhi believed that so long as humans cooperate with nature and help natural life cycle, the nature is benevolent to the requirements of the humans. He recognised the fact that human being is only a part of nature. So if he/she removes the part from the interrelationship then it will be self-destructive. In fact, Gandhi, in his life, developed an affinity with plants[33] and animals[34] to the extent that he revered them.

Gandhi's environmentalism was based on various ethical principles that he promoted to attain his political, economic social and religious ideals. Some of these principles include truth, non-violence, non-stealing, non-possession, celibacy, bread-labour, hygiene, *Swadeshi*, control of the palate, simplicity, introspection, prayer, meditation and fasting. Through these, he controlled himself by himself, because, being a *yogi*, he had complete control over his body and mind. He did not preach anything that he did not practise himself. Other ideals that he worked for were emancipation and empowerment of women, and the welfare of poorer sections of the society. All these ideals that he adopted for himself and for his followers ultimately gave him an internationally acclaimed acceptance as a great pacifist, a democrat, a defender of rights and privileges of downtrodden and of women, and an ardent advocate of environmental protection.

Conclusion

The significance of Gandhi as an environmentalist lies not in his vision and his right understanding of man-nature relationship, rather in his honest efforts to translate his precepts in actual life. His entire life viewed as an ecological treatise. His was one life in which every minute act, emotion or thought functioned much like an ecosystem: his small meals of nuts and fruits, his morning ablutions and everyday bodily practices, his periodic observances of silence, his morning walks, his cultivation of the small as much as of the big, his spinning wheel, his abhorrence of waste, his resorting to basic Hindu and Jain values of truth, nonviolence, celibacy and fasting were all exercised in tune with nature. He was able to motivate his followers to do the same. His Phoenix and Tolstoy Farms in South Africa can testify to it. His *ashrams* in India too bear the same trait. Although he eulogised the village life, it pained him to see the poverty, illiteracy and unsanitary conditions in Indian villages. Self-sufficiency of villages, promotion of small scale and cottage industries, control on the import of goods from outside, improvement in agricultural production, etc., are some of the ways that he envisaged in order to develop the villages. It is also important to note that the moralists, nonviolent activists, feminists, journalists, social reformers, trade union leaders, peasants, prohibitionists, nature-cure lovers and environmentalists take their inspiration from Gandhi's life and writings. Unfortunately, the environmentalists of today engage themselves in giving scholarly lectures and writing research papers and books on the subject. However, we can easily discern their motives—often to be prominent or for their political ambitions. This does not mean that there are no environmentalists who are activists in their own right. Gandhi, on the other hand, attempted to carry the message to the masses through the very life that he led. Hardly any political leader of his stature in the world had ever devoted so much of time and energy on these problems with so much sincerity and dedication. This is what made him an environmentalist with a difference.

Notes

1. Environmental crisis can be understood as a dramatic, unexpected, and irreversible worsening of the environment leading to significant welfare losses. Environmental crisis can adversely affect climate, conservation of species, natural resources, energy, health, soil, population, water, air, etc. which can have baneful consequences that are difficult to reverse. In his book, *Sacred Groves among Communities*, J.J. Roy Burman lists some of the environmental crisis and the reasons for them. He writes: "Today we are faced with an environmental crisis of massive proportions. The crisis of the environment involves not merely isolated and particular problems such as the pollution of our lakes, rivers, the smog of our cities and the devastating effect of pesticides on our food. It involves a threat to life on this planet and quality of this life. Alternations of the environment can destroy, and are destroying in many cases, the balance of nature, which sustains that life system. The causes of this crisis are multitude: the misuse of technology to pollute, excessive proliferation of human species, and ignorance of causal relationships in nature. The basic underlying causes of this crisis are mistaken values and attitudes." J.J. Roy Burman, *Sacred Groves among Communities* (New Delhi: Mittal Publications, 2003). According to another study, it is estimated that some 35,000 vegetal and animal species were lost by the year 2000. Tropical forests are shrinking by 11 million hectares per year. As estimated 26 billion tonnes of topsoil on croplands is lost annually in excess of new soil formation. Some 6 million hectares of new desert are formed annually by land mismanagement. Underground watertables are falling in most parts of the world and some 59 pesticides contaminate groundwater in 32 American States. About 2,500 toxic wastes need cleaning in the United States alone. It is estimated that 1.7 billion people lack access to clean water. The list is endless. And this calls for urgent responses to avert the looming environmental degradation. It becomes all the more pertinent when we consider the fact that the human being, the crown of creation, is responsible for the ill health of our planet.
2. Christoph Stueckelberger, *We All are Guests on Earth: A Global Christian Vision for Climate Justice* (Bangalore: Dharmaram Publications, 2010) 21-22.
3. Many people may not consider Gandhi as an environmentalist. This is because the environmental problems surfaced largely in

the post-Gandhian era. Although the concern for environment has assumed importance only in recent years, Gandhi made substantial contributions to the preservation of the environment through his writings, actions and by his very life. The present article is meant to understand these contributions made by Gandhi to our environment.

4. In fact, Descartes made mathematics "the measure of the inquiring mind," and he pursued a method of doubt not because he was a sceptic but because "he posits the mathematical as the absolute ground and seeks for all knowledge a foundation that will be in accord with it." In mathematics, Descartes finds "the very first and highest basic principle for the Being of beings in general." Peter J. Leithart, Farewell to Descartes? 27 February 2011. Http://www.credenda.org/index.php/Theology/farewell-to-descartes.html, accessed on 11 November 2012.
5. S. Arokiasamy, "Ecological Ethics in a Divided World," *Jeevadhara,* 21 (1991) 485.
6. Felix Wilfred, "Toward an Inter-religious Eco-theology," *Concilium* (2009/3) 52.
7. Thomas Manickam, "Holistic Ethics and Global Environmental Crises," *Journal of Dharma*, 33 (2008) 2, 129.
8. Joseph Peruma, *The Motherly Earth: An Ecological Ethics of Human-Nature Relationship* (Bangalore: Claretian Publications, 2002) 65.
9. B. Lonergan, *Insight: A Study of Human Understanding* (London: Darton Longman and Todd, 1983) 657.
10. Freya Matthews, *The Ecological Self* (London: Routledge, 1994) 118.
11. Holon is something that is simultaneously a whole and a part. The word was coined by Arthur Koestler in his book *The Ghost in the Machine.*
12. Ken Wilber, *A Brief History of Everything* (Boston: Shambhala, 1996) 38.
13. *Swaraj* means 'Self-Rule' or 'Self-Government.'
14. *Hind Swaraj* or *Indian Home Rule* was written during his voyage from England to South Africa on board *SS Kildonan Castle* between 13 November and 30 November 1909. Gandhi was disappointed at the failure of his second deputation to London meant to settle amicably the issues concerning the Indians living in South Africa. But he was determined to fight to the bitter end the battle of *satyagraha.* He was also appalled by the revolutionary views held by the Indian anarchists. While in the ship, under the impulse of a sudden inspiration, Gandhi hurried to the warm lounge,

pulled out some of the ship's stationery and began to write as one possessed. Within ten days he had covered 275 sheets with 30,000 Gujarati words of *Hind Swaraj*. It is a severe condemnation of modern civilization. The book is divided into twenty chapters dealing with *swaraj*, civilization, lawyers, doctors, machinery, education, passive resistance, etc. In the book, besides advocating the gospel of love in the place of hatred, he makes a scathing attack on modern civilization which is bereft of moral values and machinery, especially the craze for labour-saving machinery. The present article, with its focus on Gandhian perspectives on environmental ethics, is interested more in the condemnation of both modern civilization and the craze for machinery. For a reading of the book, *cf.*, M.K. Gandhi, *Hind Swaraj* or *Indian Home Rule*, 11th reprint (Ahmedabad: Navajivan Publishing House, 1996).

15. J.C. Kumarappa, *Economy of Permanence*, 5th edn. (Varanasi: Sarva Seva Sangh Prakashan, 1984) 2.
16. Oxford English Reference Dictionary, 2nd edn, 2002.
17. For example, if someone smokes in a closed room, people will feel suffocated but if he/she smokes in the open, then people will not feel suffocated. This is because the dirt gets dispersed in the atmosphere. It is cleared in the atmosphere and it gets dissipated with the good air. This means that nature has the power to dissipate the dirt and make it immobilized. But if we persistently emit the same effluent without allowing the nature to recoup herself, then the nature gets polluted.
18. Prabhu and Rao, (eds.), *Mind of Mahatma Gandhi*, 3rd edn. (Ahmedabad: Navajivan Publishing House, 1968) 189. Henceforth, Prabhu.
19. In fact, Gandhi called it as bread-labour, which is one of the vows that he stipulated for his followers who lived in his *ashrams* and took part in the Satyagraha movement. This was first stressed by a Russian writer named T.M. Bondaref. Leo Tolstoy gave it wide publicity. By bread-labour, Gandhi meant that to live human beings must work. The *Gita* enjoins in the third chapter that one who eats without offering sacrifice eats stolen food. Sacrifice here, according to Gandhi, can only mean bread-labour. If all had worked for their bread, then all distinctions of rank would be obliterated. The worldwide conflict between the capital and the labour, between the rich and the poor would cease to exist. The rich will be there but they would consider themselves to be only trustees of their property and would use it mainly in the public

interest. *Cf.* M.K. Gandhi, *From Yeravda Mandir: Ashram Observances*, trans., Valji Govindji (Ahmedabad: Navajivan Publishing House, 1932) 22. This vow also implies that every type of work is important. "No work that is done in His name and dedicated to Him is small. All work when so done assumes equal merit. A scavenger who works in His service shares equal distinction with a king who uses his gifts in His name and as a mere trustee." *Cf. Young India*, 25-11-1926; as cited by M.K. Gandhi, *India of My Dreams*, 6th reprint (Ahmedabad: Navajivan Publishing House, 1997) 63.

20. Prabhu, 490.
21. Writing in *Harijan* 26-7-1942, Gandhi presented his vision of an ideal village. "My idea of Village *swaraj* is that it is a complete republic, independent of its neighbours for its wants, and yet interdependent for many others in which dependence is a necessity. Thus every village's first concern will be to grow its own food crops and cotton for its cloth. It should have a reserve for its cattle, recreation and playground for adults and children. Then if there is more land available, it will grow useful money crops, thus excluding *ganja*, tobacco, opium and the like. The village will maintain a village theatre, school and public hall. It will have its own waterworks ensuring clean supply. This can be done through controlled wells and tanks. Education will be compulsory up to the final basic course. As far as possible every activity will be conducted on the co-operative basis. There will be no castes such as we have today with their graded Untouchability. Non-violence with its technique of *satyagraha* and non-co-operation will be the sanction of the village community. There will be a compulsory service of village guards who will be selected by rotation from the register maintained by the village. The government of the village will be conducted by the Panchayat of five persons, annually elected by the adult villagers, male and female, possessing minimum prescribed qualifications. These will have all the authority and jurisdiction required. Since there will be no system of punishments in the accepted sense, this Panchayat will be the legislature, judiciary and executive combined to operate for its year of office. Any village can become such a republic today without much interference, even from the present Government whose sole effective connection with the villages is the exaction of the village revenue. I have not examined here the question of relations with the neighbouring villages and the centre if any. My purpose is to present an outline of village government.

Here there is perfect democracy based upon individual freedom. The individual is the architect of his own government. The law of non-violence rules him and his government. He and his village are able to defy the might of a world. For the law governing every villager is that he will suffer death in the defence of his and his village's honour."

22. *From Yeravda Mandir*, (1957), p. 66; as cited by Gandhi, M.K. Gandhi, *The Selected Works of Mahatma Gandhi: The Voice of Truth*, (ed.), Shriman Narayan, Vol. 6, 4th reprint (Ahmedabad: Navajivan Publishing House, 1997) 339; Emphasis in the original.
23. To look at Gandhi in the context of technology is to understand that he was a man who had his doubts on large scale mechanisation introduced by the modern civilization. In fact, he wanted to look beyond it. When Gandhi was asked "Do you hate machines?" Gandhi answered: "No. While my body itself is nothing but meticulous machinery, how can I dismiss it? My spinning wheel or even this toothpick, for that matter, is a machine. I hate not the machines, but this growing passion for machines. I hate the passion for the machines which work upon diminishing manpower. Some talk about machine which could spare man power when thousands of people are thrown jobless on the streets. Yes, I want the human toil and time to be spared not just for a sect of people but for the humanity. I want the wealth to be accumulated not just in few hands but for all the people in the world. Today machines favour putting handful of people on top thousands." Similarly, Gandhi was not against modernization. He was against worshipping technology as a lord of salvation. As he thought salvation can never be brought from outside but attained internally. When one's soul is intoxicated by greed, Gandhi thought technology inevitably represents it. Further, he was not unaware of the role of tools in human upliftment. In fact, he had great curiosity towards tools. He had accepted many of the modern technological inventions not as a compromise but as a necessity. Thus, he travelled on trains, buses and ships. He once studied mechanism of propeller from the motor room while travelling on a ship to England. He reached out to the public through loudspeakers and printing machines.
24. Gandhi, M.K., *Young India*, 16-6-1926.
25. Gandhi, M.K., *Harijan*, 16-5-1936.
26. M.K. Gandhi, *The Collected Works of Mahatma Gandhi*, Vol. 25 (New Delhi: Publication Division, Ministry of Information and Broadcasting, Government of India, 1967), 252.

27. *World Development Report 1990* (New York: Oxford University Press, 1990), 10.
28. World Development Report 3.
29. World Development Report 56.
30. *Young India*, 27-5-1926.
31. Appropriate technology is an ideological movement originally articulated as 'intermediate technology' by the economist Dr E.F. Schumacher in his influential work, *Small is Beautiful.* It is considered sustainable as it requires fewer natural resources and produces less pollution than techniques from mainstream technology, which are often wasteful and environmentally polluting. Gandhi too advocated this form of small, local and mostly village-based technology to help India's villages become self reliant, resisting the dependence associated with colonialism and to aid in the freedom struggle against British.
32. An anecdote that explains Gandhi's meticulous use of things and the respect he owed to people who generously contributed to him for his cause is given. Soon after Gandhi's return from South Africa, a meeting of the Congress was held in Bombay. Kaka Saheb Kalelkar went there to help. One day Kaka Saheb found Gandhi anxiously searching around his desk. "What's the matter? What are you looking for?" Kaka Saheb asked. "I've lost my little pencil," answered Gandhi. Kaka Saheb was upset to see Gandhi wasting time and worrying about a little pencil. He took out his pencil and offered it to him. "No, no, I want my own little pencil," Gandhi insisted like a stubborn child. "Well, use it for the time being," said Kaka Saheb. "I'll find your pencil later. Don't waste time looking for it now." "You don't understand. That little pencil is very precious to me," Gandhi insisted. "Natesan's little son gave it to me in Madras. He gave it with so much love and affection. I cannot bear to lose it." Kaka Saheb didn't argue any more. He joined Gandhi in the search. At last they found it—a tiny piece, barely two inches long. But Gandhi was delighted to get it back. To him it was no ordinary pencil. It was the token of a child's love and to Gandhi a child's love was very precious.
33. Gandhi loved trees and did not make any adverse comments against tree worship. He wrote: "even so far from seeing anything inherently evil or harmful in tree worship, I find in it a thing instinct with a deep pathos and poetic beauty. It symbolises true reverence for the entire vegetable kingdom, which with its endless panorama of beautiful shapes and forms, declares to us as it were with a million tongues the greatness and glory of God.

Without vegetation our planet would not be able to support life even for a moment. In such a country, especially, therefore, in which there is a scarcity of trees, tree worship assumes a profound economic significance." *Young India*, 26-09-1929. To show Gandhi's love and respect for plants, the following incident is in order. While imprisoned in Yeravda Jail together Kaka Kalelkar, one day Gandhi suffered from a bad toothache. One night, he asked his friend to collect some leaves of the margosa plant so that he could crush them and put it between the teeth in order to ease the pain. To his utter dismay, Kaka Kalelkar brought a large branch of the tree. Gandhi was moved to tears. He complained that when he wanted only four leaves why did Kaka bring the whole branch that too at night while the tree is sleeping.

34 Gandhi extended his non-violence to sub-human living species, especially the animals. He abjured from eating meat and avoided animal food in any form. Gandhi once observed that the greatness of a nation and its moral progress can be judged by the way its animals are treated. To seek to reduce the suffering of those who are completely under one's domination and unable to fight back, is truly a mark of a civilized society. However, Gandhi was not fanatical. Once, with the approval of Gandhi, the Municipality killed some 60 stray dogs—some of them rabid. Gandhi received many angry letters accusing him of being violent. Gandhi in a series of articles in *Navajivan* and later in *Young India* explained the parameters of *ahimsa* in practice. "Taking life might be a duty under certain circumstances. Man destroyed plant life in order to sustain himself. He killed mosquitoes, and carnivorous beasts, which pestered villagers. Even a man who had gone mad and killed others needed to be killed. The fact is that *ahimsa* does not simply mean non-killing. *Himsa* means causing pain to or killing any life out of anger or for a selfish purpose, or with the intention of causing injury. Refraining from so doing is *ahimsa*." Sushila Nayar, *Mahatma Gandhi, Salt Satyagraha—The Watershed*, Vol. 6 (Ahmedabad: Navajivan Publishing House, 1995) 36.

References

Arokiasamy, S. "Ecological Ethics in a Divided World." *Jeevadhara* 21 (1991) 484-498.

Burman, J.J. Roy. *Sacred Groves among Communities.* New Delhi: Mittal Publications, 2003.

Gandhi, M.K. *From Yeravda Mandir: Ashram Observances.* Trans. Valji Govindji. Ahmedabad: Navajivan Publishing House, 1932.

Gandhi, M.K. *India of My Dreams.* 6th reprint. Ahmedabad: Navajivan Publishing House, 1997.

Gandhi, M.K. *The Collected Works of Mahatma Gandhi.* Vol. 25. New Delhi: Publications Division, Ministry of Information & Broadcasting, Government of India, 1967.

Gandhi, M.K. *The Selected Works of Mahatma Gandhi—The Voice of Truth.* Ed. Shriman Narayan. Vol. 6. 4th reprint. Ahmedabad: Navajivan Publishing House, 1997.

Gandhi, M.K., *Hind Swaraj* or *Indian Home Rule.* 11th reprint. Ahmedabad: Navajivan Publishing House, 1996.

Kumarappa, J. C. *Economy of Permanence.* 5th edn. Varanasi: Sarva Seva Sangh Prakashan, 1984.

Leithart, Peter J. *Farewell to Descartes?* 27 February 2011. Http://www.credenda.org/index.php/Theology/farewell-to-descartes.html, accessed on 11 November 2012.

Lonergan, B. *Insight: A Study of Human Understanding.* London: Darton Longman and Todd, 1983.

Manickam, Thomas. "Holistic Ethics and Global Environmental Crises." *Journal of Dharma,* 33 (2008) 2, 111-132.

Matthews, Freya. *The Ecological Self.* London: Routledge, 1994.

Nayar, Sushila. *Mahatma Gandhi, Salt Satyagraha—The Watershed.* Vol. 6. Ahmedabad: Navajivan Publishing House, 1995.

Oxford English Reference Dictionary. 2nd edn. 2002. Peruma, Joseph. *The Motherly Earth: An Ecological Ethics of Human Nature Relationship.* Bangalore: Claretian Publications, 2002.

Prabhu and Rao. (Eds.) *Mind of Mahatma Gandhi.* 3rd edn. Ahmedabad: Navajivan Publishing House, 1968.

Stueckelberger, Christoph. *We All are Guests on Earth: A Global Christian Vision for Climate Justice.* Bangalore: Dharmaram Publications, 2010.

Wilber, Ken. *A Brief History of Everything.* Boston: Shambhala, 1996.

Wilfred, Felix. "Toward an Inter-religious Eco-theology." *Concilium* (2009/3) 43-54.

World Development Report 1990. New York: Oxford University Press, 1990.

6

Environmental Ethics

Theory and Practice

Xavier Mao

The term environmental ethics is of recent origin. Scholars throughout the world in general and philosophers in particular have started talking about environment and environmental ethics. In what follows, I wish to clarify and expel certain confusions that becloud environmental ethics. Further in this connection, I wish to discuss and eliminate certain confusion relating to the idea of environmental ethics. In other words, this chapter is two fold; both positive and negative. In its negative aspect, I wish to dispel certain confusion that relate to the topic and its positive dimension I wish to explore various dimensions of environmental ethics in the context of north-east.

Types of Environment: Natural, political and social. In context of environmental ethics, by environment we usually mean natural or physical environment. But this is not an adequate understanding of environment. It is true that natural environment is the basic and primary, that is, to say without natural environment or nature, social and political environment will be meaningless. Therefore, it is necessary to understand environment so as to include both political and social environment within its fold.

Natural environment or nature is given to us that is to say we have not created nature. On the other hand, social and political environment are created by human beings. An individual is as much a part of political and social environment as humans are the part of nature. Political and social environment recreates human being. In other words, a human being is recreated by coming in contact with social and political order, the uncreated part of a person is our physical body but physical body becomes meaningless unless it comes in contact with social and political institutions. Institutions grow, change and evolve. What is called civilization or culture is the outcome of the contact of an individual with these institutions. It has taken thousands of years for social and political institutions to grow. Development and progress is measured only with reference to social and political environment.

Though human being is a part of nature, civilization or culture has grown in contact with physical environment from time immemorial. It is true that ancient people began their life as a food gatherer. Hunting and killing of animals for food emerged at a later stage. Settled agriculture replaced food gathering stage. Cultivation of land, planting of trees and rearing animals for various purposes introduced a new stage in human history. Human being's dependence on nature for food, shelter and survival made him/her conscious of the physical world. Perhaps, this is how gradually human being treated certain rivers, waterbodies, trees, animals, the sun, the moon and certain stars as sacred. This type of attitude towards nature is found almost in all societies whether tribal or non-tribal. It may be not out of place to mention in this context that the distinction between tribal and non-tribal is of recent origin. As a matter of fact, each one of us must have had tribal ancestry in history of civilization. Therefore, it can be said in this connection that tribal and non-tribal is not a distinction *per se*. We have made this distinction at a particular social and political development for our own purposes. There is nothing intrinsic in a tribal as a tribal. Similarly, there is nothing intrinsic in the so called entitled to that status. As a matter of fact in historical period of time some people occupied the plain land in the river basins whereas the other groups were driven out to forest, mountainous and hilly regions. This process has taken place more or less in a similar way throughout the world. Therefore, tribal and tribalism do not stand for any set of intrinsic characteristics.

As I stated earlier in this chapter humans have been conscious of natural environment from the very beginning whether at the food gathering stage or at the stage of hunting animals for food or at the stage of settled agriculture. The early human has developed a kind of reverential attitude towards nature. It may not be out of place to mention in this connection that the ancient Indian treated waterbodies as very sacred. Accordingly in Indian mythology oceans are vast bodies of water and they are classified into milk, curd, ghee, honey and even wine. It is preparation of annual *anamanag* (calculation). Indians predict intensity of rain and thunder referring to their vast bodies such as milk, honey, *ghee*, etc. Further, the Hindu mythology characterizes ocean of milk as the bedroom of Lord Vishnu in the bed of great Cobra. Further if we look at the list of incarnation ancient Indian treated creations living in water as the first incarnation of God. God incarnates from time to time. The first incarnation that God assumes is fish, second incarnation tortoise, and third incarnation is wild boar. This is how ancient Indian treated certain animals as sacred. In due course of time utilitarian consideration made them adopt worshipful attitude towards other animals like cows, cobra, certain trees like pipal, banyan, neem; rivers like the Ganges, the Yamuna, the Godaveri, the Sindhu, the Indus, the Narmada, Kaveri; and mountains like the Himalayas, the Kailash, the Vindhyas were treated as sacred. Such phenomena took place in the mainland India. Even the so called tribal living in the bush and hilly regions treated certain forested areas as sacred in Khasi Hills. Other tribal like Nagas and Mizos have mythology of furious animals like tiger having common ancestry with human beings and spirits. This clearly shows the primitive man has reverential attitude towards physical environment. In Indian tradition there is elaborate description of offering even to animals and birds.

With the advent of modern science and technology human being began to exploit and use nature to their benefit. Gradually, forests were depleted of trees, waterbodies contaminated and certain animal became extinct. Consumerism became the slogan of the day. In other words, modern science and technology has not destroyed nature but created consumerist culture, this has created dilemma before human being throughout the world. If consumerism is allowed without any restriction, physical environment is bound to be destroyed. Now what is to be done? Developed countries like the U.S.A, U.K. Germany, France and certain other Eastern European countries managed somehow the balance. They have kept the rivers Rhine, Thames, etc., clean. On the other hand, practically all Indian rivers are highly polluted. Yamuna river flowing Delhi areas is a telling example. Its water has not only become undrinkable but the area where it flows has become extremely polluted and nobody knows when things will change. So far as nature as sacred the attitude of both tribal and non-tribal is more or less the same. Reverential attitude to nature, they did not develop an ethical theory or philosophy of environment. Perhaps it is not inappropriate to say that our ancestors have developed a kind of environmental ethics. I wish to point out in this connection that our ancestors have strong moral sense towards nature or environment. In this sense, environmental ethics is of recent talks. When crisis started to develop, philosophers and intellectuals talk of environmental ethics. It is very necessary in this connection to highlight a very important distinction between morals and ethics. A moral person practicing moral attitude towards others including nature may not be a moral philosopher. Similarly a moral philosopher may be absolutely an immoral person. Some eminent philosophers in Indian Universities doing ethics made it clear that there is no affinity between moral philosophy and morality. In other words, an absolutely immoral person may do very good moral philosophy. But I wish to suggest in this connection that this attitude has made moral philosophy sterile and barren. Moral philosophy is not like physics or mathematics. A very good mathematician or a physicist may live an immoral life and yet it may not have an impact on his intellectual exercise. In the case of a moral philosopher leading an immoral life will have very bad impact in society. In this connection saying and doing or thought and action are required to go together. A physicist can afford to be immoral but a moral philosopher cannot afford to lead an immoral life.

In spite of grand ideas about the relationship between man and nature in India the natural environment is decaying very fast. Perhaps in no other country such elaborate rituals are performed towards nature. The Himalaya like other rivers is treated as sacred but due to mindless felling of trees in the region the Gangotri glacier belt has receded several kilometres. On the other hand, in the western countries such grand theories and ideas about nature are not available but they are working very hard to preserve nature. As a matter of fact, the rate of deforestation and degradation of the environment is relatively small in western countries even including China. Indians are very expert in creating theories about nature but in practice they just do the reverse. Deforestation even in tribal areas of India is very high. Rapid increase in population is one of the main reasons for this and concurrent callous attitude towards it is another reason for environmental degeneration. Both the tribal and non-tribal people stand on the same footing in this connection. I wish to point out that this is a paradoxical situation; Indians have superb and unparalleled theory building and ideas. But as regard practice they stand no where. There is wide gap or big hiatus between theory and practice in India. In Western civilization, this gap is minimal. Some overenthusiastic scholars in this country who are doing environmental ethics refer to some biblical message pointing out that the *Bible* encourages destruction and exploitation of environment, they quote wrongly or interpret wrongly on *Genesis*, Chapter I, verse 28 which only says about human's stewardship of the fish, the birds and all the wild animals.

According to these scholars Christianity *ipso facto* encourages mindless exploitation of environment, this may or may not be true but the Christians and westerners are much ahead of protecting and preserving the environment. So the ideas and theories may be the begin-all but cannot be regarded as end-all. This is the reason why in certain section of Indian tradition, great scholars are too-too ridiculed, if they have gap between theory and practice in their life. One may be a great scholar, but one may not be a great human being. As a matter of fact many great people were either illiterate or semi-educated in the formal sense of education.

It may be necessary in this connection to point out that folklores, folktales, myths, legends and mythology may be studied and researched into but unless the good ideas contained in it are put into practice, the study becomes counter-productive. Some scholars are overwhelmed by the rich traditions of folklore and folktales of tribal people. They claim that such a study will help to decipher the tribal worldview including their harmonious relationship to nature. The study is meaningful if it is conducted for the sake of scholarship and providing guidance for good living. But it is irrelevant to the protection and preservation of environment if practice is ignored. In my after serious reflection it is unfathomable greed combined with consumerist passion that led to environmental degradation among tribal and non-tribal alike. Time has come to recognize and remember the distinction between need and greed and seriously follow it. Without such adherence the earth cannot afford to meet the greed of even a section of people. Today tribal or non-tribal are all swayed away by greed. This is one of the main reasons of environmental degradation, as human greed is paramount and unfathomable.

I have already pointed out here that the concept environment includes both natural surrounding and political and social setting. In nutshell, there are three dimensions which constitute the concept environment. Therefore, while discussing environmental ethics, one should take note of both political and social dimensions. Perhaps the social environment of humankind in general is degenerating from time to time. The various wars and warfare that took place in ancient days in the world are much less than what is happening in the so-called modern world. The two world wars had stood testimony to it. Despite science and technological development and explosion of knowledge almost in all fields, man has become almost degenerated. Terrorism including religious fundamentalism is almost the order of the day. The amount spent in war preparedness and manufacture of costly and deadly weapons were unthinkable in the ancient days. The report published by UNESCO tells us that one-third number of populated people of the entire population in the world go to bed at night with empty stomach. Philosopher B. Russell vehemently argued for reduction of military expenditure. But no country paid any heed to it, as a result poverty, illiteracy; hunger and undernourishment go on increasing multifold. Of late we witness the emergence of Nasal violence by the Maoist in certain parts of the country in Andhra Pradesh, Orissa, Chattisgarh, Jharkhand and West Bengal reveals another dimension of our degenerated social and political disorder. The governments in these States including the high officials treat the violence perpetrated by Maoist as mere law and order problem which is a complete misunderstanding of the social and political problem. In the recent past in a press conference, One D.G.P. from one of the Maoist affected States argued that to solve the Maoist problem, the number of D.G.Ps should be increased to the equal number of districts in a State. I wish to point out in this connection that Maoist problem is not basically and primarily a law and order problem as argued earlier. Perhaps in due course of time, it assumes that colour. It may not be out of place to mention certain blatant facts from the Maoist affected States. People from the plains have purchased almost all lands belonging to tribal people. Clean drinking water is not available, as a result of cholera, diarrhoea and typhoid are very common in these areas. Primary schools are there but no teachers go to schools. Doctors are appointed by the government but do not join in the dispensary or hospitals. Doctors prefer to do their lucrative business in the plains. Motorable roads in the villages are almost like a dream, the supporters of Maoist movements have openly made these statements. Some supporters were arrested and jailed but subsequently acquitted of all the charges by High Court. Therefore, it is abundantly clear that Maoist movement is not primarily a law and order problem. It is primarily a social and economical problem. Politicians and people in the government are responsible for it. This type of political and social problem will destabilize the State and society. While Gandhi was struggling for independence of India an impressive idea went round that politics begins and ends with social service. But today in India politics is a very profitable and lucrative job. All facilities, benefits, lump sum pensions and other benefits are available for politicians. Such huge benefits and perks have encouraged and inspired some politicians in India to create dynastic rule in politics. Some astute politicians are very cleverly sending their family members into politics. Days are not far off, when political dynasty will be erected and replaced hereditary monarchy. Mushrooming of political parties is pointer in this direction. Disgruntled politicians are floating new political parties to fight the elections. Service to the nation and people has been pushed to the back gear. In the sixties Jayaprakash Narayan advocated partyless democracy but this message of J. Narayan has gone unheeded. Political power holds the key to economic power and with political party access to political power becomes much easier. The amount of black money that some people have including some politicians if taken away and used for the elimination of poverty would be a great improvement for the social environment of India. So much black money can lead to destabilization of any society. The advocates and practitioners of environmental ethics have not taken note of these facts.

To conclude, I wish to maintain the following: 1. Environment is wide and all inclusive term. 2. Environmental ethics should not come to end with philosophical and conceptual discussion. 3. We should put it into practice. Lastly, to quote Gautam Buddha's statement, "right understanding lead to right knowledge and right knowledge lead to liberation and emancipation" should be our guideline while doing research in environmental ethics and seminars on it.

7

Ecological Crisis and the Tribal Worldview

A Heideggerian Review

Karilemla

This chapter is a review of Heidegger's environmental philosophy and his philosophical critique of the dichotomies of modernity. Heidegger holds that since Descartes' discovery of the cogito, the modern subject has become determinative for the certainty of the realities of the objects as well. The Cartesian subject is a disengaged agent, able to reach certain knowledge of reality outside it, without any practical engagement with the world. Consequently, the modern subject becomes fundamentally disconnected from the earth. Therefore, in order to overcome this subject-object dichotomy, we need to reimagine our way of dwelling on the earth, our being-in-the-world. For Heidegger, the most ontological description of the subject is being-in-the-world. Our primordial way of accessing the world is through our involvement and interaction with the entities in the world unlike the disconnected and disengaged Cartesian subject. Heidegger notes that our forgetfulness of the engaged, embodied, worldly self, and our primordial way of accessing the world leads to contemporary environmental crisis. Hence, in this chapter, my aim is to show that for such reimagining of 'dwelling on the earth', the tribal worldview can be considered as a regulative model in fundamental respects.

I begin by showing how Heidegger turned the epistemological perspective from the disengaged agent to that of the engaged, worldly, embodied Dasein. Then I proceed to show how this changed perspective challenges the destructive nature of modern humans to planet earth and how Heidegger argues in contradistinction to this account of knowledge of the traditional metaphysics. In the second section, I discuss Heidegger's analytic of Dasein as being-in-the-world. The Heideggerian conception of the human being as being-in-the-world is understood as the referential totality of significance. For him, 'world' is the referential whole of the subject's involvements, and not the sum total of discrete objects. The analysis of Dasein as 'being in' the world and the fact that Dasein's disposing itself towards the world, the wholeness, within which it already finds itself is of importance to locate Heidegger's critique of the technological disconnection of modern humans from the earth and his understanding of dwelling upon the earth. In the last section of this chapter, I want to look at the tribal worldview of India's North-East as an exemplification of what Heidegger refers to as the engaged perspective of connectedness with nature.

The Engaged Perspective of the World

The question of human relation with the external world is central to western philosophy. Since Descartes, mainstream philosophy entertains the question of the world from a perspective of absolute disengagement and disconnection. This epistemological tradition starts with Plato's fascination with theory—the idea that one can understand the world in a detached manner and can have a theory of everything including the human beings and the world. Since the Greeks, the epistemological tradition assumed that the reality of the entities and human beings in the world can be discovered only by detaching the inquirer from the world of practical concerns.

According to this epistemology, knowledge results from a transaction between an independently given subject (knower) and object (known). In this conception of knowledge, the knower and the known are separated by an unbridgeable ontological gap. A somewhat inexplicable transaction takes place between the subject and object, as a result of which knowledge arises.

There is the world, the real world, which everyone knows, and gets to know through a kind of transaction between the real object-components of the world and the indubitable Cartesian subject. This transaction is carried out in terms of certain epistemic rules, and if these rules are correctly applied, one has achieved the production of knowledge, and if they are not correctly applied, the transaction has failed to produce knowledge. This epistemology, thus, privileges the theoretical point of view and considers it superior to practical engagement.

Such is, what might be called, a simplified account of 'the Enlightenment conception of knowledge'. The Enlightenment reified reason and fostered the presumptuous belief that the cultural progress of humanity depended on human rational efforts to perfect themselves and their institutions. This model of human progress, we need to remember, is founded on the disengaged, disconnected perspective of knowledge production.

Martin Heidegger's phenomenology begins with a philosophical critique of the modern culture's foundational notion of rational, reflective, self-conscious subjectivity. For Heidegger, the perspective of the knower as rational, reflective and self-conscious is itself conditioned on a non-reflective and non-rational dimension of human consciousness. According to him, human beings access the world in the very first place through a non-reflective, pre-cognitive understanding. For instance, Heidegger says, we hear not the scientific and theoretical dimension of a sound (as measurable in terms of these many decibels) but the humming of a cuckoo, the speeding of a vehicle, the ringing of a phone, etc. Our *zuhanden* (ready-to-hand) world is accessible to us through such a pre-reflective comportment towards things. Heidegger held the view that theoretical knowledge depended on and presupposed our pre-theoretical comportments towards the known, although the objects discovered through theoretical activity cannot be said to depend on the pre-theoretical familiarity.[1] That is, we can understand the physics of the planet we have not seen or lived in, but this understanding presupposes that we have certain involvement in the discourse of modern science and at least the minimum competence in relation to this discourse. If this is not the case, we might still understand the planet, but not in any scientific manner but, may be, as the mythical comet or as the ominous heavenly body.

The most important aspect of Heidegger's rejection of the 'disinterested spectator knower' is the collapse of the celebrated scandal of philosophy (its infamous inability to explain rationally the external world) into a pseudo problem. Heidegger argues that a correct understanding of the human being "defies such proofs, because, in its Being, it already is what subsequent proofs deem necessary to demonstrate for it."[2] Hence, the most appropriate ontological description of the subject is 'being-in-the-world'. This means the inner-outer dichotomy of the subject collapses. The human subject is ontologically no less *with* the entities outside in the world than *with* the 'I' inside.

Heidegger's well-known '*destruktion*' (deconstruction) of the history of western metaphysics lays bare the western understanding of being as constant presence right from Plato. This understanding of being is important for the modern arrival at the understanding of the subject as disconnected from the object and the object as represented in its *vorhandenheit* (presence-at-hand, roughly the objectivity of the known). In 'Metaphysics as History of Being' (1941), Heidegger discusses this progress from Plato's understanding of idea as the whatness of a thing and Aristotle's distinction between whatness (essence) and thatness (existence), to the medieval schoolmen's notion of being as actuality and the Cartesian interpretation of being as certainty. In this sense, the western history of being has only completely reified with the arrival of the scientific age the Platonic understanding of being as constant presence. This ontological movement within history has taken two remarkable momentums: (i) "man's determining the essence of certainty by himself in accordance with the essence of certainty in general (self-assurance), and thus of bringing humanity to dominance within what is real"[3] (that is, subjectivity become determinative for the certainty of the objectivity of the real), and (ii) "certainty. . .is developing its own essential fullness as the authoritative essence of truth".[4] This development in the history of being, of the subject becoming the substratum of certainty, Heidegger remarks, "First brings the trend toward the unconditionality of manipulation and positing"[5] in the modern era.

If the modern era stretches to its utmost limits the paradigm of the subject disconnected subject who objectifies the being of the real as constant presence, the results are "the darkening of the world, the flight of the gods, the destruction of the earth, the reduction of human beings to a mass, the hatred and mistrust of everything creative and free".[6] Such a perspective conceals being and its manifold revelation. Such a perspective has developed to a condition of 'devastation' which is more 'unearthly' than destruction. "Destruction only sweeps aside all that has grown up or been built up so far; but devastation blocks all future growth and prevents all building. . .establishes and spreads everything that blocks and prevents."[7] Heidegger attempts to be more faithful to our immediate access to things in the way they show themselves from themselves. On the other hand, the knower disconnected from the world of practical concerns and the earth, the dichotomous modern subject, both destroys the subjectivity of the subject and the self-emergence of nature by reducing the whole of the real to what stands before the subject as resource for use and manipulation and that alone. In this process, "both the subject and the object are sucked up as standing-reserves"[8] and the subject of the scientific age is unable to "embrace the fullness of the coming to presence of nature. . .for the objectness of nature is. . .*only* one way in which nature exhibits itself."[9]

Broadly speaking, the Heideggerian thesis admonishes the forgetting of the involved, engaged and connected aspect of our most primordial way of accessing the world. As far as the intellectual history of ideas is concerned, this forgetting is squarely blamed for the contemporary environmental crisis. Although Heidegger asserted that "I know of no paths to the immediate transformation of the present situation of the world", that is, its technologically overwhelmed condition leading to the devastation of the Planet and reduction of the human subject to mere resource, he also asserted that "it seems to me that the thinking which I attempt would awaken, clarify, and fortify the readiness [for a god who can save humanity from technological nihilism]".[10] Hence, I now turn to Heidegger's positively suggestive insights arising out of his critique of the disengaged perspective of knowledge production (which has led to absolute technological overwhelming of life and the Planet) regarding ways to subvert the destructive human comportment towards the Planet.

Dwelling on the Earth

In Heidegger's conception of the human being as being-in-the-world, the world is understood as the referential totality of significance, wherein all things with which we are engaged, the ready-to-hand, can be placed. The essence of the world means "freeing entities for a totality of involvements"[11] and all the things of the world are disclosed to us primordially as knots within this network of involvements or world. The *zuhanden* things come to the *foreground* as such and such only because of this *background*. Things are meaningful in one way or the other in terms of the world of involvement of the subject. The concept of the 'world' is of tremendous importance to locate Heidegger's critique of the technological disconnection of humanity from the earth and his understanding of dwelling on the earth. As a being-in-the-world, the human being is a "spatial" entity in the sense that space is discovered within the world understood as the background of significance wherein things appear as meaningful. Rather than being the sum total of discrete objects disconnected from the subject as in the modernist view of the world, Heidegger thinks of the world as the referential whole of the subject's involvements. In this shift of the epistemological standpoint from the spectator *of* the world to the actor *in* the world, therefore, the ontological connectedness of the subject to the world and the earth is pronounced.

In order to distance his analysis from the traditional dichotomies of subject-object and mind-body, Heidegger calls the human being "Dasein". The 'Da' of Dasein primarily signifies the contextually located character of the human being. It expresses the ontological relationship between human beings and the world. The constitutively situated, worldly, care-structured Dasein is the *fundamentum* for the Being of all other entities. 'Being' means the *thatness* of beings, the fact "that" they exist in one way or another rather than not[12] as against their whatness or essence; Being is "that which determines entities as entities, that on the basis of which...entities are already understood [by human beings]".[13] Heidegger's later sayings in the 'Letter on Humanism (1946)' that the human being is the shepherd of being and human language is the house of beings means once again that though entities exist in their thatness independent of us, we alone give articulation to and encounter the "insurrection against nothingness"[14] of Being. The term 'Dasein' underlines the fact that the exceptional human condition as the only ontological being as that entity which takes issue with Being happens in reference to a horizon or world. In an interesting study of the significance of location and place in Heidegger's understanding of Being, Jeff Malpas concludes that Heidegger's enquiry "essentially concerns the 'situated,' or better the 'placed,' character of being, and of our own being, so much so that we may describe the thinking that is associated with the name 'Heidegger' as a thinking that does indeed consist, as he himself claimed, in an attempt to 'say' the place of being—as a *topology* of being."[15] The 'Da' of Dasein is also expressed as the clearing, and later as the fourfold of the event of manifestation of being. In all these expressions, what is to be understood is the unitary background wherein entities are disclosed so that humans can understand them in their Being. Malpas argues that the 'place' of Being is not merely a locatable landscape but "that open, cleared, yet bounded region in which we find ourselves gathered together with other persons and things, and in which we are opened up to the world and the world to us."[16] But it is not merely that we can make sense of things only upon a background which Heidegger calls the 'world'. The fact that existence presupposes the world means also that the human being is an embodied self always already affected by the outside or world and thus needs a dwelling. Hence, as Gelvin stresses, dwelling or the fact that "I must have a world to live in, to dwell in, to call my home is *a priori*".[17] In the 'Letter on Humanism', Heidegger understood modernity as an experience of homelessness, which means the loss of home or ground for the understanding of Being. It is now abundantly clear that Heidegger's attempt to resolve the disconnectedness of the moderns from the earth has led him to rethink the intellectual history of the West in terms of the understanding of Being and rework that understanding of Being as one of inherent connectedness to the 'place' or earth.

Malpas's extensive study of Heidegger's ontology of place concludes that the most direct and simplest goal of Heidegger's thinking is to be understood as 'homecoming', retreating, returning back to an original dwelling place and convalescing "from the homelessness of technological modernity".[18] The recovery of human situatedness seems to be the Heideggerian project as such. It is clear from the analysis of 'being in' in *Being and Time* that human beings are 'in' the world not in the objective sense of occupying space, not in any way like water being in a bottle, but they are in the world in the sense of involvement as would be 'being in love'. 'Being in' is a way of attuning ourselves to being affected by the world. "Dasein's openness to the world", Heidegger remarks "is constituted existentially by the attunement of a state-of-mind."[19] Ontologically, the fact that we always find ourselves in one mood or another indicates for Heidegger that we are affective beings, impinged on by the world. It is immediately clear, therefore, that the fact of attunement is a pointer towards our integral existence within nature. This accessibility to nature is one characteristic of our being-in-the-world.

In the essay 'Building, Dwelling, Thinking' (1951), Heidegger asks what it means to dwell. Taken together with the explication of dwelling in *Being and Time* and in this essay[20], 'to dwell' means to be familiar with, to care for and to look after. He goes on to argue that 'to build' also originally meant 'to dwell'. Although the force of the argument here is etymological, in the overall structure of Heidegger's thought it is not. 'Being in' means to dwell upon the earth caringly. If our most primordial comportment towards the world of things and people is one of caring, mattering involvement, then 'to dwell upon the earth' really means to 'dwell caringly'. Technological modernity, on the other hand, is a mode of forgetting this primordial human comportment and being amidst the world of people and things disconnectedly and exploitatively. To dwell means to be at peace without the violence of technological modernity. To dwell negatively means to spare from harm and positively means to let be what is spared in its own nature and being, to let it be is 'into a preserve of peace'. "*The fundamental character of dwelling*", Heidegger remarks, "*is this sparing and preserving*."[21] The dwelling of human beings on the earth in this sense, Heidegger argues, means dwelling within the finite unitary fourfold of the earth, under the sky, before the divinities, and among the mortals. The divisiveness of the fourfold wrought by technological modernity can be subverted only by reflective recapturing of the fourfold. Heidegger's dense language in explicating the fourfold needs clarification. The earth and sky together stand for the natural elements of the 'world', and because they are elements of the world, their naturality is not objectness but something imbued with meaning and life. Earth and sky stand for the self-emergence of things unaided by human effort or *phusis*. Earth as such stands for elemental nature that surrounds us. Earth is what emerges in flower and fruit, rock and water, plant and animal. Sky is nature in its beyondness; the emergence of the sun and the moon, the night and the day, the stars and the clouds, the seasons and the weather. If earth stands for the spatial, rooted dimension of the world, I think, the sky stands for its temporal dimension opening towards the future of possibilities. Gods and mortals form the spiritual-cultural aspect of the world. The divinities or gods are said to be "the beckoning messengers of the godhead."[22] They are messengers from the authoritative realm of the holy, and according to the interpretation of Julian Young, they are inspirational spiritual-cultural figures, historical and mythical, who "give voice to that which is most sacred to us. As members of a given community, and whether we heed their inspiring example or not, we live our lives in the light of our gods."[23] The mortals are human beings in their finiteness and mortality. Their meaning is finite in the sense that it is constrained by the fourfold. To dwell means "to look after the fourfold in its presencing. . . . Dwelling preserves the fourfold by bringing the presencing of the fourfold into thing."[24] Heidegger means here that the fourfold is the realm wherein the meaning of things stands unconcealed. The example of the bridge across the river is meant to illustrate that modern things too are gathered in their meaning within the fourfold of the earth and sky, divinities and mortals. Things are not the Cartesian objects that are represented in the minds of the subject but are entities with independent being revealed as such to the human being. All human activity of intervening in nature, or *techne* (human assisted emergence of things like the emergence of a statue out of a piece of wood) as against *phusis*, both cultivating and constructing, in this interpretation means to gently assist things to emerge in their being or letting things appear—that is, to dwell and build or spare and preserve. In the Cartesian model these aspects of the emergence of things would appear secondary properties attached to a represented object in its materiality. However, Heidegger insists what gives rise to the Cartesian perspective is a gradual forgetting of our most primordial way of accessing the world from the engaged and involved perspective. Within the fourfold, there lies being in both its manifestness and its withdrawal. "There is much in beings," write Heidegger, "man cannot master. But little comes to be known. The known remains an approximation... Never is a being...something of our making or merely our representation."[25] What technological modernity has done is to level the hiddenness and withdrawal of Being and disallow Being its manifoldness and mystery.

The essence of technology is a particular revealing of Being as resource only reserved for human manipulation. What is dangerous in technology's essence is that it "blocks the shining-forth and holding-sway of truth... [It] threatens man with the possibility that it could be denied to him to enter into a more original revealing and hence to experience the call of a more primal truth."[26] If this were so, does a look into the world of 'primitive peoples' (in Heidegger's terms) help us either to experience or to recapture the existential condition of connectedness with the world, the authentically engaged perspective? Heidegger seems to suggest that it is the case, for he writes: "To orient the analysis of Dasein towards the 'life of primitive peoples' can have positive significance [Bedeutung] as a method because 'primitive phenomena' are often less concealed and less complicated by extensive self-interpretation on the part of the Dasein in question. Primitive Dasein often speaks to us more directly in terms of a primordial absorption in 'phenomena'."[27] However, such an approach is rejected in *Being and Time* because the science of ethnology, according to him, has not yet clarified its ground and because a general conception of the world would be sufficient to study both the 'primitive' and modern human beings. Taking a cue from this study of Heidegger's ontological interpretation of the disconnectedness of the moderns from the natural world and from Heidegger's positive observation regarding the less concealed condition of 'primitive phenomena', I now want to venture a look at the tribal worldview of North-East India as an ontic or practical exemplification of what Heidegger alludes to as the engaged perspective of connectedness with nature.

Returning to the Tribal Worldview

A plausible way of reading the huge Heideggerian oeuvre is to see it as an enormous critique of the crisis of modernity—both human (alienation, homelessness, individualism) and ecological (devastation of the earth). Heidegger's philosophical history of modernity separates modernity from other historical ages in terms of the essence of technology by way of which the whole of reality becomes material for the self-assertive production of the subject. "The earth and its atmosphere become raw material. Man becomes human material, which is disposed of with a view to proposed goals."[28] The Heideggerian enquiry is one way of answering the question of modern disconnectedness with the world. In another answer to the same question, David Abram, an American sleight-of-hand magician and phenomenologist, who travelled much among the indigenous communities of rural Asia, comes to the conclusion that contemporary western estrangement from nature is intellectually cemented by the amalgamation in the West of two divergent cultural landscapes: the Hellenistic 'rational dissociation of the human intellect from the organic world' and the Hebraic 'spiritual or religious ascendancy of humankind over nature'. Both these traditions contradicted one another in every respect but, according to Abram, except in that both these are 'profoundly informed by writing'; that is, they are profoundly literal traditions. In Abram's interpretation, upon the onslaught of the new notion of speech that floats 'free of the surrounding landscape', the oral civilizations all over the world, which lived in close conviviality with nature, began to disintegrate and disappear. As for the worldview of the oral peoples, Abram writes that:

> Long-established indigenous cultures often display a remarkable solidarity with the lands that they inhabit, as well as a basic respect, or even reverence, for the other species that inhabit those lands. Such cultures, much smaller in scale (and far less centralized) than modern Western civilization, seem to have maintained a relatively homeostatic or equilibrial relation with their local ecologies for vast periods of time, deriving their necessary sustenance from the land without seriously disrupting the ability of the earth to replenish itself.[29]

The same discord of civilizational outlooks was articulated by the Native American Chief, Seattle, when the white settlers proposed to buy their land in 1854: "We know that the white man does not understand our ways. One portion of land is the same to him as the next, for he is a stranger who comes in the night and takes from the land whatever he needs. The Earth is not his brother, but his enemy and when he has conquered it, he moves on."[30] I shall now argue that the strongly sensual affinity with the natural world has been similarly a trait of the tribal worldviews of North-East India and place this argument within the interpretation of Heidegger I have already undertaken. I shall here refer to the following: (i) the absence of the subject-object, and fact-value dichotomies in the tribal worldview, (ii) the reflection of this absence in a deep sense of connectedness with the natural environment both in respectful recognition of nature as the nurturing maternal reality and the awesome reverential reality, and (iii) the tribal conception of "the sensing body as a kind of open circuit that completes itself only in things, and in the world."[31]

A Non-Dichotomous View of Human-Nature Interaction: In an attempt to define a tribe, Mrinal Miri observes that it is, among other things, "a community which believes in an abiding continuity between nature, earth, man, and what we call the supernatural, instead of in the divisive distinctions between these that modern man makes."[32] This is the direct opposite of what Heidegger characterizes as the subject-centrism of the modern era: "Man becomes that being upon which all that is, is grounded as regards the manner of its Being and its truth. Man becomes the relational centre of that which is as such."[33] For Heidegger, the modern fact of the human being becoming the substratum of reality, however, is not the primordial event of modernity; that event, rather, is enframing, calculative, instrumental, technological rationality becoming the ground of Being as such. The human being itself is called upon by the essence of technology to take upon itself the role of the subject. But once this is done what rules is the essence of technology: "In self-assertive production, the humanness of man and the thingness of things dissolve into the calculated market value of a market which not only spans the whole earth as a world market, but also, as the will to will, trades in the nature of Being and thus subjects all beings to the trade of a calculation that dominates most tenaciously in those areas where there is no need of numbers."[34] Therefore, I need to conclude in this analysis that the absence of the subject-object dichotomy in the tribal worldview is a result of the absence of technological rationality there. The urge to reduce the whole of reality to their resourcefulness and objectness for the human subject's machination (or technological rationality) is absent in the tribal worldview.

Since nature is not 'object' for representation and manipulation, the tribals regarded nature as having life and energy with the possibility that humans could have an authentic, living relationship with nature. And because nature is imagined in this life-like, communitarian fashion (that is, as the community of life), the tribal thought of the human-nature relationship as one of involvement and interaction. Since nature is not an object out there but a being of worth, the tribal marvelled at the self-emergence (*phusis*) of nature and its inherent possibilities without any human assistance or interference. As humans sustained themselves from the bounty of nature, they in turn spared and preserved, cared for and let nature be. An integral aspect of an authentic relationship is this very 'letting the other be'. For instance, in the olden days, many Ao Naga villages maintained reserved forests because they considered these forests as the support and natural foundation for their life and livelihood. Therefore, they never cut down the trees grown in the reserved areas except to build houses for the village log drum: within the village, log drum was used for many purposes in order to convey messages to the villagers, to make the entrance and exit gate of the village, and to make coffins for the child and the widow. Children and widows were considered physically weaker than the rest of the people in the society. Therefore, the community provides the necessary things to make their coffins when they die. The protection of the reserved forest was not a utilitarian project, however, it was animated more by reverential respect of life-upholding reality. The vital exceptions to protectionism, like those mentioned, was a commemoration of the inability of humans to live unsupported by nature and, thus, only for the sake of exceptionally symbolic human purposes and not for the upkeep of the mundane, everyday aspects of life. It is to be remembered that the most central inspiration for Arne Naess's deep ecology was the notion of the 'sacred forest' among the Sherpas, a Himalayan tribe, with whom Naess as an avid mountaineer came into contact with.

The tribal did not separate between fact and value but considered whatever *is*, whatever emerges in nature (*phusis*) as already meaningful and they lived their lives engrossed in the meaningfulness of whatever *is*. The need for a separate realm of value did not occur to them as meaningful. Since nature is not an objective fact for the tribal but an intimate component of life in all its palpability, the present trend in environmental ethics to invest nature with 'a lost intrinsic value' would be completely alien to the tribal worldview. It was not the human being alone that was imbued with a moral life in the tribal worldview. The whole context of the tribal's life was imbued with moral meaning. Hence the question of speciesism or privileging the human species is an aberration from the perspective of their worldview. Heidegger mentioned that the assigning of value to a being by a subject objectifies that being and reduces its reality to the subject's representation, whether positively or negatively. Valuing in this way is yet another manner in which moderns do not let beings be. "That is to say, by the assessment of something as 'a value' what is so valued is admitted only as an object for man's estimations. . .every valuing even where it values positively, is a subjectivizing. It does not let beings: be."[35] The tribals, on the other hand, did not experience the separation between fact and value. With the modern separation of value from fact, value became a subjective project of taste and lost its reality and vitality. If the moral aspect of the world was real, true and something sensually felt for the tribals, for the moderns it is a contestable construct which needs a separate justification. And so, what failed to gather rational justification for its being was mainly the moral aspect of nature. We should say that the stripping of nature of its moral reality was a deliberate modern project for crowning the human subject as the only location of value for the sake of reducing all other beings for this being's unceasing exploitation and consumption. This view of nature does appear strange and foreign to the tribal worldview. Hence, the several efforts undertaken today to recapture in a modern idiom the premodern non-dichotomous sensual unity of all beings like that of David Abram are, in fact, returning to the tribal experience.

Respectful, Reverential Disposition towards Nature: The absence of the modern dichotomous imagination in the tribal worldview, directly invests it with a deep sense of interconnectedness of all life and the field of life—the earth as such. There is both respectful recognition of nature as the nurturing maternal reality and reverential recognition of her awesome powers. All life and non-life forms are intrinsically connected—that is, without this sense of connection there would be altogether another reality—in the tribal worldview. In practice this meant that the effortless closeness of the tribal to the environment is expressed first and foremost in a reverential attitude to nature as the source of sustenance and as a power unyielding to human machination. Hence, for the tribal, the earth is sacred, divine and holy. Among the traditional Ao Nagas, for instance, the earth or soil is believed to speak the truth and considered holy. Similar is the narrative of nature among the other hill tribes of North-East India. The awe experienced by the tribal towards the self-emergent force of nature, its presencing, withdrawing and withholding manifestations in the Heideggerian ontological parlance, can be said to be the basis of the tribal reverence for nature. In this sense, the Ao Nagas were deeply concerned about causing any harm to nature. It was believed that maintaining the peace and harmony already prevalent in nature was a human prerogative. Hence, if they were to cut down a tree in the jungle, they would first approach the trees and apologize to them in an attempt to make peace with nature before the event of apparent violence, although the violence itself was for the purpose of life-sustenance rather than for the sake of any superfluous desire. The words used in the ritual of apology were the following: "Oh handsome riverside tree, instead of letting the windstorm or landslide uproot you, or the passersby trample upon you, or the mushrooms grow wild on you, do come and guard our village. You will be honoured as we drag you along to our village. Feel not hurt and humiliated; do come to our village." The personification of the tree as the interlocutor in the ritual of apology is itself a sign of the reverential disposition of the Ao towards the natural.

In Heidegger's characterization of modernity, one of the marks of the technological society is that "even the trace of the holy has become unrecognizable"[36] and the question of the ability of the modern to experience the holy remains, for Heidegger, undecided. The 'healing' power of the holy withdraws in the modern times and together with the 'integralness of the whole'. Heidegger characterizes this scenario as 'the world's night' and 'a single endless winter'. Such withdrawal of the holy is not a mark of the traditional tribal society. The holy for the tribal, as for Heidegger, means the 'integralness of the whole'. As a knot in the web of being, the human being sustains herself from nature (the nurturing mother) and falls in adoration of nature (the awesome force). As Spinoza's God, there is no imagination of a super-natural order that oversees the natural order. What is eaten, lived with, sensually enjoyed, and adored in awe are all the same web of existence. According to the oral narratives of the Aos, during the *Longsü Putu*, known as the golden period in human history, human beings, birds, animals, trees and mountains all lived in perfect harmony. The Ao ancestors believed that this harmony can be achieved only through the possibility of *relating with* birds, trees, plants, mountains, and animals rather than *grooming them up* for human use, satisfaction and enjoyment. In this sense, the possibility of communication between them also explains the possibility of union, interconnectedness, coexistence and community. In the tribal worldview, it was impossible to see plants, animals and rivers as inert matter or objects of representation. They were sacred, inspirational forces for human edification and guidance.

Let me narrate an Ao folktale to exemplify this. According to the Ao oral tradition, during the *Longsü Putu* (golden period) there lived a beautiful girl named Matsüngchetla in *Chungliyimti* (the first Ao settlement). One day, at daybreak, while she went to fetch water from a nearby stream, she felt cheery and began to sing all alone in the stream *tsüsenjoker. tsüsenjoker* (let me be refreshed, let me be refreshed). The song was a spontaneous expression of her mood of the moment and hence an unpremeditated composition. While Matsüngchetla was engrossed in her impromptu song and was enjoying the morning in the stream, she was amazed to hear a voice responding to her song. To her surprise, a big tree, standing tall by the side of the stream, began to speak to her in a melodious tone: *Tsüsenjoker laza süremsüpang, Yongmen mezortsü, Teyongtsüko tsüsenjokang* (young lady, the one cleaning the brass ring, cleanse yourself in the middle of the stream). According to the Ao Naga tradition the overwhelming musical effect of this instruction of the majestic tree to Matsüngchetla marked the origin of musical tradition among them. The musical movements of the tree leaves, they believe, prompted Matsüngchetla's gleeful melody. In this fashion, a rich folk heritage of the Aos bears witness to the sacred, inspirational and edificatory manifestation of nature.

In Heidegger's writings, the 'holy' is a particular manifestation of being to a people and not a metaphysical object. But modern human beings are unique because they have lost the sense of the holy. An important aspect of the modern project of representation and objectification is the making of phenomena profane and thus merely useful material for human beings. The desecration of the earth in this manner is strange to the tribal worldview because it was permeated with a sense of the holy. It is to be remembered that for Abrahamic religions and for late Vedic Hinduism the earth is not sacred in this manner. The separation of the sacred from the natural (super-natural) goes together with the project of separating the subject from objects and fact from value. Hence, all ecological attempts today of recapturing the sense of the sacredness of the earth and its things are, in a way, a return to the tribal worldview and to animism in general.

Body as nature: The conception of the human being and her essence in the tribal worldview is in terms of affectedness by the world and interconnectedness with nature through human embodiment rather than as a 'spirit misplaced into a body', which is, in Heidegger's terms, the Cartesian model of the human being. The objectification and exploitation of nature is a byproduct of the mind-body dualism whereby the mind is privileged over matter in its lordship over perishable, unreal, representable matter in one form or another. For Heidegger, the human being is primordially characterized not as 'res cogitans' but as a being that is always affected by the world (state-of-mind), that understands its world in terms of its firsthand embodied practical competence (understanding), that articulates its world meaningfully in language (discourse), and that is engrossed, lost and fallen into its world in its everydayness (fallenness). Authentic way of being of the human being for Heidegger is a particular (owned-up) way of relating to one's being-in-the-world, and not returning to one's interior castle. In the words of Abram, the meaning of our embodiment is a kind of sensual openness towards the world, which means we are complete in our existence only as beings intrinsically connected to things of our world.

Abram's emphasis on oral narratives and on the detaching effect of the written word from the sensual origin of language and from our imagination of connectivity to things, speaks of a different order of life than the modern, which could generically be called 'the tribal'. I suggest that a semblance of this world can be recaptured from the oral narratives of the tribal people, where the immediacy of the narrator's connectedness to the world around her is evident. The relationship is definitive for our understanding of the being of the entities in question so that without the sensual unity of the various elements of the web of narration each of its elements would be different in their very definition. This sensual connection of the tribal narrative tradition with the world of the narration is exhibited, for example, in the vigorous gesturing of the singer and the sense of connection that these singers and their listeners are aroused to feel towards the narrative. The narratives are themselves powerful tales which arouse a realistic imagination in those involved. In these forms of art, the distinction between the real and the metaphoric collapses and the actors (narrators and their listeners) becomes protagonists and involved participants. The story becomes an event relived in an emotionally charged world of reminiscence. Moreover, what makes these narratives sensually close to the tribal world is the life-likeness of the elements of the narrative. In the above narrated apology ritual before the felling of the tree, the ritual brings out transformative effects in the real-world—that is, persuading the villagers against the destruction of nature without the necessity of prefixed exceptional circumstances.

The moment human beings imagine themselves the minded-beings, the separation from matter is instituted, and modern culture centrally means the most powerful articulation of this separation and its scheme of privilege. All forms of animism by definition means that 'anima' or soul or the vital force of life is not a human prerogative. Every aspect of modern culture centres around the separation of mind from matter and confining anima for human beings alone. Anima is constructed as instrumental rationality, which is imagined as the superior privilege of humanity. On the basis of this privileging, modern economics justifies hyper consumer economies characterized by the absolute exploitation of finite nature; modern science is driven by the Baconian desire for the ultimate human conquest of nature both intellectually and economically; modern ethics is underwritten by the Kantian imperative of dignity warranted only for humanity; modern politics safeguards each human individual's best possible liberty within a scheme of social cooperation based on self-interest. The tribal way of life is the opposite of these forms of life: its economics is one of sustenance, its science is one of praxis, its morality is one of relationship with the web of existence and its politics is one community. In all these forms, the tribal imagination extends the human body as part of the wide web of nature and animated by the same spirit that radiates in nature. In this sense, the anima is not a non-natural force but the awesome force of nature that inhabits all things natural, including the human. The tribal narrative tradition celebrates the anima in its holistic form, and the human being who articulates the anima is considered a link in the anima of nature. The very narration is both a recapturing as well as the reliving of the narrated reality. The human body is the site of this reliving, unseparated from the reality recalled by the narration.

Conclusion

The shift from the epistemological tradition from a disengaged spectator to that of the engaged actor who is within the world give positive insights regarding ways to challenge the destructive nature of the dichotomous modern subject in its treatment towards the earth. Moreover, with the changed perspective, the ontological connectedness of the subject to the world is established. Reality, in the Heideggerian discourse, can be understood only in terms of the world, understood as the totality of involvements. Reality is a mode of human interpretation of the world and depends on Dasein's existence. Traditional metaphysics, according to Heidegger, depicted reality as the aggregation of disengaged objects in their *vorhandenheit*, forgetting the fact that things or objects come across to Dasein primordially in their *zuhandenheit*. Heidegger's ontological description of Dasein as being-in-the-world erases the dichotomy between the subject and the object. Hence, Heidegger holds that this dichotomy between the subject and the object can be overcome only when the moderns reimagine their way of dwelling on the earth.

The fact that Dasein is an engaged, embodied, and worldly self, presupposes a world and a dwelling Dasein. To dwell means to have a feeling of familiarity with the world, to conserve, to preserve, and take care of the earth. Dasein not only understands the objects in its world but also *concerns* with them because Dasein is existentially constituted as 'care'. Heidegger holds that nature can neither be taken just as natural things in Dasein's environing world nor can it be taken as object within the environing world because they abound with meaning. The being of nature is said to reside in its meaning for humans.

However, the technological modern subject forgot its primordial comportment with beings in the world and they became the relational centre of everything. Human beings aim at total and exclusive mastery over all the other beings in the world and become determinative for the certainty of the realities of the objects. In this sense, Heidegger holds that the world becomes 'picture'. World picture does not mean 'picture of the world' but it is grasped as a picture when beings as a whole are taken as objects. Heidegger notes that the fundamental event of modernity is the conquest of the world as picture. For him, the openness of beings as a whole does not coincide with the aggregate of objects which are familiar to Dasein. Conversely, where beings are more remote and scarcely known by science there beings prevail more primordially. Heidegger holds that the contemporary environmental crisis is the outcome of the disconnectedness of the modern subject with the earth.

Hence, it can be safely said from the above study that to reimagine our way of dwelling on the earth is to return to the tribal worldview because the interweaving of all life forms is richly found and practiced in the tribal worldview. The subject-object dichotomy is alien to the tribals and in the absence of the subject-object dichotomy there is an interconnectedness of all life forms on earth. This is manifested in their respectful recognition of nature and their reverential recognition of the living presence of the reality of nature. However, at the present juncture, we cannot travel back in time and recapture in full the past life of interconnectedness with nature. As Mrinal Miri admits the tribal life is not available today to the tribals themselves in its palpable reality as it was before. Western modernity is no more an isolated event but through the seductive power of technological rationality, western modernity has conquered the whole world. The impossibility of going back is as real as the crisis of modernity. But regulated by the past, new narratives of interconnectivity can be imagined. The only argument of this chapter is that for such reimagining the future, the tribal worldview is at least a plausible vantage point.

Notes

1. Hubert L. Dreyfus, *Being-in-the-world: A Commentary on Heidegger's Being and Time, Division 1* (Cambridge, MA: Massachusetts Institute of Technology Press, 1991), pp. 45-46.
2. Martin Heidegger, *Being and Time*, trans. John Macquarrie and Edward Robinson (Oxford: Basil Blackwell, 1973), p. 249.
3. Martin Heidegger, "Metaphysics as History of Being", trans. Joan Stambaugh. In Martin Heidegger, *The End of Philosophy*, 1-54. (Chicago, IL: The University of Chicago Press, 2003), p. 21.
4. *Ibid.*, p. 23.
5. *Ibid.*, p. 49.
6. Martin Heidegger, *Introduction to Metaphysics*, trans. Gregory Fried and Richard Polt (New Haven: Yale University Press, 2000), p. 40.
7. Martin Heidegger, *What is Called Thinking?* trans. Fred D. Wieck and J. Glenn Gray (New York: Harper & Row, 1968), pp. 29-30.
8. Martin Heidegger, "Science and Reflection", trans. William Lovitt. In Martin Heidegger, *The Question Concern Technology and Other Essays*, 155-182 (New York: Harper & Row, 1977), p. 173.
9. *Ibid.*, p. 174.
10. Martin Heidegger, "'Only a God Can Save Us': *Der Spiegel's* Interview with Martin Heidegger (1966)", trans. Maria P. Alter and John D. Caputo. In *The Heidegger Controversy: A Critical Reader*, ed. Richard Wolin (Cambridge, MA: The MIT Press, 1993), p. 110.
11. Martin Heidegger, *Being and Time,* trans. John Macquarrie and Edward Robinson (New York: Harper and Row Publishers, 1962), p. 145.
12. Martin Heidegger, "Metaphysics as History of Being", trans. Joan Stambaugh. In Martin Heidegger, *The End of Philosophy*, 1-54. (Chicago, IL: The University of Chicago Press, 2003), p. 1.

13. Martin Heidegger, *Being and Time,* trans. John Macquarrie and Edward Robinson (New York: Harper and Row Publishers, 1962), pp. 25-26.
14. Martin Heidegger, "Metaphysics as History of Being", trans. Joan Stambaugh. In Martin Heidegger, *The End of Philosophy,* 1-54. (Chicago, IL: The University of Chicago Press, 2003), p. 1.
15. Jeff Malpas, *Heidegger's Topology: Being, Place, World* (Cambridge, MA: The MIT Press, 2006), p. 305.
16. Jeff Malpas, *Heidegger's Topology: Being, Place, World* (Cambridge, MA: The MIT Press, 2006), p. 221.
17. Michael Gelven, *A Commentary on Heidegger's Being and Time* (Dekalb: Northern Illinois University Press, 1989), pp. 58-59.
18. Jeff Malpas, *Heidegger's Topology: Being, Place, World* (Cambridge, MA: The MIT Press, 2006), p. 310.
19. Martin Heidegger, *Being and Time*, trans. John Macquarrie and Edward Robinson (New York: Harper and Row Publishers, 1962), p. 176.
20. Martin Heidegger, *Being and Time,* trans. John Macquarrie and Edward Robinson (New York: Harper and Row Publishers, 1962), p. 79-80, and Martin Heidegger, "Building, Dwelling, Thinking" (1951), trans. Albert Hofstadter. In Martin Heidegger, *Poetry, Language, Thought,* 141-160 (New York: HarperCollins Perennial Classics, 2001), pp. 144-146. See also Jeff Malpas, *Heidegger's Topology: Being, Place, World* (Cambridge, MA: The MIT Press, 2006), pp. 74-75.
21. Martin Heidegger, "Building, Dwelling, Thinking" (1951), trans. Albert Hofstadter. In Martin Heidegger, *Poetry, Language, Thought,* 141-160 (New York: Harper Collins Perennial Classics, 2001), p. 147. (original emphasis).
22. Martin Heidegger, "Building, Dwelling, Thinking" (1951), trans. Albert Hofstadter. In Martin Heidegger, *Poetry, Language, Thought,* 141-160 (New York: HarperCollins Perennial Classics, 2001), p. 147.
23. Julian Young, "The Fourfold". In *The Cambridge Companion to Heidegger,* Second Edition, ed. Charles B. Guignon 373-392 (Cambridge: Cambridge University Press, 2006), p. 375.
24. Martin Heidegger, "Building, Dwelling, Thinking" (1951), trans. Albert Hofstadter. In Martin Heidegger, *Poetry, Language, Thought,* 141-160 (New York: Harper Collins Perennial Classics, 2001), p. 149.
25. Martin Heidegger, "The Origin of the Work of Art" (1935), trans. Julian Young and Kenneth Haynes. In Martin Heidegger, *Off the Bean Track,* 1-56. (Cambridge: Cambridge University Press, 2002), p. 29.

26. Martin Heidegger, "The Question Concerning Technology", trans. William Lovitt. In Martin Heidegger, *The Question Concern Technology and Other Essays*, 1-35 (New York: Harper & Row, 1977), p. 28.
27. Martin Heidegger, *Being and Time,* trans. John Macquarrie and Edward Robinson (New York: Harper and Row Publishers, 1962), p. 76.
28. Martin Heidegger, "What are Poets for?", (1946), trans. Albert Hofstadter. In Martin Heidegger, *Poetry, Language, Thought*, 87-140 (New York: HarperCollins Perennial Classics, 2001), p. 109.
29. David Abram, *The Spell of the Sensuous: Perception and Language in a More-than-Human World* (New York: Vintage, 1996), pp. 93-94.
30. Chief Seattle, "Chief Seattle's Message: Addressed to President Pierce, 1854". In *A Peace Reader: Essential Readings on War, Justice, Non-violence and World Order*, eds. Joseph J. Fahey and Richard Armstrong, 152-156 (Mahwah, NJ: Paulist Press, 1992), p. 153.
31. David Abram, *The Spell of the Sensuous: Perception and Language in a More-than-Human World* (New York: Vintage, 1996), p. 125.
32. Mrinal Miri, *Identity and the Moral Life* (New Delhi: Oxford University Press, 2003), p. 66.
33. Martin Heidegger, "The Age of the World Picture" (1938), trans. William Lovitt. In Martin Heidegger, *The Question Concern Technology and Other Essays*, 115-154 (New York: Harper & Row, 1977), p. 128.
34. Martin Heidegger, "What are Poets for?", (1946), trans. Albert Hofstadter. In Martin Heidegger, *Poetry, Language, Thought*, 87-140 (New York: Harper Collins Perennial Classics, 2001), p. 112.
35. Martin Heidegger, *Basic Writings: Letter on Humanism*, ed. David Farrell Krell (New York: Harper Collins Publishers, 2008), p. 251.
36. Martin Heidegger, "What are Poets for?", (1946), trans. Albert Hofstadter. In Martin Heidegger, *Poetry, Language, Thought*, 87-140 (New York: Harper Collins Perennial Classics, 2001), p. 95.

References

Abram, David. 1996. *The Spell of the Sensuous: Perception and Language in a More-than- Human World.* New York: Vintage.

Dreyfus, Hubert L. 1991. *Being-in-the-World: A Commentary on Heidegger's Being and Time, Division I.* Cambridge, MA: MIT Press.

Foltz, Bruce V. 1995. *Inhabiting the Earth: Heidegger, Environmental Ethics, and the Metaphysics of Nature.* New York: Humanity Books.

Gelven, Michael. 1989. *A Commentary on Heidegger's Being and Time.* DeKalb: Northern Illinois University Press.

Heidegger, Martin. 1962. *Being and Time*, trans. John Macquarrie and Edward Robinson. New York: Harper & Row Publishers.

Heidegger, Martin. 1968. *What is called Thinking?*, trans. Fred D. Wieck and J. Glenn Gray. New York: Harper & Row Publishers.

Heidegger, Martin. 1977a. The Age of the World Picture, trans. William Lovitt. In Martin Heidegger, *The Question Concerning Technology and Other Essays*, 115-154. New York: Harper & Row Publishers.

Heidegger, Martin. 1977b. Science and Reflection, trans. William Lovitt. In Martin Heidegger, *The Question Concerning Technology and Other Essays*, 3-35. New York: Harper & Row Publishers.

Heidegger, Martin. 1977b. The Question Concerning Technology, trans. William Lovitt. In Martin Heidegger, *The Question Concerning Technology and Other Essays*, 3-35. New York: Harper & Row Publishers.

Heidegger, Martin. 1993. *Only a God Can Save Us: Der Spiegel's Interview* with Martin Heidegger (1966). trans, Maria P. Alter and John D. Caputo. In *The Heidegger Controversy: A Critical Reader*, ed. Richard Wolin. Cambridge, MA: MIT Press.

Heidegger, Martin. 1995. *The Fundamental Concepts of Metaphysics: World, Finitude, Solitude,* trans. William McNeill and Nicholas Walker. Bloomington: Indiana University Press.

Heidegger, Martin. 2001. Building, Dwelling, Thinking, trans. Albert Hofstadter. In Martin Heidegger *Poetry, Language, Thought, 141* 160. New York: Harper Collins Perennial Classics.

Heidegger, Martin. 2001. Introduction to Metaphysics, trans. Gregory Fried and Richard Polt. New York: Harper & Row Publishers.

Heidegger, Martin. 2001. What are Poets for?, trans. Albert Hofstadter. In Martin Heidegger, *Poetry, Language, Thought*, 87-140. New York: Harper Collins Perennial Classics.

Heidegger, Martin. 2002. The Origin of the Work of Art, trans. Julian Young and Kenneth Haynes. In Martin Heidegger, *Off the Beaten Track*, 1-56. Cambridge: Cambridge University Press.

Heidegger, Martin. 2003. Metaphysics as History of Being, trans. Joan Stambaugh. In Martin Heidegger, *The End of Philosophy*, 1-54. Chicago, IL: The University of Chicago Press.

J. Fahey and Richard Armstrong, 152-156. Mahwah, NJ: Paulist Press.

Malpas, Jeff. 2006. *Heidegger's Topology: Being, Place, World.* Cambridge, MA: The MIT Press.

Miri, Mrinal. 2003. *Identity and the Moral Life.* New Delhi: Oxford University Press.

Mulhall, Stephen. 2005. *Heidegger and Being and Time.* London: Routledge.

Seattle, Chief. 1992. Chief Seattle's Message: Addressed to President Pierce, 1854. In *A Peace Reader: Essential Readings on War, Justice, Non-violence and World Order*, eds. Joseph.

Young, Julian. 2006. The Fourfold. In *The Cambridge Companion to Heidegger*, Second Edition, ed. Charles B. Guignon, 373-392. Cambridge: Cambridge University Press.

Zimmerman, Michael E. 2002. Heidegger's phenomenology and Contemporary, In *Eco-Phenomenology: Back to the Earth Itself*, ed. Ted Toadvine, 73-101. Suny Press Series in Environmental Ethics and Philosophy.

8

The Metaphysical Vision of Nature: A Christian Response

Sebastian Velassery

Theories of environmental ethics may be classified as twofold: *Anthropocentrism and Non-anthropocentrism.* They contribute different approaches to the study of environmental ethics. From a cultural perspective, *anthropocentrism* has strong spiritual ties with today's Western culture, prioritizing the economic value of nature. It is conservative in the sense that it tends to maintain (and to reform, in a sense) the politico-economic world order, and to defend the dominant values of modern industrial civilization. *Non-anthropocentrism* seems to be more reasonable in the context of non-Western cultural traditions such as Hinduism, Daoism, Buddhism and Native Tribal societies. In view of the above, the present paper is concerned with principles and causes rather than contingencies and effects on a topic such as environment and the ethical issues surface therein. Accordingly, here we try to articulate (1) the problem that has resulted from the encounter of man and nature; (2) to seek the underlying causes that have brought the present ecological crisis and to reveal the principles whose neglect have made the crisis; and (3) to find out the contributions provided by Christian tradition by its deepest metaphysical principles which have been forgotten in so many circles today.

Background to the Problem: The Ecological Crisis

The ethical and political problems in relation to the environment, if they are genuine philosophical problems as they appear to be, have always been with the human subject right from the beginning of creation itself. However, recent developments, especially the speed with which they have occurred, particularly since the World War II, commonly referred to be as 'the ecological crisis' have led to an increasing number of philosophers, economists and social scientists, to give a special reflection upon this matter and offer certain answers to these problems. The publication of Rachel Carson's *Silent Spring* in 1962, warning the dangers to humans in general and to the wildlife in particular from toxic pesticide residues, is widely recognized as the spark that kindled the environmental movement as it is known today. In 1971, the first conference on environmental philosophy was held at the University of Georgia, U.S.A.[1] and in 1973, Richard Sylvan wrote an article "Is there a Need for a New, an Environmental Ethics?" a question which he answered positively. In the same year, a Scandinavian philosopher Arne Naess published his article "The Swallow and the Deep, Long-Range Ecology Movements" in Inquiry which provided certain admired momentum later and paved way for the group that may be called deep ecologists. Arne Naess, the Norwegian philosopher who first outlined this shallow-deep split in environmentalism advocated the development of a new eco-philosophy or "ecosophy"to replace the destructive philosophy of modern industrial society.[2] In the field of environmental law, Christopher Stone published an essay entitled "Should Trees have Standing?" wherein he argued that 'environmental issues should be litigated before federal agencies or federal courts in the name of inanimate objects about to be despoiled. . . . and where inquiry is the subject of public outrage'.[3] Stone's article, though could not be considered as a profound philosophical piece on environmental ethics, yet has provided a platform for appropriating the language of 'rights' for the non-human world. In fact, Stones article is the background that has provided many to think about the interconnectedness between ecological movements and human rights movements, which is not the concern of this chapter.

Today, most of us who are living in the urbanized centres of Independent India and who had a fairly village background feels intuitively that something is lacking in their lives. We are living in the 'city centres' which were created out of an artificial environment from which nature has been excluded. As Mircea Eliade says, even the religious man in such circumstances has lost the sense of the spiritual significance of nature. According to Eliade, the cosmic liturgy, the mystery of nature's participation in the Christological drama, has become inaccessible to Christians living in a modern city. The religious experience is no longer open to the cosmos. In the last analysis, it is a strictly private experience; salvation is a problem that concerns man and his God; at most, man recognizes that he is responsible not only to God but also to history. But in these man-God-history relationships there is no place for the cosmos. From this it would appear that, even for a genuine Christian, the world is no longer felt as the work of God.[4]

The dangers brought about by man's domination over nature are too well known to need elucidation. Nature has become desacralized or desanctified for modern man. Eliade explains that 'experience of a radically desacralized nature is a recent discovery; moreover, it is an experience accessible only to a minority in modern societies, especially to scientists. For others, nature still exhibits a charm, a mystery, a majesty in which it is possible to decipher traces of ancient religious values".[5] Regrettably, nature has come to be regarded as something to be used, manipulated and enjoyed in its fullest possible way without having any accountability towards it. Such senses of domination over nature combined with a materialistic conception and greed have generated a loss of the meaning of nature. As Schuon argues, 'in a certain external sense, it may be said that the great social and political evil of the West is mechanization, for it is the machine which most directly engenders the great evils from which the world today is suffering. The machine is, generally speaking, characterized by the use of iron, of fire and of invisible forces. To talk about a wise use of machines, of their serving the human spirit, is utterly chimerical. It is in the very nature of mechanization to reduce men to slavery and to devour them entirely, leaving them nothing human, nothing above the animal level, nothing above the collective level. The kingdom of the machine followed that of iron, or rather gave to its most sinister expression. Man, who created the machine, ends by becoming its creature".[6] As a result, we have neglected concepts such as ideology, doctrine, representation, *Weltanschauung*, spirit, ethos and spiritual significance of everything including nature. The result is the eulogization of an impersonal model of culture, which has inevitably changed humanism into utilitarianism and anti-humanism. Our external nature has been obliterated; it no longer determines the conditions of survival. The fact of the matter is that the harmony between man and nature has been destroyed. How did we lose that harmony (between nature and man) is the ethical question of the present century?

The debate about ethics as applied to nature (often thought of as "natural resources") posits the question whether the primary values about which we should be concerned are cultural, that is, anthropocentric, or whether there is also intrinsic natural value, independent of humans, which humans ought to consider. Asking such a question is quite outside the capacity of plants and animals. Only human beings have conscience enough to do this. Though human beings are evolved out of nature, but they have evolved *out* of it is a matter of ethics and philosophy. It means, otherwise, that there is a concomitant relationship between man and nature. Hence, man's ideal condition is a union with nature just because he is really a part of it. In thinking of him as somehow apart from nature or superior to it is a violation of the deepest laws of his own being. What is intended to argue here is that the domain of nature should not become a 'thing' devoid of meaning. To answer the above question, I would like to introduce two types of rationality, which stamp our civilization and culture, the analyses of which can be a good starting point to reveal a very decisive influence upon the occurring processes of the loss between man and nature. The two classical types of rationality, which have existed till now in the Western civilization are *metaphysical rationality* and *instrumental rationality*. The sources of metaphysical rationality can be traced back to Greek philosophers, mainly Parmenides, Plato and Aristotle. Later, in the Middle Ages, metaphysical rationality was echoed in the views of St. Augustine and St. Thomas Aquinas, and, further, it found its classical expression in philosophical systems of the 17th and 18th centuries, including the system of Hegel. Before Hegel, metaphysical rationality found its strong grounding in the philosophical systems of Descartes, Spinoza and Leibniz.

Metaphysical Rationality

Metaphysical rationality possessed a number of distinctive features. The most important of them was the conviction of the necessary connection between reason and being and assumed that the world was organized wisely and purposely, because it owed its existence and ordering to the existence and efficient power of the divine Absolute. This absolute is variously called as the *Being* identical with reason by Parmenides, the *Nous* by Anaxagoras, the *Divine builder - Demiurge* by Plato, the *First substance* by Aristotle, the *God* by Christian philosophers, the *Substance* by Spinoza, or the *Absolute idea* by Hegel. In every case, it was dependent upon the existence of an objective cause that warranted law and order to the temporal world. Despite certain imperfections, the world/nature as a whole appeared as a reflection of the divine Absolute in this philosophy. In other words, metaphysical rationality excluded any accidentality. Everything that exists has a meaning and is purposeful, which can be analyzed into exact logico-mathematical or natural laws originating from the objective reasonableness.

In metaphysical rationality reasonableness is an attribute of both being and man. The human intellect, *ratio*, is a particle and man is equipped with reason with an end in view of comprehending and disclosing the reasonableness of the whole being. "The reason, wrote Hegel, is the certitude of the consciousness that it is all-embracing-reality."[7] Rationality belongs to the being itself, where objective rationality warrants law and order to all that exists; the thinking which takes place in human mind displays the truth of being and in the final account it is a road on which being itself is reached at the true knowledge about himself.

From the standpoint of metaphysical rationality the nature or the cosmos is full of meaning; all that exist are endowed with meaning including nature and human history. In this image of rationality, knowledge is an activity, which mirrors the objective meaning of things and, therefore, it acquires a positive moral value. The rational behaviour, being compatible with an objective order, is always moral and it directs towards more and more new values. Perhaps one of the most important features of metaphysical rationality is that ideas of truth and goodness are related with themselves. Once this is applied to nature, it implies that man is intimately related with nature and the cosmos conveys to man a meaning that concerns him. What is that meaning is the primal question that concerns again the ethical dimensions of environment and nature. It is true that a majority of people live in a desacralized world of phenomena whose only meaning is either their quantitative relationships expressed in mathematical formulae that satisfy the scientific mind or material usefulness. Beyond this phenomenality of 'things', there is a symbolic world of meaning that these phenomena convey. What I am trying to emphasize may be summarized in the following way: The phenomenality of things should be integrated into the dimension of metaphysics so that its undisputed facts could also gain a spiritual significance. This task can only be accomplished by rediscovering the spiritual meaning of nature which has certain metaphysical basis and Christianity was able to appropriate the same till the middle of the 19th century.

Instrumental Rationality

From the historical viewpoint, instrumental rationality is the result of the destruction of classical rationalism on the one hand and as the effect of positivistic phenomenalism on the other; it got eventually combined with the scientific attitude with its cult of techniques together with the widespread technocrat ideologies. It lost the transcendent and objective references, e.g., to God, Logos, objective reason, objective order etc. and, instead, it became exclusively connected with a human subjective reasoning subordinated in the form of instrumental tools to the realization of aims whose reasonableness nobody inquires. The transition from objective to subjective reason caused reason to become exclusively an instrument; its only value became the utilitarian one. The results and consequences of the transformation of the instrumentalization of reason enabled the human subject to plunder the nature for his/her own personal motifs.

The criteria of instrumental rationality found its wide application in all spheres of human activity in science, techniques, economy, organization of collective life, etc., and rationality has been universally identified with perfection, splendour, profit and material abundance. As a consequence, one feels obliged to rationalize one's own existence, thinking and acting. In the stereotype of instrumental rationality, the qualification "rational has also meant consistency with scientific methods, resting on the knowledge about causality and other laws of nature" and thereby in conformity with established aims such as bringing profitable results and to foresee future events optimizing human actions in all forms of life. Hence, instrumental rationality affirms on the model of most efficient instrument for the creation of conditions of a 'prosperous' life of people. As Herrigel says, "if one really wishes to be master of an art, technical knowledge of it is not enough. One has to transcend technique so that the art becomes an 'artless art' growing out of the unconscious".[8] The visible sides of this moral degeneration are alienation within oneself, rudeness toward nature, indifference to ecological issues, apathy for the coming generation and cruelty. The distraction of the old and proven traditional means gave birth not only to a spiritual vacuum but also to the forced introduction of values and norms which do not correspond to the real social conditions in our society. In other words, we are victims of a degenerated self which has lost its authentic self which was in communion with the nature. Hence, we need the recovery of metaphysical thinking and transcend ourselves from the instrumental or means-end rationality. It is pertinent here to recall the words of Heidegger: "The approaching tide of technological revolution in the atomic age could so captivate, bewitch, dazzle and beguile man that calculative thinking may someday come to be accepted and practiced as the only way of thinking. What great danger then might move upon us? Then this might go hand in hand with the greatest ingenuity in calculative planning and inventing indifference toward meditative thinking, total thoughtlessness. And then? Then man would have denied and thrown away his own special nature that he is a meditative being. Therefore, the issue is the saving of man's essential nature. Therefore, the issue is keeping meditative thinking alive."[9]

Metaphysical Rationality and Christian Response

If the loss of the metaphysical rationality is responsible for the loss of harmony between man and nature and of the role of the sciences of nature in the total scheme of knowledge, then we may have to admit that this knowledge and rationality has been nearly forgotten in the West while it has continued to survive in the traditions of the East. Lynn White. Jr, in his famous article on "The Historical roots of our Ecological Crisis" published in 1967, argued that the crisis in ecology is Christianity's fault because Christianity taught that man had dominion over nature and man has treated nature in a destructive way[10]. This accusation, though valid in a certain sense, cannot be accepted in its face value. When we turn our attention to the *Bible*, especially in the Old Testament, there are certain references to the participation of nature in the religious view of life such as in the vision of Hosea in which God entered into a Covenant with beasts and plants in order to secure peace, or when Noah was ordered to preserve all animals whether they were clean or unclean, that is, irrespective of their usefulness or relation to man.[11] When God flooded the earth he took pains to ensure the preservation of every creature as much as men. After the flood he instructed every type of living creature not man alone to be fruitful and multiply upon the earth. The co-called covenant of the rainbow was a promise not only to Noah and his descendants but to every creature of the earth. These observations obviate the necessity to argue that dominion of man on nature/earth cannot be understood as governing with force and cruelty but in the manner of a good shepherd anxious to preserve the earth in the best possible way. Man must treat nature with an overwhelming respect. Likewise, virgin nature or wilderness is conceived as a place of trial and punishment as well as refuge and contemplation or as the reflection of paradise. This vision and tradition of the contemplative view of nature was to survive later in Judaism in both the Kabbalistic and Hassidim schools. As for the *New Testament*, the death and resurrection of Christ is accompanied by a withering and rejuvenation of nature pointing to the cosmic character of Christ. St. Paul also believed that all creation shares in the redemption.

Gradually in the Western Church, the selective character of salvation became more emphasized and virgin nature and wilderness became interpreted as a domain of warfare and combat rather than of peace and contemplation. Even the geographic expansion of the Renaissance and the conquest of the New World were accomplished with this motif in mind.[12] In the Eastern Church, however, the contemplative view of nature was emphasized and made much more central. Nature was considered as a support for the spiritual life and the belief was held that all nature shares in salvation and the universe is renovated and reconstructed by Christ in his second coming. Among the early Christian fathers like (Greek) Origen, Irenaeus, Maximus the Confessor and Gregory of Nyssa who were so influential in the formation of orthodox theology developed a theology of nature. It may be emphasized here that Christian fathers like Origen and Irenaeus have applied the Logos doctrine not only to man and his religion but also to the whole of nature and all creatures. Their followers too showed much sympathy for a spiritual vision of nature.[13]

With the spread of Christianity into Northern Europe, new ethnic groups entered the fold of Christianity. History says that these groups though infected with paganism of the Mediterranean world yet were keenly concerned with the spiritual relation between man and nature. In this connection, it may be recalled that there was a strong awareness of the harmony between man and nature among the Anglo-Saxons. A historical trajectory of the characters who have contributed to the strong connection between man and nature are the names of Johannes Scotus Erigena and Dionysius the Areopagite. Erigena, it is often said, was deeply aware of the interlinking connection between man and nature which made him to talk about the transcendent origin of the Universe. According to him, all things in the universe come from God and are created through Christ.[14]

Erigena, following Gregory of Nyssa, held a conception of matter according to which matter rather than being an opaque quantity is a combination of incorporeal qualities, while form is all that gives existence to corporeal bodies and relates this domain to higher planes of existence. Thus, Erigena argues in the following way: "The space of a point is not space perceived by the senses, but a space understood by the intellect. So a point is incorporeal and the beginning of lines; a line is incorporeal and the beginning of surfaces; a surface is incorporeal and the beginning of solidity and solidity is the perfection of matter. Matter, therefore, is really a combination of incorporeal qualities. It is form which constitutes and contains all material bodies and form is incorporeal'.[15] These observations suggest that the Christian thinkers vehemently argued for the interconnectedness between man and nature. According to them, human subject stands between the spiritual and material creations and partake the nature of both. The *Bible* says that man is created in the image of God; yet he/she is an animal so that from one side the spiritual world is reflected in him and from the other side what is observed is his world of 'animality'. In the light of this spiritual conception of nature, Erigena possessed a strong symbolic vision of things. He also expounds a doctrine of the states of being and the interrelation between levels in the hierarchy of existence. This interrelation or inter-connectedness among things resembles the universal metaphysical doctrines of the Orient. One of the eminent examples of the Christian contemplative vision of nature is Saint Hildegard of Bingen. She is a great visionary whose exposition of the structure of the cosmos is combined with remarkable miniatures going back to St. Hildegard herself.[16] What is observed in her is a Christian cosmography and cosmology expounded through the means of the sacred art of Christianity which was conveyed through the medium of traditional art. She had a vision of nature and in her vision she is addressed by the Spirit in these remarkable words: "I am that supreme and fiery force that sends forth all the sparks of life. Death has no part in me, yet I do allot it. . . . I shine in the water, I burn in the sun and the moon and the stars. Mine is that mysterious force of the invisible wind. I sustain the breath of all living. . . I am the force that that lies hid in the winds, from me they take their source, and as a man may move because he breathes, so doth a fire burn but by my blast. All these live because I am in them and are their life.[17] If Erigena expounded a metaphysical doctrine of nature and Saint Hildegard a vision of a Christian cosmos expressed on terms of Christian iconography and symbolism, Rogen Bacon was a scientist and experimenter. He was also an illuminationist and Pythagorean who tried to cultivate the sciences of nature in the matrix of supernatural knowledge and conceived of mathematics in a symbolic sense. It is said that he experimented not only with nature but also with Holy Spirit within himself. He possessed a vision of the hierarchy of knowledge much like that of Avicenna who was a Muslim and whom he greatly admired.

We also find in the figure of St. Francis Assisi a most startling reminder of the possibility of a reverential attitude towards nature within the aura of Christian saintly life. His life among the birds and beasts that he addressed was a concrete example of the Christian belief that through holiness man can gain a relationship with nature. Francis Assisi's addressing of birds as his brothers reflected this stewardship that men must not see himself as conqueror of the earth but as a steward to preserve the nature. This is a return to conditions before the fall with its ensuing disruption of harmony between man and nature.[18] In the *Canticle of the Sun* and in many other sermons, St. Francis displays a disinterested contemplative view of nature outside all human utility. He was able to get a deep rooted intimacy with the nature as he was able to get himself identified with the Spirit that breathes within it.

As in the case of St. Francis of Assisi, we see an eminent example in Dante of the integration of all knowledge—scientific, theological and philosophical—into the total structure of Christianity. In the *Divine Comedy*, the cosmos is a Christian one; the seven liberal arts correspond to so many levels of existence which the soul must realize; the plight from the summit of the mount of Purgatory symbolizes the departure of the soul from the pinnacle of human perfection. The point is that one must actually traverse the cosmos, or the levels of existence, to realize that the force that pervades all things are the 'love that moves the sun and the stars'.

Unfortunately, after the Middle ages, the visualization of nature based on the metaphysical doctrine is more difficult to observe in the Christian tradition; it continued to show its presence here and there till the nineteenth century. Among those who talked about the metaphysical vision of the nature, the names of John Ray and Jacob Bohme deserves to be mentioned. Jacob Bohme, who is known as the last Christian agnostics, continued the alchemical tradition of the study of nature. According to him, man cannot see the inner forces of nature as well as its primordial pristine purity because of the darkness within their souls. He has sought to reclaim this pristine purity of nature by removing the darkness within our souls.

Metaphysical Vision of Nature and the Shift of Outlook

So far, we have been tracing the historical trajectory of Christian vision of nature which is based on its metaphysical principles. Such a metaphysical vision emphasizes a change of attitude, an attitude of intimacy with nature as cosmos conveys to man a meaning that concerns him. We have lost such a sense of meaning and contemplation as we have lost the contemplative and symbolist spirit which sees symbols rather than facts. It is a true statement if I say that the West has already forgotten the symbolic view of things. Thus, the modern West live in a desacralized world of phenomena whose only meaning is either their quantitative relationships expressed in mathematical formulae that satisfy the scientific mind or their material usefulness. This is to suggest that we have made an extreme effort in emptying the sacred character of the cosmos and made it to become profane. Thus, the symbols in the nature became facts and spiritually meaningless. What I am arguing for is the resurrection of a metaphysics that emphasize on the contemplative and symbolist rather than the passionate and the factual mentality which can revitalize the lost connection between man and nature. As opined by Guenon, the quantitative character of modern science must be pointed out in particular because it exists as a general tendency which seeks the reduction of all quality to quantity and all that is essential in the metaphysical sense to the material and substantial.[19]

In accord with Christian spirituality and philosophical vision, Christianity till the nineteenth century advocated a philosophy of nature based on the principles of metaphysical rationality that advocated a harmony between man and nature. They were happy with nature because they accepted its norms and its rhythms, so to say, its *dharma* (metaphysical rationality) rather than to seek to dominate and overcome it. Put the same differently, they have not judged nature according to human utility (instrumental rationality) nor have they made earthly man as the measure of all things. They had followed the *dharma* of nature and the *ṛta* of the cosmos by accepting and following the nature of things and have not sought to disturb nature by artificial means. That is why Christianity as an integral tradition has developed diverse cosmological and natural sciences and even spiritual techniques tied intimately to the use of the energy within nature. Thus man was considered a channel of grace for nature because man only can cast light into the world of nature through his active participation. But only he who has turned toward the inward dimension of his being can see nature as a symbol, as a transparent reality and come to know and understand it in the real sense. This excellence was especially evident in some of the saints, mystics and theologians who visualized direct symbols of the spiritual world in the virgin nature, trees, streams and the sky, in birds and buffaloes. With the strong symbolist spirit with which nature was endowed, they saw everywhere images of celestial realities. For them, nature was sacred (not profane) and there was a definite disdain of the artificialities of sedentary life. This is what I understood as the visible expression of the implication of metaphysical rationality. We may also add here that from the point of view of metaphysical rationality, the reality of a species is not exhausted by its purely material manifestations. The metaphysical approach undergirds the idea that the species ultimately are the manifold ideas in the Divine Mind which at a particular cosmic moment have become imprinted in the corporeal world and retain their reality on other planes of existence. This dimension of the metaphysical vision of nature is asserted by St. Paul in his *Epistle to the Romans*. According to St. Paul, the total salvation of man is possible when not only man himself but all creatures are redeemed.[20] We forget conveniently that the divine response to the making of the world is to confirm the reality of diversity and alternatives in human habitat. In brief, Christian tradition and its metaphysically based doctrines on the vision of nature must be considered as a tradition whose foundations were built on a concomitant relatedness between man and the cosmos.

This new ethics of conscientiousness emphasizes on accountability and commitment which is the outcome of metaphysical rationality. On the contrary, the results and consequences of the transformation of the instrumentalization of reason have resulted to the loss of spiritual roots in human understanding on freedom, nature, other creatures in the planet, happiness, tolerance, etc. Consequently, we have lost the 'human' in human settlements, in family relations, in neighbourhood, religion, economy, ecology and polity. The shaping of the present rationality within a span of 150 years was able to bring forth a number of negative phenomena in science, techniques, art, concepts of development and sustainability, philosophy, literature and practically in all spheres of social and cultural life and rationality has been universally identified with perfection, splendour, profit and material abundance. In the stereotype of instrumental rationality, the qualification "rational has also meant consistency with scientific methods, resting on the knowledge about causality and other laws of nature" and thereby in conformity with established aims such as bringing profitable results and to foresee future events optimizing human actions in all forms of life. The underlying point is that instrumental rationality affirms on the model of most efficient instrument for the creation of conditions of a 'prosperous' society wherein we have lost 'the nature'. Therefore, it is argued that only the revival of a spiritual conception of nature that is based on the metaphysical doctrines and rationality can hope to neutralize the havoc brought about by the applications of modern science and integrate science into more universal perspective.

Notes

1. The conference, Philosophy and Environmental Crisis, was held at the University of Georgia, February 18-20, 1971. Proceedings were published in William Blackstone (ed), *Philosophy and Environmental Crisis*, Athens, GA: University of Georgia Press, 1974.
2. (Naess, Arne, "The Shallow and the Deep, Long-Range Ecology Movements", *Inquiry* 16 (1973): 95-100.
3. Christopher Stone, "Should Trees have Standing?"Southern California Law Review 45, No. 4(1972): 462.
4. M. Eliade, *The Sacred and the Profane, The Nature of Religion*, New York, 1959, p. 179.
5. M. Eliade, *ibid*., p. 151.
6. F. Schuon, *Spiritual Perspectives and Human Facts*, trans. D. M. Matheson, London, 1953, p. 21.
7. Hegel, G.W.F., *The Phenomenology of Mind*, 2: 269.
8. Herrigel, E., Zen in the *Art of Archery*, trans. R. F. C. Hull, 1953, New York, Random. 71 (V-VI).
9. Heidegger, M., *Being and Time*, trans. J. Macquarie and E. Robinson, 1962, New York, Harper & Row, 56.
10. Lynn Townsend White, Jr, "The Historical Roots of Our Ecologic Crisis", *Science*, Vol. 155 (Number 3767), March 10, 1967, pp 1203-1207.
11. Williams, George, H., *Wilderness and Paradise in Christian Thought: The Biblical Experience of the Desert in the History of Christianity*, Harvard Divinity School, 1962, Introduction, p. x.
12. This development is fully traced in William's book, *Wilderness and Paradise in Christian Thought, op. cit.*, p. 118.
13. Raven, Charles E., *Natural Religion and Christian Theology*, Cambridge University Press, 1953, p. 47 where it is quoted thus: 'A single blade of grass is enough to occupy your whole mind as you contemplate the skill that produced it'. The first chapter of the book, 'Biblical Attitude towards Nature' is an excellent exposition of Christian understanding of Nature from a biblical perspective.
14. Erigena followed the view of Clement of Alexandria who asserted thus: 'The Son is neither absolutely one, as one; nor yet many, as parts; but one, as all things; for from Him are all things; and He is the circle of all powers collected and united into one's' quoted in H. Bett, Johannes Scotus Erigena, *A Study in Medieval Philosophy*, Cambridge, 1925, p. 32.

15. *Ibid.*, p. 40.
16. For a detailed understanding, refer to "The Scientific Views and Visions of Saint Hildegard" in the book C. Singer, Studies in the *History and Method of Science*, Oxford, Vol. 1, 1917, p. 33.
17. *Ibid*; p. 33.
18. Williams, George. H., *op. cit.*, p. 42.
19. For a detailed analysis of this question in all aspects see R. Guenon, *The Reign of Quantity and the Signs of the Times* (trans. Lord North Bourne), London, 1953.
20. St. Paul, *Epistle to the Romans*, Chapter VIII.

9

Some Reflections on Environment

Shephali Vidyanta

A troublesome thought which has shaken the whole of humanity is climate change. The temperature of the atmosphere is increasing. According to a recent study made by world-ecologists and some economists published in an All India Daily—'more than 100 million people will die and global economic growth will be cut by 3.2 per cent of gross domestic product (GDP) by 2030 if the World fails to tackle climate change. As global average temperatures rise due to greenhouse gas emissions, the effects on the planet, such as melting ice caps, extreme weather, drought and rising sea levels threaten populations and livelihoods.

These dreadful pictures of environment are necessary consequences of modernization and industrialization. It is a serious challenge to the ecologists, and scientists to tackle the situation and find a way out to protect the nature for the future generations. Economists are, on the other hand, worried about declining features of economic growth. Philosophers may lack expertise to tackle the environmental situation, or may not have ability to expedite the economic growth; they may still be able to say something useful, something essential for mankind to understand.

Let us have a quick look at nature; it may help us to assess the present ecological situation better. Man is one of the evolutes of the planet earth and he is the latest among all. Whether it is the result of the ideas found in Old Testament or Greek thoughts, is a point to be discussed separately. Today's fact is that man keeps himself at the centre, treats himself as all in all. He segregates himself from the rest of the evolutes in the planet and is solely concerned with his own interest. His primary concern has been to satisfy his material needs, and bodily pleasure has been the sole aim of the whole process. Growth, for him, means the economic growth; science and technology are used to achieve the same. The idea which induces and nourishes material flourishment is the belief that if only there were more wealth everything else would fall into place. In his constant race after material gain and bodily comfort it is not merely that man ignores his relationship to other (other than man) natural objects but uses them in a rather destructive manner if needed.

Man by his natural power of intelligence makes constant attempt to grasp the laws of nature. His knowledge of natural laws helps him to control the nature and use it to satisfy his own selfish desires. For example, man constructs a dam and controls the natural flow of river-water, and then he produces electricity from it. Invention of electricity has opened up new dimensions in the process of industrialization and development of agriculture. The result is material prosperity.

The craze of material prosperity is frantic and bridleless. While absorbed in the race man misses the distinction between his need and his greed. In the pride of material achievement he constructs high-rise buildings by destroying forests and wilderness. He cuts trees and uses them to satisfy his hobby and have amusement. He kills birds and animals to satisfy his stomach. The whole edifice of this man-made modernization, thus, stands on the use of nature and natural objects.

At this juncture man fails to get one point; he forgets that, in spite of his distinctive characteristics, he himself is nothing but a nature's product only. Nature is the whole system and man is only a part of it. Nothing goes incoherent or irrelevant in Nature. The previous evolutes constitute the platform for the next. Man's appearance on the planet depends necessarily on the previous ones like soil, water, plants and animals. Any kind of disorder in any state of existents would affect the whole system. We can compare it with a multi-storey building in which the residents of the top floor are busy in new construction, extension and beautification. This might have brought some damage to the ground floor. May be the soil, or the plinth of the building cannot bear the extra weight put on the top floor. The building collapses. The residents of the whole building suffer. Same is the case with man. He is the latest evolute on the earth. To satisfy his selfish interest he uses and destroys the rocks, soil, water, plants and so on which are just like the plinth, pillars and the ground floor of the building. If its plinth, pillars are not taken care of, as the building collapses, so would happen with the whole system of planetary evolution (necessarily including man), if soil, water, plants are not taken care of.

The situation (ecological imbalance) stands as a challenge to the leading thinkers of the world. Their centre of attention is—'How to save the planet'! While discussing the problem Albert Schweitzer and Paul Taylor would say that it is not the inanimate objects but the living ones are to be paid proper importance. This idea may be thought to take support of the fundamental principle of morality which holds "it is good to maintain and cherish life; it is evil to destroy and to check life. A man is really ethical only when he obeys the constraint laid on him to help all life which he is able to succour, and when he goes out of his way to avoid injuring anything living". But there are others who would not accept this. For them 'Living objects are not something special which need exceptional care.

They hold that it is possible to give a purely physical explanation of what is happening to living things like plants and trees. There is no good reason why we should have greater respect for the physical processes that govern the growth and decay of living things than we have for those that govern non-living things. It is at least not obvious why we should have greater reverence for a tree than a stalactite or for a single celled organism than for a mountain.

Deep ecologists, in this respect, hold it necessary to preserve the integrity of the biosphere for its own sake. According to them every organism and entity in the ecosphere is equal in intrinsic worth. The planet has to be saved in its totality. To quote from Bill Devall and George Sessions "the intuition of bio-centric equality is that all things in the biosphere have an equal right to live and blossom and to reach their own individual forms of unfolding and self-realization within the larger self-realization. This basic intuition is that all organisms and entities in the ecosphere, as parts of the interrelated whole, are equal in intrinsic worth". To put the view of Leopold "a thing is right when it tends to preserve the integrity, stability and beauty of the biotic community. It is wrong when it tends otherwise".

If, as this quotation appears to suggest, bio-centric equality rests on a basic intuition—one can surely pull the idea ahead to raise question against the prevailing notion that human beings' rights to live and blossom ought to be preferred. Man's essential abilities of being able to think, to decide, to plan for the future and to make moral deliberations are, like any other natural object, necessarily integral to the self-maintaining system of nature. Then man's capacity to desire to maintain itself is also a natural evolutionary product of Nature. Now the question arises as to if man's essential but distinctive characteristics are natural expression of integrity of Nature then why do the integral parts of it build up a situation which goes against the Nature itself? Is it not self-contradictory for the integral components of a system to go against the system itself?

There may be many answers to these questions. In my humble attempt I would try to hold that, it is a matter of common sense that when I make use of my abilities of making plans and decisions I must not ignore the foundation, on the basis of which I have been able to do so. It is the integrity of Nature that has brought these capabilities (e.g. the capacity to decide) to me. It would be self-killing if my decisions go against the sustainability of nature. Nature, the enduring mother, must be preserved and respected. We have to cherish and nourish the natural resources, and hand them over to generations that follow.

Now, if it is the case that the integrity of nature has given us the power of moral deliberations, a right choice, and an action with a proper dimension would only enrich the wholeness of nature. Any endeavour, if goes against Nature's integrity, would be nothing but self-defeating—either nature would not accept it, or nature would be damaged by it.

It is at this stage that some thinkers find it necessary to develop an environmental ethic in which a set of virtues are praised and a set of ethical prohibitions are adopted by the individuals and societies. Environmental ethics ideally rejects the idea of a materialist society in which success is measured by the number of consumer goods one can accumulate. Instead, it judges development in terms of real fulfilment. In this connection environmental ethics encourages the idea of frugality and temperance. It finds virtue in saving and recycling the natural resources and vice in extravagance and unnecessary consumption.

The ideas surely are helpful to save the Nature, if they could be applied in our practical life. But the present socio-economic structure shows a different picture. The economic structure of our society is constituted by the intentions of the commercial enterprise. Our needs today are not dependent on physical scarcity of an object, the feeling of need and want is created and pampered in the mind of the consumer by the selfish interest of the corporate sector. The entrepreneur produces a commodity and motivates the society, through various advertising devices, to consume the same. In case, the feeling of the want is suppressed because of the lack of purchasing power, credit cards and debit cards are supplied to the people so that they can immediately buy the commodity without worrying about their pockets. The financial inability of the buyer is tactfully disguised and the commodities are sold. The system of production and consumption is fully controlled by the profit-makers and businessmen.

Where would be the room for frugality then? Why should one practise self-control? Things are available, one has capacity to purchase them, and then why should one control the desire to buy It? In this scenario frugality, as held by the environmental ethics, remains nothing but an ideal which ought to be practised to save the nature. Environmental ethics holds that their advocating frugality does not mean that they negate achievement of pleasure. Pleasure, according to them, does not come from consumption of material goods, it is an emotion which is developed through warm personal relationships. Being close to children, to parents, to friends, having conversations and sharing every little thing with near ones, according to environmental ethics, constitute the edifice of a pleasant satisfied life.

Today's socio-economic system aims at producing only material goods, and if consumption of material goods cannot give 'pleasure', then what does the present system aim at? What the whole endeavour is up to? On the other hand, where lies the source of pleasure, if it is not to be found in consumption of material goods? The source of pleasure, according to environmental ethics, then, lies somewhere beyond this socio-economic framework. The experts say this pleasure comes from personal relationships. Concept of 'personal relationships' need further clarification, because commonly our personal relationships are matters of experience. My point here is to ask the environmentalists whether the 'pleasure' they speak about, is only an experience limited by empirical boundary! Would the environmentalists limit the foundation of their ethic in experience alone?

Once we accept the need to preserve our environment seriously environmental ethics would hold that our choice of recreation is also not ethically neutral. If we have to choose between motor-car racing or cycling, we should go for cycling because motor-car racing requires the consumption of fossil fuels and discharge of carbon dioxide into the atmosphere.

Now the point is practice of frugality, recycling the natural resources or opting for cycling as a form of recreation instead of motor-car-driving—all are temporary arrangements to avoid immediate environmental crises. If this is the sole point which the environmental ethics wants to make, then it becomes a shaky and superficial attempt which depends solely on a utilitarian ground. I feel even the term 'ethic' needs clarification here. Acceptance and appreciation of others and adequate concern for them build the ground on which environmental ethics has to set up its foundation.

Now the situation is that scientists, ecologists, and even the experts of environmental ethics-whoever is trying to find out some means to overcome the crises of Nature, accept the scientific and mechanical progress as the only kind of progress possible while reject some consequences of the progress. The fact is that remaining within the system of mechanization it is rather impossible to deny the effects coming out of the system. Is it not paradoxical to talk of sustaining Nature while we are encouraging a developmental procedure which stands on destructive use of natural objects?

The North-East region is still on the lap of Mother Nature. The trees and creepers, insects, birds and animals are still intimately inter-dependent. One protects, the other is protected; one is the food and the other is its consumer. Soil, water, forest are tied by the same thread in which one is saved by the other. Fortunately, North-Eastern States are free (to a great extent) from the grip of modernization. People living here still lead a simple life surrounded by Nature and natural objects. Nature, here, still supplies abundant resources in charity. We have to use them in proper dimension so that nature is not exploited. The economic developments are to be brought in a friendly relation to objects of nature. Our enjoyment and recreations are to be experienced in harmony with the environment.

In the attempt to pursue a progress in the dimension mentioned above, people of North-East may turn to the tradition (for guidance) in which we find reverand vedic thinkers, the Bauddhas, Jainas and M.K. Gandhi. Self-restraint and the capacity to withdraw oneself from material satisfaction lie at the root of frugality. Self-control which is the presupposition of frugality is a matter to be achieved through sincere and constant attempt of the practitioner. The great thinkers of the world have paid much importance to temperance by characterizing it as a cardinal virtue. Our forefathers have taken us one step ahead of them by making self-restraint a way of life. Achievement of bodily comfort and material prosperity (*artha* as a purusartha) are attainable goals only under strict vigilance of morality (*dharma*). Actually the whole endeavour lies in our return to the tradition, its reassessment and practice. If a well-thought and systemically programmed strive in this line would be devotedly applied in the lives of the people of North-East, then they could be at the fore-front in the line of the savers of the planet.

10

The Interconnectedness Sensibility

Tribal Ethos and Environmental Ethics

Siby K. George

In these times of global warming and technology-aided devastation of the earth, there is a widespread sense of deep crisis. A common response to the crisis insistently articulated with increasing frequency is the necessity for a moral revolution that radically decentres the obsession with humanity and its interests in modern ethics. This call for revolutionary transformation of morality understands the ecological crisis as originating from the loss of the interconnectedness sensibility. In the four sections of this chapter, I shall argue for the following four philosophical contributions to the desired moral revolution: (i) moral philosophy may focus on contributing to revive our lost moral sense of interconnectedness with nature in a phenomenologically evocative sense rather than by way of producing rational arguments for the intrinsic value of nature, (ii) moral philosophy may perform its equally important critical task by unveiling the untenable moral structures of modern consciousness, (iii) because the task of recapturing a lost sensibility is to be historically contextualized, the mythical category of 'the tribal' may be considered as the vantage point for understanding and recapturing the lost human sensibility of interconnectedness with nature, and (iv) from the vantage point provided by the mythical reformulation of the cultural vision of the many tribal worldviews of the world, a moral sense of connection with nature can be articulated as real hybrid cultural possibilities available in myriad vernacular modern traditions. The attempt here is not so much to explicate the conceptual textures of the notion of interconnectedness with nature; rather, I shall invoke the tribal world as the moral-phenomenological site of such a sensibility. I now proceed right away to the first section on my understanding of moral philosophy's task in revolutionizing ethics in response to the ecological crisis.

Being Moral

The transcendental human condition for the possibility of morality is often subjected to rigorous philosophical scrutiny. In this scrutiny, the question 'how is morality possible?' is strenuously distanced from the question 'how what is morally right is distinguished from wrong?' Modern philosophy gave common answers for both these questions. For Kant, we are moral on account of our rational nature and so the criterion for distinguishing moral action from its opposite is also rationality, that is, the universalisability of action as a rule for all rational humans of all times and places. For Mill and the utilitarians, on the other hand, we are moral owing to our hedonistic, happiness-seeking nature and, thus, the morality of our action can be judged only on the basis of the measure of happiness it gives rise to the maximum number of humans around us. In the contractarian political morality of Hobbes, humans are self-interested egoists, and so, egoism is also the moral basis for the political state, which negotiates self-interest to the best possible extent. Such explanatory apparatus for the phenomenon of morality, and also for the humanity of the human being as such, is viewed as problematic by several philosophers of the continental tradition in the recent past. I want to look at this problem in order to raise a fundamental objection to the way environmental ethics is conceived today in response to what is widely perceived since the 1960s as the human-generated ecological crisis.

After Rachel Carson's *Silent Spring* most dramatically presented to the American public the depth of the ecological crisis in 1962 and the ensuing launch of the modern environmental movement in America, a host of ethicists have begun to speak of vesting nature with intrinsic moral value. For these ethicists, the comparable intellectual background is the articulation of the intrinsic moral worth of the human being since the seventeenth century by philosophers like Locke, Rousseau and Kant. As humanity could suddenly—in a matter of a few centuries—imagine that every human person of every colour, race, language, class and caste is of intrinsic moral worth during the age of reason, humanism and the scientific revolution, so too, humanity today in the post-industrial age, vividly aware of the ecological crisis and the need to extend the moral compass to all beings in order to stem the tide of the devastation of the earth, actually can swiftly begin to imagine that all reality has intrinsic moral worth. This quick transformation of the moral imagination is not because morality is something closely linked to human imagination, culture and way of being but because what is exceptional about human beings is their rational capacity, and so, through the right use of reason, they can be led to see the intrinsic moral worth of all beings. What is required for any moral transformation is a set of clear arguments of reason which can persuade human beings everywhere, for arguments of reason, when most abstractly framed in their ideality, ahistoricity and universality, are like mathematical formula, which could persuade all persons who have achieved 'rational adulthood', that is, completion as human beings. Those that cannot be so persuaded by reason are rational children, awaiting full humanity. In this conception, earlier moral arguments, like that of Kant regarding the instrumental moral worth of non-human reality, are rational errors that can now be corrected and, thus, humanity can be effortlessly pushed towards a moral view of the earth and all beings by such production of reasons. This great transformation can be envisaged almost acontextually and without overlapping relations to other human actions and comportments.

Such philosophical-ethical theories, it can be argued, do not distinguish between conditions for the possibility of morality and the normative questions of morality. All such views make the fundamental assumption that morality arises from the rational nature of humans, and so, the criterion for distinguishing moral actions from their opposite is also rationality. In such moral conceptions, a major moral paradigm shift is a matter of producing a set of new rational arguments, and no further fundamental questioning, painful transformations in overlapping layers of the human condition or radical rejections of cultural/philosophical vantage points is required.

The western intellectual tradition, as is well known, turned from an inordinately other-worldly, spiritual worldview of the medieval era towards a radically humanistic (human-centric) worldview of the modern era definitively by the end of the eighteenth century. Let us now consider that the intellectual momentum of the western cultural horizon is now supposedly, though not yet definitively, shifting gradually towards an ecocentric worldview. If this latter cultural arrival of the west is an absolute point of universal morality, it is then the case that the earlier theocentric and anthropocentric worldviews of the west have been absolutely wrong and a whole civilization has been morally in the dark in an absolute sense. And, by contrast, consider the fact that according to this conception of moral progress the world's indigenous and tribal communities, which the west has always been caricaturing as living in civilizational childhood, awaiting moral light and reason, with their animistic worldviews, would now appear to have been always on the right side of the moral divide. A deeply problematic and contradictory side of the absolutist strain of thought hidden beneath the acultural, ahistorical, acontextual view of morality can, thus, be brought to the fore. The Canadian philosopher, Charles Taylor, points out at least two problems with such a stance. First, such acultural stances are ethnocentric in their view of other cultural and moral phenomena. From such stances, one judges and sees the other through the prism glass of the self.[1] Second, such views overrule the possibility that one's own cultural landscapes are products of powerful moral visions, and hence, its historical deviances from that vision could be rectified from time to time.[2]

A second problem with the acultural view of morality, and I think the more fundamental problem, is a grossly inadequate and partial picture of the human being that it gives rise to. I will now very briefly elucidate how an alternative and richer view of the human being, which, I think, can better account for the phenomenon of human morality and, thus, can also explain the contemporary ecological crisis and the complex requirements demanded by the new moral revolution pertaining to nature, could be brought to the fore from the phenomenological tradition.

Husserl's phenomenology is the descriptive science of the intentional structure or the object-directedness of consciousness. The fact that every case of consciousness is a consciousness of some object—be it perceived, imagined, remembered, dreamt or desired object—is the animating insight of Husserl's method of the first-person account of the objects of consciousness. The genetic and anatomical structure, and the life pattern of a sparrow would interest biology, but phenomenology's interest is in how the sparrow comes across to an experiencing human consciousness. Similarly, while for the physicist the earth is spherical and mobile, from a phenomenological perspective it is the firm basis on which my feet stand. According to Husserl the success of the description depends on the subject's ability to bracket her/his natural attitude towards the world—our implicit everyday convictions about ourselves and our world—and look at phenomena as they appear to our consciousness in a theory-free or presuppositionless fashion. Hence, phenomenology will not be troubled by how things or matters are in themselves or how they are from a scientific point of view. Phenomenology, on the other hand, attempts to lay bare the universal structures of consciousness in general or the structures of specific conscious experiences in the way we live them through. Husserl himself did a great deal to explicate the noetic (the *act* of consciousness intending its object) and the noematic (the *experience* of object) structures of consciousness, besides its several other aspects. According to Simone de Beauvoir's account, young Sartre's excitement for phenomenology began when a friend told him that he could phenomenologically describe the glass of apricot cocktail that was in front of him because Sartre always wanted to speak philosophically of things 'as he touched them'. The phenomenological method suited his preoccupation "to transcend the opposition of idealism and realism, to affirm at the same time the sovereignty of consciousness and the presence of the world as given to us."[3]

Although phenomenology opened up the Continental philosophical scene for themes that are generally considered outside the philosophical terrain, Husserl's prodigy and heir, Heidegger, comprehensively rejected his master's central thesis of the theory-freeness of intentionality. For Heidegger, consciousness is always contextualized and involved within a network of practical engagements before any Husserlian-style theoretical approach to things can be undertaken. In fact, theoretical approach is conditioned by our primordial comportments, which are guided by a pre-cognitive awareness of our world. In Heidegger's idiom, we, as engaged, conscious beings, are directed not towards the objectness of entities but towards their being—the way entities are understood by us, the manner of their presencing and, thus, appearing to our consciousness. Heidegger was always fascinated by the way the world affects us. Being is revealed to the seeker of being, the human being, not only by that agent's active pursuing but also by the thing's or the world's active manner of affecting the agent. Hence, in the hands of Heidegger, phenomenology becomes the description of how the being of entities are seen by the human being in the very way as it shows its being from itself. Thus, phenomenology is nothing but ontology or the description of the being of entities. Heidegger, unlike Husserl, admits that our sight is already theory-laden and so, when phenomena make their appearance to our already affected consciousness, there is always an element of concealment of their being. Phenomenology is practised as the way of steering clear of these concealments to describe phenomena just as they show from themselves.

An important consequence of Heidegger's interpretation of phenomenology is the abandonment of the assumption of theory-free description. "Our thought and speech," says Dermot Moran while explicating Heidegger's notion of intentionality, "is determined by engagements with the world, which themselves are not static, but mediated by tradition, by culture, by 'what one says' about things."[4] Description of the forms of consciousness is not culture-free but culture or horizon-dependent. This is what is meant by the hermeneutical turn of phenomenology with Heidegger. In the post-*Being and Time* writings, Heidegger began to delve deeper into the radical meaning of his discovery of the theory-ladenness of experience. He began to notice that the western ontological tradition in each historical era broadly interpreted the meaning of being in general in a particular way, and it was on account of this broad interpretation of being that entities in their being made sense to the westerner. By the later Heidegger's 'history of being' is meant this historicizing of the hermeneutical horizon of the western understanding of being in various historical epochs, especially of his own age, late modernity.

I began to speak of phenomenology with the justification that it strives to give us a richer conception of the human being. The phenomenologists, for example, reject the very essentialist philosophies of the human being like that of Descartes (thinking thing) or Kant (autonomous knowing and moral agent). Husserl's transcendental ego only means that consciousness is an independent entity which does not ontologically depend on nature; rather, nature is an intentional correlate of consciousness. Not that nature is denied by Husserl; what he denies is naive philosophical naturalism, according to which consciousness is ontologically dependent on nature.[5] In Heidegger, the separate consideration of consciousness as the ontologically independent 'pure' entity is replaced with the a richer notion of intentional consciousness as 'care', a term which captures the ontology of the human being as an entity for which the being of entities matters. In all our meaningful relation with other entities, 'care' is our existential mode of being towards them. What strikes Heidegger is not the fact that we are knowers but that we are affected by our world in each case as expressed in our moods (state-of-mind), that we have a pre-cognitive way of making sense of our world (understanding), and that we are engrossed and lost in our world (fallenness). Our being is manifested in these three ways because ontologically we are characterized by care and because our care-structure is primordially temporal. We relate in the present to things that matter to us, others and ourselves in terms of our having been and by projecting further possibilities into the future.

The phenomenology of Merleau-Ponty enriched our understanding of the human being in yet another fashion. As a critical follower of Husserl like Heidegger, he begins by rejecting the Husserlian assumption of the disengaged, disembodied transcendental ego. He proceeds from the intuition that it is the body that enables our insertion into the world in order to experience it, and hence concludes that the subject of experience is this very 'body subject' and not a disembodied transcendental ego. While Heidegger emphasized how the world impinges on the located experiencer of things, he too did not clarify how we, as sentient, embodied beings, let the world affect us. David Abram, whose project is to formulate an ecology from the threshold of phenomenology, relies heavily on the insights of Merleau-Ponty to regain the bond that western humanity has broken with the earth since the scientific revolution. The insight is this: "at the heart of even our most abstract cogitations [is] the sensuous and sentient life of the body itself."[6] I am not merely a Heideggerian being-in-the-world; I am an embodied being-in-the-world. I am affected by the world, the earth and everything living and non-living around me in and through the threshold of my body. It is because I am a body subject that I have a close bond with all the living and the non-living material world. For Merleau-Ponty, perception is the dynamic, reciprocal exchange through which we access our world and its things. Things, whether living or non-living, are not passive matter that the active intellect comes into contact with. They are dynamic entities participating in the unfolding of perceptual experience. Perception happens through a coordinated, complementing flourish of the body subject. Merleau-Ponty later began to speak of the elemental power of the world and matter as 'flesh' because there was no name for such a notion in western history.

Another phenomenologist, Emmanuel Levinas, began noticing an ethical structure in pre-intentional consciousness, even before we could speak of the freedom or unfreedom of consciousness in the Sartrean fashion. For Levinas, consciousness, which is usually characterized in the Husserlian way as the ego, is already infested with alterity or otherness. It is such pre-reflective receptivity towards otherness that acts as a native obstruction to the ego's spontaneity and imperial freedom to conquer and smother the other's alterity. This openness to otherness, which Levinas unfortunately formulated only in terms of intersubjectivity, is the condition for the possibility of any ethical gesture, even the little there is.

From these inadequate excurses into the rich phenomenological conceptualization of the human being in contrast to the Enlightenment notion of the subject as an autonomous freedom, a spectator over the world who can disinterestedly abstract universal features of the essence of reality, I want to suggest, we need at least to start trying to formulate a richer understanding of our moral sensibilities. Levinas's wonderful insight that it is otherness that is the condition for morality, I think, is a rejuvenating vantage point to start rethinking our morality. The ethical sensibility of the human being arises not from the autonomous rational freedom of the disengaged subject, but from the limit posed to the free subject by the ontologically inescapable otherness that is constitutive of subjectivity itself. Husserl, Heidegger, Merleau-Ponty and Levinas analyzed the structure of experience as inextricably tied up with otherness, whether human or non-human. The Cartesian chasm between matter and consciousness cannot stand if we are radically body subjects inalienably bound up with the world and other body subjects. Neither self, which is a drive towards satisfaction and fulfilment, nor reason, which is a drive towards measuring, calculating and ordering, can be the ground of the moral sensibility, which is a drive towards the other in goodness—a fundamental movement towards the other in negation of self. Reason is not the negation of self but a restraining drive for the self, as Levinas never tires of emphasizing, which orders the upsurge of the moral as law, politics and convention. The moral sensibility is an unbounded movement towards otherness in the Levinasian idiom, which is restricted in its profundity by the rational order of the state and its institutions, law and culture. If ethics is conditioned on our openness towards otherness, this openness itself is possible because we are embodied, experiencing being-in-the-world. The moral revolution demanded by the ecological crisis can be inaugurated only with such an understanding of the human being and her moral sensibility.

But the existentialist phenomenological thinking of the

Sartrean variety exemplifies the opposite of this possibility. Sure, he did not conceive of the human in the mechanistic, robotic fashion as the scientific strain of thought during his times was prone to do. Rather, he juxtaposed the lonely, arbitrary freedom of the human being (being-for-itself) against the absurd orderliness of lifeless, meaningless reality (being-in-itself). According to Erazim Kohák, existentialism was popular in the mid-twentieth century because it mirrored the western humanity of the age of war and self-doubt: "the humans of the West in the mid-twentieth century indeed perceived themselves in a great part as perplexed, perhaps defiant aliens in a strange, meaningless universe."[7] Kohák, like the phenomenologists we have looked at, does not subscribe to high spiritualism (religious humanism), human exceptionalism (existentialist humanism) or exaltation of the producing, labouring human being (Marxist humanism). For him, the ecologically sensitive moral revolution can begin only with a specifically naturalistic understanding of the human being. By naturalism Kohák means any philosophy of the human being which relates the being of the human integrally to nature and treating them as distinct only in as much as any species is distinct. A naturalistic understanding of the human being, Kohák contends, will not conceive the human being as thrown into an alien world against which she/he is to defiantly struggle. Instead, in a naturalistic conception of Kohák's nuance, as Husserl, Heidegger, Merleau-Ponty and Levinas acknowledge, the human being is at home in the cosmos as she/he is its integral part. Modernity is problematic because its essential tendency is to deny the human sense of at-homeness in the world.

This also means that though ethics should be formulated in a normative format, the moral sensibility itself is not a 'rule'. Rather morality is a sensibility that arises from the limits posed on the self's freedom in its confrontation with otherness as such, human and non-human. The moral sensibility is groomed and reinforced by cultural developments that happen in close affinity with the natural as well as human environment. In other words, our moral development does have a context and history, and so, moral norms are neither universal nor absolute, even though we should never cease dialoguing with moralities of all contexts and histories to broaden and further radicalize our moral horizon. This view, therefore, has an unsettling bearing on the universalistic, all-conquering, absolutist strain of thought in modern moral theory (of which the contemporary attempts in environmental ethics to produce arguments for the intrinsic value of nature is a reflection) that attempts to formulate a single, universal moral norm under the assumption that there is a single moral reasoning.

I shall argue in the remaining portion of this article that the relativist consequence of the view I am trying to articulate is a blessing in disguise. As for the next section, I shall argue that the modern human condition which has brought about a definitive severing of the natural bond between the human being and nature is the unfortunate consequence of the inadequate Enlightenment conception of the human being, which itself was the crowning arrival of the western philosophical thinking since the ancient Greeks with its inherent tendency to capture the exceptionality of the human being in her rational capacity as opposed to her natural, animal condition.

Being Modern

The modern sensibility is exceptional for a variety of reasons. I shall only deal with the exceptional new human relation with nature that modernity inaugurated around the seventeenth century. Despite half a century of vigorous intellectual debate, we must note, the modern vision of human-nature relation still stands good—challenged and vilified but disinclined to bow out.

The central or essential drive of the modern western worldview, according to Heidegger, is the technological comportment towards all that is. What makes modernity distinct from all other historical epochs in the west is this belief and capacity to transform the real into material for human manipulation through the use of technology and technical ways. The whole sphere of modern approach to the real, thus, has come to be called technological or instrumental rationality in the words of Herbert Marcuse. Heidegger ontologizes technology. He calls the essence of technology *Gestell* or framework. The essence of technology, in this sense, means the whole approach of modern humans towards all that is real, propelled by the desire to reduce the real into a frame so that they can be called upon at will to be resource for human machination. The whole of nature, animate and inanimate nature, thus, becomes a huge pile of resource, reserved and standing ready to be transformed into useful material at the beck and call of the human being. For Heidegger, technology is not a technical piece or machinery; it is the concealed ontology of the modern age. Each age, for him, is defined by a specific ontology. The specific ontology of modernity compels human beings to look at the river not as the fountain of water, flowing down from the woods, taking so many wonderful twists and turns on her path to the ocean, blessings the living population all across her fertile banks. The river, which might have been once thought of as dynamic and lively, having a life of her own, becomes for the modern a passive site for hydroelectric power, a picnic spot, a supplier of water for irrigation, and the locale for so many other innovative uses. Heidegger's *Gestell* is this particular ontological interpretation modern humans undertake when they look at reality; it is a particular way in which being as such is interpreted. Technology, then, is the general ontology of the modern age.

The ontology of the modern age has several specific manifestations in Heidegger's account. In the 1938 essay 'The age of the world picture', a specific aspect of modern ontology is noted as the objectification of all that is by the subject. According to him, subject-object divide was unknown to the pre-moderns. The uniqueness of the subject is that she is able to represent to herself the whole world, indeed all that is, as picture, as representation, as object that can be carefully scrutinized, studied and have control over. But in this process of objectifying, according to the 1954 essay 'Science and reflection', the subject herself is not spared. She is also sucked up into the technologically representing act and is produced as the technicized animal (as detailed in the 1938 work *Contributions to Philosophy*). In fact, the human being as the producer-labourer turns into human material, human resource par excellence (see the 1946 essay 'Why poets?). The subject of the scientific times can objectively look at everything: life (biology), the physical universe (physics), the chemical structure of the universe (chemistry) and even God (theology), human mind (psychology), society (sociology), non-modern societies (anthropology), and politics (political science).

However, Heidegger untiringly stresses the most specific fallout of the technological age as the devastation of the earth. In 'Why poets?', he remarks that 'the open', that is being as such, is objectified in the technological age and the human being asserts her dominion over the object field as the subject. Through self-assertive, willed production, all elements of the object field, plant and animal, water and the earth, are diverted towards the desire of the subject. The produced are then delivered to users through the market as calculable material in terms of its commercial value. The market realm of the produced reversely dominates the human realm in its totality, even where there is no need of numbers. It is in this way that the hidden essence of technology rules everything.

In the 1946 essay 'Letter on Humanism', Heidegger questions Christian, Marxist and existentialist humanism as moral theories which uncritically assume the metaphysical definition of the human being as 'rational animal'. The essence of the human being, for Heidegger, is this: she is the only being capable of articulating being, its revealing-concealing play, in language. There is no other specific essence that separates the human being from nature. All else, including reason and science, held as sacred essences of the human being by the modern imagination, are its own cultural, historical products. In the 1955-56 lecture course, called *The Principle of Reason*, the Leibnizian principle of sufficient reason is itself interpreted as a product of technological rationality. The modern rational ethics which seeks the one universal principle that can judge all human action in its morality is itself a product of the hidden essence of technology. For Heidegger, ethics means closeness to the dwelling, the open, which is the home of being. According to him, caring for the whole earth and all its elements in response to the finite revealing of being is ethics.[8] Humanism, on the other hand, is the underlying ethical philosophy for the modern moral normativism, which has led to the devastation of the home of life in the name of various humanistic justifications.

Humanism, we cannot forget, achieved several great wonders for humanity during the modern age. It was in the name of humanism that such hallowed modern ideals as freedom, democracy, equality, rule of law, rational science and the like became an ingredient of everyday life for western humanity first, and now promising to be for every human being anywhere on earth. The miracles of modern medicine, agricultural techniques, and even space science have a humanistic underpinning. At the same time, it was never without a humanistic justification that some humans were enslaved by others, some nations colonized by others, and some cultures overrun by others. Not surprisingly, every form of modern violence was heaped on sections of humanity or on animals or the earth under the pretext that an object of violence was overtly natural and not yet civilized or humanized. The big modern project, therefore, was one of coercing what was conceived to be inordinately natural to be humanized. Non-western peoples, indigenous/tribal communities, women, peasants, *dalits*, poorer people, people of non-western religious traditions, animals, plants and nature itself were subjected to untold violence in the name of their lack or absence of humanity as understood by the modern west. Those in the animal and plant kingdoms that humanity was less familiar with in its dealings, like fishes in the seas and trees in the forests, could be more callously violated, for they were farthest away from human dealings.

This inordinate preoccupation with the human, a human-centrism in fact, has not ebbed with the incoming of modern environmentalism. Even today, the question of relevance to many environmentalists is: how much economic growth could nature possibly sustain, or what is the manageable extent of the growth-oriented, consumer economy. That is why postdevelopment critics like Arturo Escobar think that the discourse of sustainable development is about "what kind of new manipulations can we invent to make the most of the Earth's 'resources'."[9] The global march of capital many times seems to be the driving force behind such discourses of managing the earth's finite resources. Escobar insightfully dwells on the two contradictions of capital in two of its global phases: (i) in the modern phase of capital, the contradiction of the exploitation of its social condition, labour, came to the fore, and was 'managed' through various rationalizations and methods that finally benefited capital itself; and (ii) in the postmodern phase of capital, the contradiction of the exploitation of its environmental condition, nature itself, came to the fore, and is now being 'managed' through the discourse of sustainable development, which too, finally safeguards the interests of capital itself. In Escobar's analysis, technology is the medium of the entrenchment of capital's often elusive representation—'hard' technologies in its modern phase and predominantly 'soft' technologies in the current ecological phase. In both Heidegger's and Escobar's analysis, it appears to me that the human is taken possession of by forms other than human, technology and capital, in the name of a humanistic ethic. The human being herself appears to be duped by the triumphalist ethics of modernity, the only rational moral possibility within its universalistic logic.

Technological rationality, subject-object dualism, self-assertive productionism, humanistic ethical universalism—if these are fundamental to being modern, we can speak of these ways of being modern as a whole in terms of a certain privilege granted to the ahistorical, acontextual generic stance. While pre-modern life was lived close to nature and animatedly intertwined with it without drawing a clear distinction between the natural and the cultural or human, the modern vision first and foremost strove to tear the human being away from its ground. The modern subject is called upon to clearly distinguish herself from her context, go above it, take as much distance as possible from her ground, and thus come up with, what is called, the objective or disinterested perspective, something which the pre-moderns could not have arrived at. Philosophers and scientists of the seventeenth century invented several methods for achieving such a perspective, which was not culturally predominant at the time. Galileo held that without the language of mathematics it was impossible to understand the hidden mysteries of nature. Francis Bacon called upon intelligent minds to create knowledge that is useful for humanity (as against the useless and imprecise philosophical knowledge) on the basis of the inductive method. René Descartes asked the observant to withdraw from the sensual world to the world of the mind so that things would appear to them without their accidental sensual characteristics but in their essential substantiality. The achieved disconnection of the moderns with the earth that sustains them is founded on this assumption that knowledge produced in these ways of objectivity and scientific precision is the only form of authentic knowledge. Other forms of knowledge, if they can be called knowledge at all, are imprecise and merely subjective. This is the basis of the current anxiety of every form of enquiry, whether it be philosophy or social science, to be like a physical science that has the highest possibility of accuracy.

The phenomenologists we have referred to above have all been bothered about this curious development within the modern culture. David Abram's attempt to articulate a new, revolutionary ecological philosophy begins with such an assumption: "Our spontaneous experience of the world, charged with subjective, emotional, and intuitive content, remains the vital and dark ground of all our objectivity."[10] The point is not simply that we need to take a position of antagonism towards the ahistorical perspective. Rather, the point is that the ground of scientific abstraction and modern knowledge, its primordial base, is the world of our experience. Charles Taylor questions the economist's claim to have arrived at the status of accurate science as if by crossing over from a condition of error to a condition of truth. It is impossible to achieve conditions of objectivity in a field of enquiry without, what Heidegger calls, the ground plan already laid for it. That is, objectivity itself is a cultural product. Economics has been able to develop its present degree of exactness because modern culture prepared the conditions for human beings to behave predictably in terms of a certain 'calculable considerations of instrumental rationality'. "Economics can aspire to the status of a science, and sometimes appear to approach it, because there has developed a culture in which a certain form of rationality is a (if not the) dominant value".[11] In this view of engaged, historical rationality, the world of experience and practice, meaning and value, is the ground of all our theoretical endeavours and abstractions, and—this is important—their guide and corrective agent. In this view, again, moving from one form of moral sensibility to another is not a passage from truth to error, but a necessary dialectical movement within the dynamic terrain of culture, morality and meaning. This movement, since it happens in close proximity to context and experience, meaning and interest, there is no necessary universal telos guiding it, though the experiential realm, since it is not walled off to an outside, is always in dialogical engagement with other such realms. Universal agreement is not a necessary rule, not even a regulative ideal. When they come, universal agreements in moral and cultural matters are never blind to the necessary differences and contestations upon which they make their open claims of possibility. Without this realization deliberately guiding our projects of rule making, rules and norms become abstract operative matrixes of regimes of power and dominion.

I shall now look at the strikingly contrasting possibility of existence to the modern, the tribal, with the view that the denial of its authentic possibilities by the modern cultural horizon in fact, and paradoxically, reveals a certain moral sensibility within its complex cultural texture, which modernity has denied itself. That is, the tribal as a dialogical interlocutor to the modern.

Being Tribal

The contrast between the modern and the tribal ways of being are striking because their perspectives of looking at the world, explaining and understanding phenomena, and making sense of the reality around them are strikingly the opposite. Because the tribal worldviews did not consider knowledge production as a definitive, self-conscious possibility, set up within established institutional apparatuses as in the Greek or the Vedic Indian cultures, I shall not refer to these stances of looking at the world and making sense of phenomena as epistemological perspectives. I shall, rather, call them 'semantic standpoints' because the indigenous people, who did not think it necessary to produce concrete, written deposits of organized knowledge, as if knowledge were a commodity to be produced, stored and sold, still made sense of themselves and their relation with others, animals and nature by way of these orally and metaphorically organized standpoints. They were meaning systems rather than epistemological perspectives. These did not contradict other competing standpoints as would happen in the modern world, where the scientific standpoint constantly gets into conflicts with, say, religious and ethical standpoints. Their approach to life was not fragmentary as would be in the modern world but holistic and internally non-conflictual.

I must insert a cautionary remark here. 'Tribal' is a very generic category with a great deal of internal diversity. The danger of bypassing these real differences and naively homogenizing what is in fact filled with distinctions is rather unavoidable when we speak of 'the tribal' in general terms as it is the case with all such generalities. However, it is to be noted that the liberty taken here is a philosophical one of constructing the category of the tribal, and to the extent that it is constructed, 'the tribal' is a myth, the bearer of a possible and alternative world, as Paul Ricoeur holds. As myth, the truth of it is immortal and always points to a possible way of living our lives. In the context of the present book, the ethos or general spirit of the myth of the tribal spoken of here should apply authentically to the several tribal communities of North-East India, which are fast losing their traditional worldview with the onslaught of modernity. At the same time, because of its mythical character, truer than fact, this construction should be excused of literal inaccuracies. I justify the present construction, 'the tribal', in the belief that the myth retold is resolutely positive and to a certain extent romantically nostalgic because neither the fast modernizing tribal communities talked about in this volume nor the already modernized peoples can authentically immerse themselves today in the mythical tribal life. There is no possibility of a total going back. However, this very disappearance, the absence, is the moment for freshly constructing the positive tribal life. Here I do so with the specific aim of recapturing what I have called in the title of this chapter 'The Interconnectedness Sensibility'. In short, I am not at all blind to the fact that I am actually working with and coproducing the binary of the tribal *versus* the modern. The Derridian objection that such absolute binary opposites that do not contain each other in some form do not exist in purity and detachment from each other is accepted by positing that 'the tribal', conceived here in opposition to the modern, is a construct, a myth. However, this admission does not reduce the significance of the construction but opens up its positive possibility of entering contemporary cultural forms and producing feasible modern hybrid ecological visions. So, I use 'tribal' like the anthropologist David Maybury-Lewis to mean "small-scale preindustrial societies that live in comparative isolation and manage their affairs without a central authority such as the state... however diverse, such societies do share certain characteristics that make them different from 'modern' societies."[12]

At least two blockbuster (non-documentary) Hollywood movies, which had an environmental message, were, in parts, about recapturing the tribal past, and both bagged several Academy and Golden Globe awards. The awards and the popularity of these movies, I think, at least partly speak about the impact and power of the theme in contemporary imagination, and thus, evoke the anxiety about the destruction done to the earth and a certain helplessness in the face of the inability to bring about a reversal. *Dances with Wolves*, the 1990 Kevin Costner drama in the western genre, filmed the mindless destruction of the nature-friendly, communitarian worldview of the Sioux or Lakota Indians of North America by the conquering whites. The story is about an American civil war hero who chooses to be posted to the frontier near to the abode of the Lakota Indians "before it's gone", and the film ends with the note that the whites had indeed subdued the Indians after thirteen years, destroyed their habitat and the buffaloes in the prairies on which they lived. Nature, animals and the Lakotas, who are 'nature' itself, have to be eliminated and reproduced as environment, resources and moderns. *Dances with Wolves* does not compromise on the reality of annihilating from view whatever remains of the authentically ecological worldview. *Avatar*, the 2009 James Cameron science fiction drama, on the contrary, celebrates the myth of the tribal and its impossible victory over the modern. However, the impossibility of this victory is underlined by the fact that it is set up in another planet. Though

Cameron's story ends with that improbable victory, according to him, the message is all about learning to seek the hard way "a life that's in balance with the natural cycles of life on earth"—fundamentally, then, a tribal life. And, like Costner, Cameron is also telling the story of the history of America, indeed of colonization in general, of invading and obliterating the tribal worldview, of taking without asking, of displacement and marginalization of the indigenous, of a 'long, wonderful history of the human race written in blood'.[13]

I have evoked the category called 'the tribal' to recapture what is being referred to as the 'interconnectedness sensibility'. The construction of the 'myth' of the tribal is justified here on account of the difficulty of recapturing in any meaningful sense the interconnectedness sensibility from within the modern condition, itself constituted on the foundation of a deep, dichotomous split between the human (subject) and the natural (object), and between fact and value, with meaning and value invested solely on the subject. In this conceptual landscape, nature and whatever is imagined as resource for human machination, is to be 'objectified', neutralized and considered morally invalid, in order to accomplish the project of human machination. The tribal, therefore, is imagined as that spiritual ethos constituted without the divisions between fact and value, and subject and object, and hence, imbued with a sense of interconnection, cooperation and reciprocity between human beings and nature. In the first section, I stressed the importance of the moral sensibility rather than reason. I will here link the interconnected sensibility, which environmental ethics visualizes, as the definite possibility of tribal life, which somewhat artificially and forcibly the modern will have to inculcate if the supposed revolutionary environmental ethical sensibility is to begin. Without going into the details of the debate regarding the necessity of the interconnectedness sensibility for the new environmental ethics, I take it that such *a sense of connection* with nature is necessary to feel morally for nature.[14] It is not enough to enumerate and parade 'reasons' for ethical action. This would have been enough if ethical action were to follow from a rational calculus. On the contrary, the transcendental condition for ethical action is otherness constitutive of our selfhood, as Levinas holds. However, unlike what Levinas argues, for tribal life, the otherness constitutive of self is not merely human otherness; otherness for tribal life is constitutive of all that is not self; nature that challenges the ego's spontaneity just like the human other, is also constitutive of otherness. Interconnectedness sensibility, which was integral to tribal life, asserted nature as constitutive of authentic (moral) humanity. As an identity, a self is constitutive of its other, the non-self, and as that which challenges the ego's spontaneous life, the other evokes ethical responsibility from the self.

Instead of producing reasons for interconnectedness sensibility, though such an exercise is valuable in itself, we may look at this possibility, which is alien to modern life, within the tribal ethos. The inspiration for this search is Ricoeur's argument that every myth hides within itself a possibility of authentic life for others, who are outside the world of that myth. Ricoeur told in an interview: "The important point here is that the original potential of any genuine myth will always exceed the limits of a particular community or nation. The mythos of any community is the bearer of something which exceeds its own frontiers; it is the bearer of other possible worlds."[15] Ricoeur looks to language for recapturing and reviving the lost tribal world. Linguistic forms can 'open up possible worlds'. More than merely being the articulation of the lost, the nostalgia for what might have been, powerful linguistic forms can formulate the new in authentic conversation with the possibilities hidden in the mythical world. "Poetry and myth," argues Ricoeur, "are not just nostalgia for some forgotten world. They constitute a disclosure of new and unprecedented worlds, an opening onto other possible worlds. This is what I mean by the re-creation of language."[16] A sensibility is revived gradually in response to a crisis by way of articulating new discourses, very often, in dialogue with possibilities that are available. I am trying to show that within what is called 'the tribal', interconnected sensibility is available as a real form of the moral life.

In both the movies I have referred to above, a deep sense of connection with nature is an integral part of what is represented cinematically as the tribal ethos. In *Dances with Wolves*, more than any direct mention of the interconnectedness sensibility, what is portrayed is life lived within the rhythm of nature, a sensibility that speaks to the viewer silently and directly. But in *Avatar*, Cameron projects the same sensibility much more overtly. The idyllic Pandora, very much like the landscapes of the American West in *Dances with Wolves*, does speak to us. But more directly, Jake Sully, in his efforts to enter into the cultural world of the Na'vi, recollects what Neytiri tells him of the Na'vi worldview of deep connection with nature: "She talks about a network of energy that flows through all living things. She says all energy is only borrowed and one day you have to give it back." Alluding to the Native Indian hunting ritual, Jake speaks to the killed animal: "I see you Brother, and thank you. Your spirit goes with Eywa. Your body stays behind to become part of the people." Moreover, Jake learns the Na'vi cultural vision in a gradual process of sensitizing himself, and not through a process of rationalization. He recollects that "everyday it's reading the trails, the tracks at the water-hole, tiniest scents and sounds... the flow of energy, the spirits of animals." Dr. Grace's advice to Jake is revealing. According to her, his entry into the Na'vi cultural world is not merely about 'eye-hand coordination' but about seeing the forest through Neytiri's eyes. The supposed revolution in environmental ethics, I think, can happen only with a reawakening of the interconnectedness sensibility, at least in modern hybrid forms. Psychologists have been arguing for some time now that it is possible to cultivate such a sensibility as the child develops from her infancy. The project of ecopsychology, according to Martin Jordan, is: "coming into relationship with nature in ways that celebrate the complexities of our emotional worlds, acknowledging not only the destructive tendencies of the human race, but also its capacity for love and reparation, and directing this capacity toward the natural world."[17] Jordan, having done with the modern split with nature and its psychological underpinnings, evokes optimism from the tribal spirit of reciprocal relationality. They did not see what the moderns see as 'environment' but 'a profoundly metaphysical landscape capable of expressing their deepest spiritual yearnings'. The tribals teach their children from their infancy that they are an integral part of nature, and not independent self-sites vested with the right to use and abuse nature. To cultivate the interconnectedness sensibility, the moderns need to experience it as a moral sensibility contrary to their human-centric sensibility of separation and independence.

The problem with moral reasoning is the tendency to see contradictions without any authentic appreciation of the notion of 'degree' in morality, and, thus, the consequent resignation to the belief that a moral relationship with others (including nature) is not really possible because any intervention appears to be violent. A look at the tribal ethos helps us in the face of such moral tangles. The tribal sense of interconnectedness did not, for example, mean that they did not hunt animals. Most tribes lived off the animals they hunted. But they did not draw any conclusion of lordship over animal kingdom from their cleverness in hunting those animals. In fact, like the Na'vis of *Avatar*, they felt obliged to the animal for becoming their food and parts of themselves—a sensitivity that comes from their feeling of connection with the animal kingdom. Murbury-Lewis recounts the outrage of the Native Americans, when they first encountered the colonizers' wanton killing of the buffaloes, which they hunted only for their sustenance needs. The famous speech of Chief Seattle, Murbury-Lewis reminds us, recounts the Chief's anxiety about the supposedly civilized attitude towards animals and nature: "If all the beasts were gone, man would die from a great loneliness of spirit... All things are connected... We know that the white man does not understand our ways... The earth is not his brother, but his enemy, and when he has conquered it, he moves on... His appetite will devour the earth and leave behind only a desert."[18]

The tribal vision, on the other hand, is concerned with the essential unity of everything. No exalted status is invested with the human being that allows her/him to lord over the earth. The tribal sense of human-nature-God continuum is often disparagingly referred to in the term 'animism' to mean that while the supposedly more advanced religions strictly demarcated between nature and spirit, the sacred and the profane, animism did not, and saw spirit in what it was not. This cultural divide wrought by what are called advanced religions obstructs our appreciation of the alternative tribal worldview. Sujata Miri, who has studied the tribal worldviews closely for long, objects to the disparaging tenor in the use of the term 'tribal animism'. The dichotomy between the sacred and the profane, which the advanced religions introduced, has disappeared with modern secularism because, as philosophers like Heidegger assert, the moderns have lost the sense of the holy altogether. Whereas, according to the tribal vision, "man, God and nature are necessarily bound together with each other. Man and Nature share a common life, which incidentally includes a common moral framework."[19] What Miri calls 'the religious ecology' of the tribes of North-East India is today strange to the tribals themselves. The animistic, reverential, tribal ecology also points toward the possibility of considering nature sacred and, thus, appreciate the interconnectedness of everything. Miri poses the tribal people of North-East India as the interlocutors and exemplars of the radical shift from an anthropocentric to ecocentric environmental ethics. In the tribal vision, she argues, "[i]f all creatures including man are animated by a common indwelling spirit, then no one species could conceivably assume that the whole existed for its benefits alone."[20] For the tribals, connection with nature was not a rationally argued contrivance but a real experience, a sensibility they lived and breathed. Hence, there was a natural mechanism of questioning human exploitation of nature. If killing more buffaloes than required was unthinkable for the Native Americans, the same was the case for most tribal people. In *Dances with Wolves*, the camera lingers long on the wanton killing of the buffaloes by the whites with a tacit question posed on the modern attitude towards nature. Without the interconnectedness sensibility, there is no argument to stop such wanton destruction. If the beast is made for man and only for him, what would limit his desire to destroy the beast for meat as well as for sport and fun? It is useful to remember that the Himalayan Sherpa's practice of reluctance to climb the mountains they considered sacred was the inspiration for the mountaineer philosopher Arnae Naess's radical environmental philosophical theory of deep ecology. Such practices are found among many hill tribes like the Khasis of North-East India, who call their sacred grove *law kyntang*, from where it was a taboo to pick even a leaf.

To briefly elucidate the expressive traditions of the tribal sense of interconnectedness with nature, epically achieved in the cinematic forms of *Dances with Wolves* and *Avatar*, let me refer briefly to the Garo and Naga tribal myths of North-East India. The Garo creator God Dakgipa-Rugipa is conceived as the great mother of the 'universal household' or *Nokdang*, where all creatures, irrespective of their species specificity, are siblings. Like the *Nokna* or mother of the household, Dakgipa-Rugipa nurtures all her children. The *oikos* imagery in the Garo myth refers more to the interconnectedness and interdependence of everything rather than to their common origin. Every being within the *Nokdang* is conceived as playing out a specific role. According to modern Garo scholars, the myth implies that although there is a responsible nurturing role for the human being within the God-world-human continuum, the Garo creation myth is a powerful expression of the impossibility of human existence apart from the natural order.[21] The sense of cooperation with the natural order evoked in the myth was an integral aspect of traditional Garo consciousness. In a similar vein, the earth is called Mother or *ayi* in several Naga languages. According to Naga myths, *ayi* and *atsang* or the sky (male) complement each other in the flourish of life. The Naga oral lore speaks of the spirit, the human being and nature belonging together to the Mother Earth, until they broke off to initiate a lasting animosity between each other. What led to alienation, disharmony and disorder was the death of Mother Earth. Modern Naga scholars think that this worldview was not human-centric, but conceived the land as holding together the clan, the village, the tribe, the supreme being, spirits, ancestors and the whole ecosystem as one family.[22]

An element of violence is always present in our technological intervention in nature, however rudimentary. What was absent in tribal societies was a lack of triumphalism in regard to the necessary violence inherent in human intervention in nature. Interventionist violence was not glorified and a sense of proportion and balance was spontaneously maintained. The strongly communal nature of tribal social organization disallowed individual excesses and greed. In short, the view that nature is out there as a reserve of resources and energies at our beck and call is a typically modern cultural attitude cultivated over at least four centuries since the seventeenth. To sixteenth century westerners this attitude was absolutely strange and unwarranted as it is to the tribal vision everywhere even today.

The interconnectedness sensibility allows human beings to restrain their technological rationality to intervene in nature violently and reduce nature to artifact. The tribal sense of connection with nature did not lead to prohibition of the technological drive in human beings, but its balanced, restrained use. It is this sense of balance that the moderns have lost. I shall now turn to the possibility of reimagining modern life ethically with the tribal myth as the exemplar of such reimagination.

Being Moral, Modern and Tribal

Human beings are not rational spirits misplaced into body but are sensual, embodied, 'othered', beings-in-the-world, who in everyone of their waking moments access their world in a sensual-emotional-embodied-moral-rational continuum: such is the proposition with which I began this chapter. Morality itself is positive restraining of the self's egoistic project (of disallowing the other's alterity and totalizing her/its otherness in the self's terms) in sensual assertion of the other's presence (face). I went on to argue that this holistic picture of the human being was lost with a particular cultural development in seventeenth century Europe, which, fortunately is being revived in the same European tradition of philosophical enquiry by such figures as Husserl, Heidegger, Merleau-Ponty, and Levinas. I have emphasized that reviving a moral sensibility is not primarily about producing rational arguments for or against an ethical position. It is, rather, about articulating a cultural change, gradually beginning to see a new world through a new pair of eyes, and instituting new possibilities in our 'world' with sensitivity. Without being produced as new moral beings, there is little possibility for the success of a new moral code. As Dr. Grace advises Jake Sully, the humanoid Na'vi *avatar*, entering a strange cultural world is not merely about the mechanics of learning a new set of codes and rules; it is about *seeing the earth 'through Neytiri's eyes'.* Hence, as Maybury-Lewis suggests, "we need an ecosophy of our own, imbued with moral commitment and emotional power, if we are to protect the resources on which we depend and ensure not only our own survival but also that of our fellow creatures on this earth."[23] (up to here)

The job of the moral philosopher also is to evoke the moral sensibility, whether new or lost, through critiques of established and dominant moralities difficult to dislodge. An established morality produces ourselves as moral subjects through already laid out, uncompromising institutional forms. But it does so more powerfully by means of surreptitious, indiscernible representations not easily visible. They cancel out and slowly remove from view, from the realm of the possible, moral forms that challenge the dominant view of the world by their constant accusatory gaze and weaving a web of incredulity around them. Penetrative deconstruction is required to unearth these stealthy forms that create our contemporary moral objects. Such deconstructions are routinely performed today, both philosophically and otherwise, which can be seen as evidence for the anxiety about the destructive potential of modern culture. What, I think, now required is the movement to the next stage of critique, which is constructive and productive of new forms. Active visualization of newer forms of the moral life is called for.

In this, the philosophy of the human being as a much more complexly constituted being than the traditional '*Zoon logon echon*' (rational animal) is the starting point. For a moral revolution to unfold, a cultural change is necessary because the moral agent is an embodied, embedded, othered identity, a culturally constituted being-in-the-world. The Enlightenment imagination that the moral agent is the acultural, ahistorical rational agent, able to revolutionize its morality when she/he sees the moral world with rational clarity and accuracy is rejected thereby. The Age of Reason and its morality is to be understood as a path-breaking cultural revolution that unfolded in seventeenth century

Europe in the background of a particular response to phenomenal interpretation, cultural transformation, material changes and the tremendous possibilities that became visible in Europe's cultural horizon in terms of the new fascination with instrumental rationality—a view of the external world as resource for the self's machination. The modern worldview does not recognize this cultural element in its history, but interprets its own cultural transformation as the rational ideal, the perfect a historical model, that humanity everywhere should gradually come to realize, when it progresses from civilizational childhood to adulthood, aided by the universal light of reason. It is in this context that I spoke in the first section of this chapter about the contribution of philosophers like Husserl, Heidegger, Merleau-Ponty and Levinas.

Visualization of new forms of moral life, however, has to be contextualized in a definite historical setting. The contemporary ecological crisis can be seen as such a setting. Moreover, imagining new forms of moral life itself has to refer to a set of possible moral forms in response to the historical fact of the ecological crisis. I have been arguing that the tribal sense of interconnectedness is such a moral form. Maybury-Lewis calls us to remember that tribal people, if they are still living the tribal life, are not like the moderns in that they have not tried a different form of life unsuccessfully. Their form of life is sustainable, ecofriendly and satisfying to them. They have chosen to live a different life. They have not met with the modern problems of alienation, loneliness, family disintegration, ecological devastation and spiritual famishment. So he posits the tribal life as that possible form of moral life which moderns could authentically dialogue with. He writes: "It is critical that we examine the roads they took that we did not; only then can we get a clear insight into the choices we ourselves make and the price we pay for them. . . Only then can we consider the possibility of modifying some of those choices to enrich our lives."[24] This is the possibility I now am referring to.

Every authentic historical cultural form, in Heidegger's terms, is a possibility that we choose and yet inherit from our own cultural horizon.[25] Every such form is historically rooted and yet new in terms of what it asks its adherents to see and do. There is a continuity rather than an abrupt rupture with the current cultural vision. This is the only way of escaping the cultural trauma of engaging with alien phenomena. Tribal scholars of the North-East have repeatedly pointed out the trauma of sudden, imposed modernization and Christianization,[26] which trivialized and negated their long-standing cultural vision. Everything different and new has to be reproduced in the cultural world of the people in order for them to own up to the new form. Heidegger's insight that there is no separate form of understanding a bare world or an alien other means that everything alien is still looked at, that is, otherness is always interpreted, from the vantage point provided by 'my world'. If all understanding is a modification of the context and self-understanding of the one who understands, then we cannot understand any phenomenon by overlooking the hermeneutical context of our interpretation. Consider that we are trying to understand a person from a completely different cultural context than our own. "I understand him from the world in which he is with me," Heidegger asserts, "a world which is discovered and understandable through the regard in being-with-one-another. It is because understanding is drawn from the world that there is the possibility of understanding an alien world or a world mediated by sources, monuments, and ruins."[27] Hence, although I want to positively admit the credence of the alternative, tribal, ecological vision, this vision, strange as it is to the moderns, has to be reinterpreted from within the modern hermeneutical context. Spaces for the new have to be opened up within our own worlds.

I have already discussed Ricoeur's important idea that mythical forms can exceed the boundaries of their world because every authentic myth bears within itself something that can ignite the imagination of other possible worlds. He looks toward the expressive traditions of cultures to make possible the transition of one mythical form from its original world to another. That is, expressive traditions of modern cultures will have to powerfully recreate the tribal sense of interconnectedness if there is any hope of its revival. Ricoeur refers to Jaspers' notion of the limit or boundary situation as the inescapable point when a culture experiences a fundamental existential crisis, and puts itself into question. Threats of destruction that come from within or without are the most apt situations for cultural questioning and radical transition. According to Ricoeur, "[i]n this way, we become aware of our basic capacities and reasons for surviving, for being and continuing to be what we are."[28] The contemporary ecological crisis is such a limit situation and calls for a moral, cultural transition to a vision of ourselves as beings connected to the earth and all other creatures, modelled on the tribal vision. The transition cannot happen in a day; it has to happen over a great deal of time and thought; it has to happen through revolutionary linguistic forms of all types that will invite the moderns to see reality differently. According to Heidegger, our understanding of reality, being as such, changes over historical periods he calls 'epochs'. What happens with these epochal changes is: with them we will begin to interpret being differently and articulate a different moral, cultural vision. An understanding of being is housed in language and in human beings whose existence is inextricably tied to their language. It is in powerful linguistic forms like poetry, thought and other evocative expressive traditions that an ontological change of vision is inaugurated and instituted. Consider the forceful tide of philosophical expressions of the seventeenth century that legitimated the new scientific view of the world, which came to infest the cultural psyche of the European with a reductive view of reality.

Hence, we should say that the tribal interconnectedness sensibility has to be reincarnated in modern forms, in various modern contexts variously, for it to become a modern moral sensibility. As the post-structuralists tirelessly remind us, every yearning for a pure form is doomed to fail; indeed, when we think that such a form is pure, a serious deconstruction would in fact unveil its 'other' hidden within its own supposedly pure identity terrain. Hence, my insistence that 'the tribal' is a myth has this additional significance. We are not referring to a pure cultural form for the sake of transporting it in its purity to an alien cultural context. We are, rather, looking at a cultural possibility, variously internalized by tribal societies of yore, so that its moral potential could be feasibly evoked in different modern contexts, in line with the specificities of those contexts.

This attempt, therefore, is not a going back; the attempt is not to recapture pre-modernity. The attempt, if at all, is post-tribal, post-modern or alternatively modern. The experience of the tribal people all over the world can, in some form, become different experiential vantage points for the moderns. While 'connect' is a catchword, we need to remember that there are myriad cultural forms of connecting with the earth and other beings. In Ashis Nandy's idiom, this turn to the tribal can be seen as holding in trust the rejected selves of the first and the erstwhile second worlds[29] —but most authentically the selves of the tribal worlds rejected by the modern civilization. To this extent, invoking the tribal ethos for the moral transformation of the ultra-modern world is also civilizational justice done to peoples all over the world, who have been denied legitimacy for their moral view of the world. The turn to the tribal interconnectedness sensibility is, therefore, an assertive turn towards the cultural visions rejected by the first world and turn away from the central vision of that world—a driven, consumer economy, based on the sanctity of the atomistic individual, that lays waste to the planet.

Several scholars, especially anthropologists, are speaking today about the porous nature of our concepts, the possibilities of inhabiting alternative worlds from our own, and of hybridization in general. To illustrate, after a devastating deconstruction of the notion of development and of the third world, Arturo Escobar turns to 'hybrid cultures' for solace. Looking away from grand, modernist alternatives, he looks towards "alternative representations and practices in concrete local settings, particularly as they exist in contexts of hybridization, collective action, and political mobilization."[30] He remarks that the proposal is made in the context of the ecological phase of capital and the struggles over the world's biological diversity'. What he means by these hybrid forms are "negotiated realities in contexts shaped by *traditions, capitalism, and modernity*. . . It is a 'transcultural between-world reality' that requires travelling *simultaneously backward*—into cultural heritage, oneself, one's social group—and *forward*, cutting across social boundaries into progressive elements of other cultural formations."[31] At the same time, Escobar warns that the new cultural form that it gives rise to should not be considered a new, unchanging essence, a constant presence. Hence, what I have evoked here as 'interconnectedness sensibility', in place of the modernist ecological vision in order to look at the place of the human being within the world, in terms of the materiality, embodiment, embeddedness and historicity of that being, is *not a new essential condition* but merely new moral spaces that moderns need to occupy in response to new situations of crises, new narratives of post-humanity, and a new world coming forth from the old. What we are sure about in this proposal is: *these sensibilities of connection with the natural world, envisaged in new, hybrid cultural forms, and the rejection of visions of progress that destroy that world, holds within itself a rich repository of moral meaning.*

Hybrid linguistic forms of cultural expressions can be of a variety of types, styles and sites. They can be poetry and other forms of literary expression; they can be theological, philosophical and scholarly work in various disciplinary domains; there can be cinema, music and other forms of art. The evocative power of creative expression is the grooming ground for gradual cultural transformation. These are not, however, the only forms of expressive traditions. There can be, and should be, a variety of well-articulated political, cultural and alternative economic movements to bring change. Changes within the institutions of modernity can only appear gradually with the expressive tradition laying the ground for lifestyle and institutional metamorphosis, for we are linguistically structured, culturally webbed, socio-historically constituted beings.

While I do mean to say that what we have called the tribal form of interconnectedness with nature is a valuable moral sensibility, an alternative response to the ecological crisis, I do not mean at all to say that the actual 'tribal' of today should remain tribal for all times, nor do I say that today's tribal has no reason to aspire for a better life. Ramachandra Guha argues that the moderns, who have exploited the natural environment to their advantage, cannot today assume, except for their own comfort, that tribal people or ecosystem people want to remain where they are.[32] Instead, he suggests responsible, austere political allocation and use of the world's resources under the basic assumption that all cultural groups, given a chance, would like to be like the American consumer. Whether Guha is right or not, it is not fully right to assume that the colonization of the mind is a one-way traffic that starts off from the global north to the south. There is this extraordinary phenomenon of the internalization of the colonizer's moral universe and his historical and cultural spaces. *The Development Dictionary*, compiled by radical post-development advocates in 1989, asked for writing the obituary of the post-war discourse of development. However, in the *Dictionary*'s second edition of 2010, its editor correctly diagnoses the development dilemma as a politics of either equity without ecology or ecology without equity, but admits that in 1989 the contributors to the *Dictionary* had not appreciated how far the idea of development had got entrenched in the mind of the third world itself: "across the world hopes for the future are fixed on the rich man's patterns of production and consumption. The longing for greater justice on the part of the South is one reason for the persistence of the development creed—even if, in this century, neither the planet nor the people of the world can any longer afford its predominance."[33] China's development success and its sense of having arrived on the world scene is the paradigm case. Unlike Guha, the *Dictionary*'s editor advocates delinking the desire for equity from economic growth and relinking it with culturally specific notions of wellbeing in Escobar's vein. But Guha, I think, would agree with this proposal, provided there is political justice rather than the operation of the exploitative mechanisms of power in these claims of small-scale cultural visions.

Guha's assumption that people everywhere do desire a better life is right, but this can generically mean only a sense of wellbeing in relation to the imageries of her/his cultural landscape. He does not do enough to deconstruct and dethrone what he calls 'the American way of life', which, he agrees, brings doom for the planet. Hence, it is necessary to assert the possibility of fragmenting the grand narrative of a single consumerist notion of wellbeing and articulating culturally specific, less resource-intensive visions of wellbeing more in connection with nature and its rhythms for encountering the ecological crisis. However, the necessity to restrain and hold back the modern paradigm everywhere, even if variously, is called for because of its tendency to trivialize all other cultural visions and posit itself as the only pivot of moral legitimacy. All these various attempts to subvert the hegemony of the modern paradigm, I argue, should be underlined by the moral sense of interconnectedness with nature, modelled on the tribal vision, without thereby essentializing 'the tribal' as a historical category with no hope of dynamism in terms of further possibilities of wellbeing within itself. On the contrary, various forms of culturally sensitive and ecologically aware new articulations of wellbeing are necessary, but all of them variously conceiving their own sense of connection with the natural environment.

The interconnectedness sensibility cannot be articulated in structural affinity to yet another modernist grand narrative. Rather, research should bring forth several vernacular visions of the interconnectedness sensibility from various linguistic traditions, both oral and written. Vernacularizing these sensibilities is a way of subverting the modern tendency to essentialize them as grand narratives.

The hybrid forms, thus, are those wherein neither the 'real tribal' nor the 'real modern' is essentialized. The happy news is that such forms, in their impurity and diversity, hybridity and internal differentiation, are available today all over the world. The Amish community of North America, the several hybrid traditions in Latin America that exist within nebulous spaces of premodernity, modernity and post-modernity, which Escobar tirelessly illustrates in *Encountering Development*, and the several tribal communities in the North-East and other regions of India could be spoken of in this vein. But we need to be cautioned here that the hybrid forms are creative manners of encountering modernity rather than sealing oneself off from the modern. Keeping this in mind, I will now very briefly refer to one such attempt, as the scope of this chapter is far from empirically surveying such forms.

The Timbaktu Collective, a utopian commune in rural Andhra Pradesh, led by the activist couple Mary Vattamattom and Bablu

Ganguly, organizes the farmers of Anantapur district "to work for the regeneration of wasteland and start organic farming, soil conservation, and propagation of traditional food crops. They have also taken steps towards women's and *dalits'*... empowerment as well as the improvement of rural health."[34] Bablu and Mary were inspired first by Marx; gradually they turned to Gandhi for inspiration, and adopted the methods of the Japanese philosopher-agriculturalist Masanbou Fukoka (of 'one straw revolution' fame that advocates do-nothing farming).[35] Uma Das Gupta has argued that Tagore's Sriniketan experiment could have been an equal inspiration for Mary and Bablu.

Going through the well-articulated philosophical note of Timbaktu Collective on its website, one finds an authentic hybrid of the type I have evoked in this chapter, though we need to be aware that the reality of the activities of the Collective would be further hybrids of its given vision as is the case with all forms of authentic praxis. The note reads in parts:

> We want to green the hills and the land. We want to develop alternative lifestyles. Lifestyles that are sustainable and provide more liberty and happiness, than those based upon exploitation... Timbaktu is envisaged as an agro-forest habitat. It is an attempt to create an alternative eco-sensitive community. A community while caring for nature and tending to its basic needs can demonstrate a sustainable, alternative, decentralized, self-respecting, non-alienating way of life for all sections of the society. Such a community can be the only starting point for building a just and peaceful world, as any vision of such a world, without an ecological perspective is vacuous.[36]

Timbaktu Collective's farming is organic, its structure is cooperative and communitarian, and its goals deeply imbued with a sense of connection to the land that the farmer works with. At the same time, Timbaktu Collective is not a premodern form; it is formally organized, scientifically informed and erected on the basic philosophy of helping people to reconnect "with their environment, with their land, with their tradition and culture, with nature and their community".[37] If Timbaktu Collective lives up to its announced vision, as the several first-person accounts of its activities I have heard of seem to testify, these bold efforts can be seen as at least one of the many hybrid forms of evoking the tribal sense of interconnectedness with nature in contemporary terms. However, as a moral way of relating to non-human reality, the sensibility to feel connected with nature and the animal world is a personal human comportment. Institutional forms like that of the Timbaktu Collective are important, for they historically institute cultural forms as the open site of moral-political possibilities for individuals and social actors to enter and be.

In conclusion, moral philosophy's important task of revolutionizing ethics at critical historical junctures may be restated. This function is different from listing logically transparent rational arguments for the same purpose with no reference to context, history and the non-rational aspects of human constitution. Evoking a moral sensibility philosophically is, on the other hand, deconstructive intellectual/cultural critique, phenomenological illumination and hermeneutical unconcealing. The modest attempt of the chapter has been to invoke 'the tribal' as a mythical category for locating interconnectedness sensibility, lost with modernity's introduction of radical separation between humans and non-human reality, nature and culture, fact and value. The tribal is the moral site of the interconnectedness sensibility. Tribal ethos, uninhabited by such dichotomies, viewed nature with reverence, thankfulness and a deep sense of connection, in the awareness that the human being was its integral part rather its lord. A new environmental ethics can be articulated, it is argued, only if cultural groups everywhere recapture, if variously in hybrid forms, this lost interconnectedness sensibility, for which the tribal ethos is the exemplar.

Notes

1. Charles Taylor, 'Two Theories of Modernity', *The Hastings Center Report* 25:2 (1995) 26.
2. *Ibid.*, 28.

3. Ethan Kleinberg, *Generation Existential: Heidegger's Philosophy in France, 1927-1961*. Ithaca, NY: Cornell University Press, 2005, 116.
4. Dermot Moran, 'Heidegger's critique of Husserl's and Brentano's accounts of intentionality", *Inquiry: An Interdisciplinary Journal of Philosophy* 43:1 (2000) 60.
5. Herman Philipse, 'Transcendental idealism', in *The Cambridge Companion to Husserl*, eds. Barry Smith and David Woodruff Smith. Cambridge: Cambridge University Press, 1995, 250-1.
6. David Abram, *The Spell of the Sensuous: Perception and Language in a More-than-human World.* New York: Vintage, 1996, 45.
7. Erazim Kohak, *The Embers and the Stars: A Philosophical Inquiry into the Moral Sense of Nature.* Chicago, IL: The University of Chicago Press, 1984, 5.
8. See Julian Young, *Heidegger's Later Philosophy*, Chapter 8: Being a guardian. Cambridge: Cambridge University Press, 2002, 105-121.
9. Arturo Escobar, *Encountering Development: The Making and Unmaking of the Third World.* Princeton, NJ: Princeton University Press, 1995, 193.
10. David Abram, *The Spell of the Sensuous*, 34.
11. Charles Taylor, 'Social theory as practice', in *Philosophical Papers, Vol. 2: Philosophy and the Human Sciences.* Cambridge: Cambridge University Press, 1985, 103.
12. David Maybury-Lewis, 'On the importance of being tribal: Tribal wisdom', in *The Environment in Anthropology: A Reader in Ecology, Culture, and Sustainable Living*, eds. Nora Haenn and Richard R. Wilk. New York: New York University Press, 2006, 390.
13. Film news: 'James Cameron says Avatar a message to stop damaging environment' [online], *The Telegraph*, UK, 11 December 2009. Available at: <http://www.telegraph.co.uk/culture/film/film-news/6782339/James-Cameron-says-Avatar-a-message-to-stop-damaging-environment.html> [Accessed 3 December 2012].
14. This debate is not closed. For example, Martin W. Lewis, author of *Green Delusions: An Environmentalist Critique of Radical Environmentalism* (1992), argues that the fear of civilization corrupting humanity has always been a prevalent view since Greek antiquity. Reconnecting with nature is envisaged in this view not for the sake of nature but for healing humanity from its aberrations, and hence a veiled anthropocentrism. Economies that are deeply embedded in nature rather than disconnected from it, Lewis argues, would accelerate environmental destruction. Lewis seems to imply that the interconnectedness sensibility

may not necessarily lead to environmentally helpful human action. "Contrary to eco-radical expectations," he writes, "living in the midst of nature does not necessarily make people appreciate it, while being largely disconnected from nature on a daily basis actually seems to make many individuals more concerned about its preservation, and willing to act on those beliefs." [Martin W. Lewis, 'On Human Connectedness with Nature", *New Literary History*, 24: 4 (1993) 807.] I think, it is important to think about the consequence of moral action. If moral action leads to consequences that are the opposite of the intended results, I think, we need to be bothered about such a morality. Hence, interconnectedness sensibility, while a good in itself, should be finally good for nature and the human being. But, I believe, the sensibility is a good in itself and without it, the revolution intended in environmental ethics is flawed from the start. Interconnectedness sensibility does not necessarily mean non-technological, non-modern lifestyle. I shall argue in the forthcoming section that returning to the state of nature is not a possibility for humans. Recapturing the interconnectedness sensibility can mean only a hybrid form of life for us moderns.

15. Paul Ricoeur and Richard Kearney, 'Myth as the Bearer of Possible Worlds', *The Crane Bag* 2: 1/2 (1978) 117.
16. *Ibid.*, 118.
17. Martin Jordan, 'Nature and Self—An Ambivalent Attachment?", *Ecopsychology* 1:1 (2009), 30.
18. David Maybury-Lewis, 'On the Importance of Being Tribal: Tribal Wisdom', 396.
19. Sujata Miri, *Communalism in Assam: A Civilizational Approach*. New Delhi: Har-Anand Publications, 1993, 123.
20. Sujata Miri, *Ethics and Environment: Theory and the Adi and Khasi Practice*. New Delhi: Spectrum Publications, 2001, 65.
21. Sahilendra R. Marak, 'Nature and Culture: The Garo Perspective', in *Rationality and Tribal Thought*, ed. Sujata Miri. New Delhi: Mittal Publications, 2004, 147-8.
22. Tezenlo Thong, 'A Clash of Worldviews: The Impact of the Notion of Progress on Naga Culture, 1832-1947', *Journal of Race, Ethnicity, and Religion*, 2: 5 (2011) 34.
23. David Maybury-Lewis, 'On the Importance of Being Tribal: Tribal Wisdom', 395.
24. *Ibid.*, 395.390.
25. Martin Heidegger, *Being and Time*, trans. John Macquarrie and Edward Robinson. Oxford: Blackwell, 1962, 435.

26. Charles Chasie, 'Nagaland in Transition,' in *Where the Sun Rises When Shadows Fall: The North-East*, ed. Geeti Sen. New Delhi: Oxford University Press, 2006, 257.
27. Martin Heidegger, *History of the Concept of Time: Prolegomena*, trans. Theodore Kisiel. Bloomington, IN: Indiana University Press, 1985, 243.
28. Paul Ricoeur and Richard Kearney, 'Myth as the Bearer of Possible Worlds', 114.
29. Ashis Nandy, 'Shamans, Savages, and the Wilderness: On the Audibility of Dissent and the Future of Civilizations', *Alternatives*, 14: 3 (1989) 273.
30. Arturo Escobar, *Encountering Development*, 19.
31. *Ibid.*, 220 (my emphasis).
32. Ramachandra Guha, *How Much Should a Person Consume?: Thinking through the Environment*. Ranikhet: Permanent Black, 2006, 242-3.
33. Wolfgang Sachs, 'Preface to the new edition', in *The Development Dictionary: A* Guide to Knowledge as Power, ed. Wolfgang Sachs, Second Edition. London: Zed Books, 2010, ix.
34. Uma Das Gupta, 'Tagore's Ideas of Social Action and the Sriniketan Experiment of Rural Reconstruction, 1922-41', *University of Toronto Quarterly* 77: 4 (2008) 1003.
35. D.V. Sridharan, 'No stops anywhere, after Gandhi', [online] *GoodNewsIndia*. Available at: <http://www.goodnewsindia.com/index.php/Magazine/story/timbaktu/> [Accessed 9 December 2012]. The online magazine 'GoodNewsIndia' is the effort of Mr. D V Sridharan to publicize the many new initiatives in contemporary India. See: www.goodnewsindia.com.
36. Available at: <http://www.timbaktu.org/philosophy.html> [Accessed 8 December 2012]. For a 30 minutes English documentary on the Collective's activities and philosophy, named 'Tmbaktu' and narrated by Bablu Ganguly, see: <http://www.youtube.com/watch?feature=player_embedded&v=aOWp-5Mjs7Y> [Accessed 8 December 2012]. For another story on Timbaktu's farming philosophy, see: Madhavi Tata, 'The forest comes alive: Timbaktu? Arcadia!', [online], *Outlook*, 22 August 2011. Available at: <http://www.outlookindia.com/article.aspx?278010> [Accessed 22 August 2012].
37. *Ibid.*

11

Disaggregating the Discourse of Man *vs.* Nature

A. Raghuramaraju

This chapter brings into discussion three interrelated themes on the issue of the relation between man and nature. The discussion on the topic of ecology brings into centre stage the recent discussion of deep and shallow ecology, and sometimes Heidegger on ecology and technolcgy. In this context there is an important thesis advanced by Lyn White Jr. White traces the roots of ecological crisis not to technology but to Christianity. He says that it is Judo-Christian concept of anthropocentrism that is responsible for ecological crisis. Judo-Christianity by establishing dualism between man and nature made it God's will that man use nature for his ends. This according to White laid the foundation for the recent ecological crisis. I disagree with this contention, as while White is right in his reference to Christianity, what he however misses is the relation between indulgence or creed and ecological crisis. Use of nature does not lead to the ecological problems, rather it is intrinsically related to over use, or greed *a la* Mahatma Gandhi, of human being that causes ecological crisis. Though it is true that God made nature for man to use, He according to Christian theology did not mean it for man's indulgence. Indulgence, not use that causes ecological crisis. Franciscans, the ascetic school bears witness to this limited and minimum use of nature by man. Further, though man can use nature, there prevails the overall supervision of God who is the creator of both man and nature. Therefore, it is not proper to trace ecological crisis to Judo-Christianity. With this background let me begin my analysis.

With this beginning let me bring three more thinkers from the west including Husserl, Descartes and Aristotle, to thicken the plot as it were on this theme. The reason why I bring these is to show the limitations in the present discussion on ecological crisis. The present discussion, at least one dominant part largely conducts the debate along the axis of man *versus* nature. What I want to highlight in this chapter is the idea of man in man-centred universe, which is the discourse of modernity. Descartes laid foundation to modernity by institution the centrality of man. His concept of man is not been clearly discerned in the scholarship. We have taken it for granted that it is the empirical man. On a closer scrutiny what we can see is not empirical man but rather cognitive individualism. Descartes achieves this feat of individualism through an interesting logic of exclusion.

The Enlightenment formulated a man-centred universe, a centrality unprecedented in human history. This formation was possible through a unique logic of exclusion authored by Descartes, this logic is the logic of exclusion, excluding through the criterion of certainty all that are given, the whole past. This logic is so powerful its impact can be seen even in the contemporary natural science disciplines like artificial intelligence, which inhabit this logic. This idea of centrality has two aspects to it: (i) What the self asserts its nature to be; and (ii) What it excludes from its domain. The self in the Enlightenment anthropocentrism asserts its nature as being independent from its immediate and mediated surroundings, locating itself outside history. The Cartesian self refuses to have any relation with the empirical man. To borrow a term from Alasdair MacIntyre, the Enlightenment has no account of 'man-as-he-happens-to-be.' (1985). The Enlightenment self, therefore, is purely and exclusively a cognitive self—a self privileging its claims to centrality, certainty, universality, rationality, etc. Within the Enlightenment theories the non-cognitive comes to be constructed as something 'other', to be excluded.

If we take Descartes as one of the important formulator of the discourse of modernity, he at the outset declares his normative scale, which is *cogito*, reason and certainty and embarks on excluding, at the outset, the following. These are: childhood (as it is the domain governed by appetite and teachers rather than reason, the latter he identifies as the domain of adults. (1985: 117), language (1985: 113), history (for him past is like travelling which takes us away from the present), oratory, poetry (poetry is the 'gift of mind rather than fruits of study' 1985: 114), moral writings of pagans (1985: 114), customs, evolutionary growth of societies (he rejects gradual growth of societies 1985: 116), he even rejects classical logic and mathematics as they are 'mixed up with' all sorts of things. (1985: 119-120). All aspects that Descartes excluded form part of the Western social reality. It is this exclusion and their subsequent inclusion, some by Descartes himself through modification such as logic, mathematics, language, and other aspects by subsequent thinkers such as history by Hegel, evolution by Darwin, unconscious by Freud which constitutes the major preoccupation of Western modernity.

The modern self is exclusively cognitive and entirely autonomous. Let me also clarify that the point is not about the identification of cognitivity in human beings, but to a view, which determines human beings as thinking beings devoid of non-cognitive aspects. Before discussing the relation between the cognitive and the non-cognitive realms, let me digress and clarify the ground—a plausible ground-making for the emergence of a self centred universe. Quite often, the project of modernity is characterised as a radical project. There is no doubt that it is radical indeed. What is not reckoned is that this radicalness is a self-proclamation. This form of proclamation like self-justification has its own limitations and vulnerabilities.

So what is threatening the nature today is not the real and empirical individual—who uses, even at times misuses nature but in a limited volume also nurtures it—but the cognitive self. It is this cognitive rather exclusively cognitive individual who threatens to devastate nature. So there are two notions of the self, the cognitive self and the empirical self. The former not only threatens the nature but also threatens the latter. This has not been accounted for in the main discussion on ecology. This is largely because they inhabited a terrain of man *versus* nature and assumed the former to be unproblematic. This included Heidegger who in the context of locating the rise of technology which contributes to the ecological crisis to 'subjectivistic-metaphysics' In contrast I take the former to be both complex and problematic and would seek to disaggregate—following Plato's definition of justice, which is distinguishing principle of complementarity—what is taken to be a homogeneous concept. Now let me discuss another important move in this direction within western philosophy.

This is found in Husserl who in his *Crisis in European Sciences* makes available a distinction between rationality largely associated with sciences and individual self that form the foundation for modernity. He highlights how rationality and its associated corollary modern science have developed in such a way and in such proportion that strongly but substantially undermines the self. He through this distinction between self and rationality points how the uneven proliferation of the latter threatened the very existence of the former. Taking a clue from Husserl and even extending his thought or rather valuable caution ask what is central to modernity, is it, self or rationality? If the latter threatens the former what should be done. He seems to make an appeal to bring back into the centre stage, the self. Phenomenology initiated by Husserl has favoured the self. What is to be noted here is that how do we ensure the safety of the self which was and is being threaten by rationality through modern science. What is the guarantee that the same thing will not repeat. In this context I want to bypass a little the preoccupation of phenomenology with transcendence, or even with the empirical self. I want to offer two moves: one to disaggregate the self as cognitive self authored by Descartes and ordinary self (from now on wards use this to make my point more forcefully than empirical self of phenomenology). I also want to bring the western tradition to highlight this difference. In this context I want to bring Aristotle into the discussion. It is Aristotle, who while laying bare the nature of the polis says that the whole is prior to the parts. He in this context also says that for analytical though not for ontological purpose the whole may be disaggregated into smaller units. What is important in this context is that he says that the purpose of the family as an institution is to attend to the daily recurrent needs of the society. Let us discuss Aristotle.

Aristotle

In Aristotle, there is an ontological argument where he maintains that the whole is prior to the parts. There is yet another explanation, which he calls 'analytical' which has not caught the attention of many, where he does allow the possibility of analysing a whole into its simple and uncompounded elements. He uses number and biology in the following passage in *Politics*. He says:

> "Just as, in all other fields, a compound should be analysed until we reach its simple and uncompounded elements... so we must also consider analytically the elements of which a polis is composed.... First, there must necessarily be a union or pairing of those who cannot exist without one another. Male and female must unite for the reproduction of the species.... Next, there must necessarily be a union of the naturally ruling element with the element which is naturally ruled, for the preservation of both.... The first result of these two elementary associations [of male and female, and of master and slave] is the household or family... The first form of association naturally instituted for the satisfaction of daily recurrent needs is thus the family... The next form of association... is the village... When we come to the final and perfect association, formed from a number of villages, we have already reached the polis... as association which... while it *grows* for the sake of mere life... it *exists*... for the sake of a good life. (1986: 7)

What is important here is that in analytically reaching the simple in the Polis which is the whole, Aristotle stops at the level of pair thereby obstructing the possibility of one, the individual, a necessary requirement of modernity? To obstruct this he employs biological argument and a different philosophy of number.

As long as these are accepted there is no possibility of eliciting one, the individual, which is the foundation of modernity. Aristotle would argue that two or the pair cannot be further divided as for the one to come into existence, two, namely, the male and the female, should have come into sexual union. So analytically two is a fundamental category, it can even be said to precede one, unless one relapses into creationism and its associated theology. Therefore, in Aristotle, it is neither zero, as in the Indian mathematical tradition, nor one, which is the beginning of arithmetic. His argument presupposed two to be the basic and prior number. In my reading, as long as we remain within the domain of biology and adhere to his philosophy of arithmetic there is no way to arrive at the one which is the prerequisite for individualism, the bedrock of modernity. Aristotle very ingenuously stymied the possibility of individualism. Centuries have passed in following this fundamental and indomitable format. It is against this that we have to read the crucial passages in Descartes. In his *Discourse on Method* Descartes first attempts not to engage with Aristotle, which is almost impossible, but bypasses him.

Inevitability of Disinheriting

Descartes accomplishes this by bypassing the biological domain when he says:

> . . . I reflected that we were children before being men and had to be governed for some time by our appetites and our teachers, which were often opposed to each other and neither of which, perhaps, always gave us the best advice; hence I thought it virtually impossible that our judgments should be as unclouded and firm as they would have been if we had had the full use of our reason from the moment of our birth, and if we had always been guided by it alone. (1985: 117)

Here he is identifying appetites with childhood, reason with adulthood. While privileging the latter he is marginalising the former. He seems to suggest how it is not philosophically interesting to examine how children are born to parents who are a pair. Rather, what is important is when do they become rational which is identified with adulthood. This bypassing of the biological domain facilitated, as it were, the possibility of one, the individual who is embellished by two associated features, namely, reason and adulthood. This by implication keeps the domain of childhood outside the purview of modernity because it is the domain of non-reason and is guided by appetites and teachers, which are unreliable. The foundation for this is clearly laid down in Descartes. To get one you need to bypass the biological domain and childhood and present the adult domain with rationality. So, it is this problem with the predecessors that informs the nature of modernity. Thus, there is a need to take into consideration this inevitability rather than mere radical posture of modernity.

Second Innings in Rousseau

Subsequently, we have in Rousseau a move to finish off in the second round, so to say, the privileged domain of family, which inhabits the childhood. He says:

> The most ancient of all societies, and the only one that is natural, is the family: and even so the children remain attached to the father only so long as they need him for their preservation. As soon as this need ceases, the natural bond is dissolved. The children, released from the obedience they owed to the father, and the father, released from the care he owed his children, return equally to independence. If they remain united, they continue so no longer naturally, but voluntarily; and the family itself is then maintained only by convention. (1952: 2)

If we closely read this passage, there is an important sub-text that, in addition to dismantling family as an institution, introduces a linear notion of time that replaces the circular notion of time. The child is free after he or she attains adulthood. But this leaves the deal not complete. One might ask why the father should spend time and resources on the child. What does he get in return? The account is not settled. In a traditional paradigm, the account is settled when children take care of their parents in their old age. This is not acceptable to Rousseau as that would make the contract brief and put the child in debt. This also will legitimise the return to the family, which he is seeking to dismantle. So how does one settle this deal? If we read the passage carefully, the sub-text reveals that children need not take care of their parents. Father takes care of children until they become independent, yet the account is settled. It is settled because the father is only paying off his debt to his father by bringing up his own children. Therefore, it is more in the form of paying a debt than making his children indebted to him. It is this that legitimises the institution of old-age home in the modern times. So to conclude, it is this inevitability of the pair in Aristotle that may have forced Descartes to formulate the thematic of modernity in this way. So modernity viewed in relation to tradition can reveal elements of desperation rather than radical postures of power. So western nation has to inevitably disinherit the past, dismantle it. But this is not governed so much with power but with desperation.

The reason to bring Aristotle into the discussion is to show how the self of the modernity is not the ordinary self of the individual but a mere cognitive self who not only threatens nature but also other ordinary individuals. The ordinary individual is a part of a family. The purpose of family is to attend to the daily recurrent needs. This is a major purpose of family as a social institution. Now to this major purpose of family let me add another aspect of a family or even a village which bring to the theme of the seminar, Environmental Ethics in Tribal Communities. Like in the family, and unlike in the concept of the individual self, daily recurrence is very constitutive aspect. I propose here that the other constitutive element in a family or a community is the availability of an exemplar. Akeel Bilgrami in an interesting paper says that Mahatma Gandhi is an exemplar. Unlike Western moral philosophy that gives moral principles which by their very nature eschew violence, exemplar on the other hand maintains Bilgrami while setting moral standards does avoid eschewing violence. Without going into the merits of Bilgrami, let us use his insight to re-recognise that there are examplars in every village, particularly in the pre-modern tribal villages. We must recognize the importance of examplars. In this context there is a need to distinguish between political leaders and exemplars that people respect and draw inspiration from.

Now let me quickly make brief comments on the existing views on understanding pre-modern societies. There are those who argue that they all must navigate towards the modern ways of life. These form the modern radicals. They see nothing substantially good in the pre-modern life and, therefore, suggest the need to discard them and move towards the modern way of life. On the opposite side is the other extreme that stubbornly advocates the need to retain the *status quo*. Both the sides seem to essentialise and fail to capture the reality. I want to argue against both the views. In this context to begin with I want to ask whether there have been instances where these tribal societies have given themselves to changes, what are the terms of these changes and why did they give themselves to these. I want to make this point to historicize the so called stagnant view of society. I also want to ask if these societies have now become stagnant making it a historical phase or has been like this since the beginning. I also want to remind in this context that the west has taken so much of time to change. The voting right to women was given in the early twentieth century. So we must not force change but make a case for gradual process. In this context let me propose the following as a part of this different understanding of the relation between man and nature, thus avoiding conflating cognitive self or cognitive nude along with ordinary man-as-he-happens to be self to use MacIntyre's phase:

1. There is a need to get rid of routing complaint made where the modern state is seen as oppressing the pre-modern society along the oppressor and oppressed route. While accepting the fact that the modern state indeed is oppressing, and continues to oppress the pre-modern

state let us simultaneously theoretically recognise and acknowledge that the pre-modern does not and has not been succumbing at least frequently and often to the pressures of the state. The pre-modern unlike in the west where there is a sequential relation between the pre-modern and the modern, in India they are positioned simultaneously thus proving us a different combination. Further, the pre-modern too interrogates the modern in India. In the west there is no pre-modern to interrogate the modern, what they have is dissenting the modern that is available in romanticism, in Tolstoy, Ruskin, Thoreau and others. There is a significant difference between dissenting and interrogating. What one should recognise particularly in this part of the country is the tremendous resource to interrogate not merely negatively but positively with instances of good life outside the modern and liberal framework. Not merely to attack the state and get into the combative mode but to offer positive and real instances of good life. This will enable providing an alternative to the critique of modern by the high tradition. This alternative coming from the pre-modern can also be critical of traditional discourse and point out evil in it.

To embark on this project I suggest that we begin with at least sometimes to set aside the oppressive and oppressed formulate. To reclaim that the village or the tribal communities not only get oppressed but also resist it. To theoretically formulate it there is a need to get out of the mere political or moral of being good or bad, or right or wrong, and enter into the domain of cognitive competence. In this context one can elucidate different capabilities of the villages and tribal communities. (Telling truth and telling a lie.)

2. As part of recognising the cognitive competence of these communities let me bring to the notice of those who are critical of these communities for not modernising, let me remind that the people from these communities while being critical of modern do send their children to study

in faraway places and stay back where they are. This provides, both those who stay back and those who go outside an opportunity to evaluate and not merely to become stagnant or be swept away by the outside.

3. In this context let me use this metaphor of Buffet to elucidate the symbolic changes that are taking place in the societies in front of us. Symbolically one way of elucidating the community life of pre-modern society it is used to eat the food that is served. Rather than choice of what to eat more importantly members eat what is served to them. From this we are slowly gravitating towards buffet where one chooses from verieties of dishes. While it gives variety and choice, it also increases responsibilities such as: learning to hold the plate in hand, choosing the right food and its combination, choosing the right order of dishes, avoiding serving right quantity lest you go hungry, or over eat or waste. This requires different competence and it is necessary to make note of it and make suitable changes. We also need to see how these two modes are hybridising each other issuing out different combinations.
4. The last point that I want to make is there is an actual tendency that makes a present majority into minority in the future. This tendency has to be critically evaluated before giving oneself either to this or that option.

I have began by making a claim to shift the present day preoccupation with Man *vs.* Nature paradigm and pointed out how there is a need to disaggregate the self as cognitive self that is modern one and the ordinary self as available in the community life, in tribal societies. In order to highlight this distinction I have discussed the views of Husserl and brought Aristotle to make a contrast. In this context together with the daily recurrent needs that village as a community takes care of, I, following Akeel Bilgrami added the need to look at moral exemplars in these communities, who can provide moral resources to promote the values and morals in these societies. I in the conclusion made some brief remarks about crucial aspects such as avoiding essentialism of stagnant pre-modern and vibrant modern, to step outside the oppressor and oppressed; the symbolic modes of the pre-modern and modern life; and the ongoing process of present majority becoming a minority in the future. The overall purpose of appealing to set aside the man *vs.* nature trajectory is to diminish the importance of the cognitive self of modernity and elevate through highlighting the virtues of tribal and pre-modern societies so that we can get a better picture of this modern tension which at present seems to have poised one sided.

12

Man and Nature

R.K. Behera

Today it is realized that a growing concern for the environment is an integral part of the overall process of sustainable development. The result of this chapter reveals that a sound ecological wisdom or 'Ecosophy' is needed to preserve the stability, integrity and beauty of the biotic community. It also shows that it is the need of the hour to consciously be aware of our ecosystem. A sound environmental ethics is the moral basis of our responsibility towards environment. Human beings live in the realm of nature, they are constantly surrounded by it and interact with it. The most intimate part of nature in relation to man is the biosphere, the thin envelope embracing the earth, its soil cover, and everything else that is alive. Our environment, although outside us, has within us not only its image, as something both actually and imaginatively reflected, but also its material energy and information channels and processes. This presence of nature in an ideal, materialised, energy and information form in man's Self is so organic that when these external natural principles disappear, man himself disappears from life. If we lose nature's image, we lose our life.

Man is constantly aware of the influence of nature in the form of the air he breathes, the water he drinks, the food he eats, and the flow of energy and information. And many of his troubles are a response to the natural processes and changes in the weather, intensified irradiation of cosmic energy, and the magnetic storms that rage around the earth. In short, we are connected with nature by "blood" ties and we cannot live outside nature. During their temporary departures from Earth spacemen take with them a bit of the biosphere. Nowhere does nature affect humanity in exactly the same way. Its influence varies. Depending on where human beings happen to be on the earth's surface, it assigns them varying quantities of light, warmth, water, precipitation, flora and fauna. Human history offers any number of examples of how environmental conditions and the relief of our planet have promoted or retarded human development.

At any given moment a person comes under the influence of both subterranean processes and the cosmic environment. In a very subtle way he reflects in himself, in his functions the slightest oscillations occurring in nature. Electromagnetic radiations alone from the sun and stars may be broken down into a large number of categories, which are distinguishable from one another by their wavelength, the quantity of energy they emit, their power of penetration, and the good or harm they may do us. During the periods of peak solar activity we observe a deterioration in the health of people suffering from high blood pressure, arteriosclerosis or infarction of the myocardium. Disturbances occur in the nervous system and the blood vessels are more liable to suffer from spasms. At such times the number of road accidents increases, and so on. It has been noted that there is dependence between any weakening in the Earth's magnetic field and acceleration of growth, and *vice versa*, growth is retarded when the magnetic field becomes stronger. The corpuscular, radioactive irradiations, cosmic dust, and gas molecules which fill all universal space are also powerful creators and regulators of human existence in biological life. The universe is in a state of dynamic balance and is constantly receiving various forms of energy. Some forms are on the increase or decrease, while others experience periodic fluctuations. Each of us is a sensitive resonator, a kind of echo of the energy flows of the universe. So it would be quite wrong to regard only the energy of the sun as the source of life on earth and humanity as its highest manifestation. The energy of distant cosmic bodies, such as the stars and the nebulae, has a tremendous influence on the life of man as an organism. For this reason our organisms adjust their existence and development to these flows of external energy. The human organism has developed receptors that utilise this energy or protect themselves from it, if it is harmful. It may be said, if we think of human beings as a high-grade biological substance, that they are accumulators of intense energy drives of the whole universe. We are only a response to the vibrations of the elemental forces of outer space, which bring us into unity with their oscillations. Every beat of the organic pulse of our existence is coordinated with the pulse of the cosmic heart. Cosmic rhythms exert a substantial influence on the energy processes in the human organism, which also has its own rhythmic beat.

Man is not only a dweller in nature, he also transforms it. From the very beginning of his existence, and with increasing intensity human society has adapted environing nature and made all kinds of incursions into it. An enormous amount of human labour has been spent on transforming nature. Humanity converts nature's wealth into the means of the cultural, historical life of society. Man has subdued and disciplined electricity and compelled it to serve the interests of society. Not only has man transferred various species of plants and animals to different climatic conditions; he has also changed the shape and climate of his habitation and transformed plants and animals. If we were to strip the geographical environment of the properties created by the labour of many generations, contemporary society would be unable to exist in such primeval conditions.

Man and nature interact dialectically in such a way that, as society develops, man tends to become less dependent on nature directly, while indirectly his dependence grows. This is understandable. While he is getting to know more and more about nature, and on this basis transforming it, man's power over nature progressively increases, but in the same process, man comes into more and more extensive and profound contact with nature, bringing into the sphere of his activity growing quantities of matter, energy and information.

On the plane of the historical development of man-nature relations we may define certain stages. The first is that of the complete dependence of man on nature. Our distant ancestors floundered amid the immensity of natural formations and lived in fear of nature's menacing and destructive forces. Very often they were unable to obtain the merest necessities of subsistence. However, despite their imperfect tools, they worked together stubbornly, collectively, and were able to attain results. This process of struggle between man and the elements was contradictory and frequently ended in tragedy. Nature also changed its face through interaction with man. Forests were destroyed and the area of arable land increased. Nature with its elemental forces was regarded as something hostile to man. The forest, for example, was something wild and menacing and people tried to force it to retreat. This was all done in the name of civilisation, which meant the places where man had made his home, where the earth was cultivated, where the forest had been cut down. But as time goes on the interaction between man and nature is characterised by accelerated subjugation of nature, the taming of its elemental forces. The subjugating power of the implements of labour begins to approach that of natural forces. Mankind becomes increasingly concerned with the question of where and how to obtain irreplaceable natural resources for the needs of production. Science and man's practical transforming activity have made humanity aware of the enormous geological role played by the industrial transformation of earth.

At present the interaction between man and nature is determined by the fact that in addition to the two factors of change in the biosphere that have been operating for millions of years—the biogenetic and the abiogenetic—there has been added yet another factor which is acquiring decisive significance—the techno genetic. As a result, the previous dynamic balance between man and nature and between nature and society as a whole, has shown ominous signs of breaking down. The problem of the so-called replaceable resources of the biosphere has become particularly acute. It is getting more and more difficult to satisfy the needs of human beings and society even for such a substance, for example, as fresh water. The problem of eliminating industrial waste is also becoming increasingly complex. The threat of a global ecological crisis hangs over humanity like the sword of Damocles. His keen awareness of this fact has led man to pose the question of switching from the irresponsible destructive and polluting subjugation of nature to a reasonable harmonious interaction in the "technology-man-biosphere" system. Whereas nature once frightened us and made us tremble with her mysterious vastness and the uncontrollable energy of its elemental forces, it now frightens us with its limitations and a new-found fragility, the delicacy of its plastic mechanisms. We are faced quite uncompromisingly with the problem of how to stop, or at least moderate, the destructive effect of technology on nature. In socialist societies the problem is being solved on a planned basis, but under capitalism spontaneous forces still operate that despoil nature's riches.

Unforeseen paradoxes have arisen in the man-nature relationship. One of them is the paradox of saturation. For millions of years the results of man's influence on nature were relatively insignificant. The biosphere loyally served man as a source of the means of subsistence and a reservoir for the products of his life activity. The contradiction between these vital principles was eliminated by the fact that the relatively modest scale of human productive activity allowed nature to assimilate the waste from labour processes. But as time went on, the growing volume of waste and its increasingly harmful properties destroyed this balance. The human feedback into nature became increasingly disharmonized. Human activity at various times has involved a good deal of irrational behaviour. Labour, which started as a specifically human means of rational survival in the environment, now damages the biosphere on an increasing scale and on the boomerang principle—affecting man himself, his bodily and mental organization. Under the influence of uncoordinated production processes affecting the biosphere, the chemical properties of water, air, the soil, flora and fauna have acquired a negative shift. Experts maintain that 60 per cent of the pollution in the atmosphere, and the most toxic, comes from motor transport, 20 per cent from power stations, and 20 per cent from other types of industry.

It is possible that the changes in the chemical properties of the biosphere can be somehow buffered or even halted, but the changes in the basic physical parameters of the environment are even more dangerous and they may turn out to be uncontrollable. We know that man can exist only in a certain range of temperature and at a certain level of radiation and electromagnetic and sound-wave intensity, that is to say, amid the physical influences that come to us from the atmosphere, from outer space and from the depths of the earth, to which we have adapted in the course of the whole history of the development of human life. From the beginning man has existed in the biosphere, a complex system whose components are the atmosphere, the hydrosphere, the phytosphere, the radiation sphere, the thermosphere, the phonosphere, and so on. All these spheres are and must remain in a natural state of balance. Any excessive upsetting of this balance must be to the detriment not only of normal existence but of any existence at all, even human vegetation. If humanity does not succeed in preventing damage to the biosphere, we run the risk of encountering the paradox of replacement, when the higher plants and animals may be ousted by the lower. As we know, many insects, bacteria, and lichens are, thanks to their relatively simple structure, extremely flexible in adapting to powerful chemical and even physical factors, such as radiation. Mutating under the influence of an unfavourable environment, they continue their modified existence. Man, on the other hand, "nature's crown", because of the exceptional complexity of his bodily and mental organization and the miraculous subtlety and fragility of his genetic mechanism may, when faced with a relatively small change in the chemical and physical factors of the environment, either produce unviable progeny or even perish altogether.

Another possible result of harmful influences on the environment is that the productivity of the biosphere may substantially decline. Already we observe unfavourable shifts in the great system of the universe: Sun-plants-animals-plants. Much more carbon dioxide is being produced on earth than plants can assimilate. Various chemical preparations (herbicides, antibiotics, etc.) affect the intensity of photosynthesis, that most subtle mechanism for the accumulation of the vital energy required by the universal torch of life. Thus, not only progress but even human life itself depends on whether humanity can resolve the paradoxes in the ecological situation that have arisen today.

Modern technology is distinguished by an ever increasing abundance of produced and used synthetic goods. Hundreds of thousands of synthetic materials are being made. People increasingly cover their bodies from head to foot in nylon, Capron and other synthetic, glittering fabrics that are obviously not good for them. Young people may hardly feel this and pay more attention to appearance than to health. But they become more aware of this harmful influence as they grow older. As time goes on the synthetic output of production turns into waste, and then substances that in their original form were not very toxic are transformed in the cycle of natural processes into aggressive agents. One gets the impression that human beings are working harder and harder to organize bits of synthetic reality by disorganizing the systems evolved by nature. Emphasizing man's hostility to nature—hostility armed with the vast achievements of modern technology—both natural scientists and philosophers are today asking themselves the pessimistic question: Is it not the fatal mission of man to be for nature what cancer is for man himself? Perhaps man's destruction of the biosphere is inevitable?

One would like to think that the limited capacities of nature do not signify a fatal limitation of civilization itself. The irrational principle, which once permeated human nature, still exists in human behavioural mechanisms, as can be seen, for instance, in the unpredictable consequences of their individual and concerted efforts. Much in human activity goes beyond the limits of the predictable, even when it is humanely oriented.

The man-nature relation, the crisis of the ecological situation is a global problem. Its solution lies in the plane of rational and humane, that is to say, wise organization, both of production itself and care for mother nature, not just by individuals, enterprises or countries, but by all humanity, linked with a clear awareness of our planetary responsibility for the ecological consequences of a civilization that has reached a state of crisis. One of the ways to deal with the crisis situation in the "man-nature" system is to use such resources as solar energy, the power of winds, the riches of the seas and oceans and other, as yet unknown natural forces of the universe. At one time in his evolution man was a gatherer. He used the ready-made gifts of nature. This was how human existence began. Perhaps even today it would be wise to resort to this method, but on a quite different level, of course. The human being cannot restrict himself to gathering, any more than he could in primitive times. But such a shift in attitude could at least abate the destructive and polluting principle in civilization.

As cybernetic methods and principles in the various fields of knowledge and practice develop, control theory has been widely applied in many spheres. Its aim is to ensure the optimal function of a system. A humanely oriented mind should be able to transfer the idea of optimality and harmony to ecological phenomena.

In their production activity people are mastering more and more new materials and learning to replace one with another. In the long term this could lead, as the alchemists once believed, to production on the principle of everything out of everything. Moreover, our planet has an active balance—it loses less substance in the upper layers of the atmosphere than it receives from outer space. It would, therefore, appear that the amount of substance available as a whole will not place any radical limitation on material production. Life, including human life, is not only metabolism; it is also a form of energy transformation and movement developed to degrees of subtlety that are as yet beyond our comprehension. Every cell, every organ and organism as a whole is a crucial arena of the struggle between entropic (dispersing) and anti-entropic processes, and the biosphere represents the constant victory of life, the triumph of the anti-entropic principle in the existence of the living.

Losses of living energy from our organism are constantly compensated by various forms of energy flowing from the vast expanses of the universe. We need not simply energy, such as electromagnetic radiation or heat, but radiant energy of the finest quality. The struggle for the existence of living creatures, including man, is a struggle not so much for the elements that compose his organism—they are abundantly available in the air, water and underground—not for solar energy in its direct, electromagnetic radiation, but for the energy that is captured by the mechanisms of photosynthesis and exists in the form of organic, particularly plant structures. When we consume vegetable food, we take the energy of nature particularly that of the sun, at first hand, so to speak. But plants are also the food of herbivorous animals, and when we eat meat, we take this energy at second hand.

So the biosphere is not a chaotic conglomeration of natural phenomena and formations. By a seemingly objective logic everything is taken into account and everything mutually adapts with the same obedience to proportion and harmony that we discern in the harmonious motion of the heavenly bodies or the integral paintings of the great masters. With a sense of wonder we see revealed before us a picture of the magnificent universe, a universe whose separate parts are interconnected by the most subtle threads of kinship, forming the harmonious whole which the ancient philosophers surmised when they viewed the world with their integrating, intuitively perceptive gaze. We are part of the ecological environment and it is a part of the universe. It contains myriads of stars and the nearest of them is the Sun. The Sun is the master of Earth. We are, in a certain sense, its children. Not for nothing did the rich imagination on whose wings mankind flies ever further and higher in the orbit of civilization portray the Sun in ancient legends as the highest deity.

But to return to our theme, the bitter truth is that those human actions which violate the laws of nature, the harmony of the biosphere, threaten to bring disaster and this disaster may turn out to be universal. How apt then are the words of ancient Oriental wisdom: live closer to nature, my friends, and its eternal laws will protect you!

'Environment' in general refers to the surroundings of an object. Today it is realized that a concern for the environment is an integral part of the overall process of sustainable development. Environmental ethics which is a part of environmental philosophy examines how human beings should interact with the non-human world around them. American ecologist, forester, and environmentalist Aldo Leopold suggests that our legislations and policies must be in conformity with a set of ethos or guiding beliefs. These beliefs are associated with biodiversity and environment as a whole. He stresses on the point that ethic is needed to preserve the "stability, integrity and beauty of the biotic community." It is the need of the hour to consciously be aware of our ecosystem. Joel Feinberg in his essay The Rights of animals and Unborn Generations emphasizes the interests of future generations to preserve endangered species. He says, "Surely we owe it to future generations to pass on a world that is not used up garbage." A human centric environmental ethics based on a traditional western approach poses a threat to environmental values. A nature centric system of ethic opposed to human centric ethics is the need of the hour. Norwegian philosopher Naess, the founder of "deep ecology movement" maintains that every being, whether animate or inanimate has an equal right to live. Ecology teaches us a beautiful symbiotic interrelation and interdependence between the members of the biotic community. Population growth at a very high rate is now a threat to the ecology. We need to take programmes for reduction of population. Professor Paul Ehrlich suggests the 'I = PAT' formula in relation to the impact of environment. Here, I = environmental impact, P = population, A =consumptive affluence, T = technology. describe the impact of human activity on the environment.

Conclusion

It is the human behaviour and not the environment that needs to be managed. To control population size, level of affluence, dependence on technology and thereby to modify our societal attitude towards environment, Cairns suggests that the formula, i.e. I = PAT can be taken into consideration while taking up the issue of man-environment interaction. Man must learn how to use scientific and technological knowledge to fulfil their needs without causing any harm to the natural environment. Hinduism lays much importance on the unity between man and nature. According to Hinduism, men are neither separate nor independent of nature, but constituent part of nature. M. K. Gandhi says that the earth provides enough to satisfy every person's need but not every person's greed. Love for nature cannot be brought about by laws. It must come from within because we love the earth and living beings thereof.

References

1. Shrivastava, A.K. (2004), *Environmental Ethics*, p. 186, A.P.H. Publishing Corporation.
2. Feinberg, Joel (1994), "The Rights of Animals and Unborn Generations," in James E. White (ed.), *Contemporary Moral Problems*, New York: West Publishing Company, p. 434.
3. Satyanarayana, Y.V. (2010), *Ethics Theory and Practice*, Dorling Kindersley (India) Pvt. Ltd., p. 109.
4. Cairns, J. (1995), "Respect for the Inherent Worth of Each Individual *Versus* the Web of Life: an Unresolved Conflict," *Speculations in Science and Technology*, Vol. 18, pp. 294-301.
5. Sharma, P.D. (2001), *Ecology and Environment*, p. 623, Rastogi Publication.

13

Applied Ethical Issues in Environment

General Observations

Vanlalngbak

The importance and urgent need of applied ethical issues in environment today cannot be ignored. The more it is ignored the more degradation in environment will take place and consequently the earth will be unfit for human habitation. This chapter is not an attempt to defend any particular position or theory as such but just to throw some important issues and raised questions concerning how it is important and relevant today. Philosophical reasoning and approaches to the issues will definitely enhance understanding and possible move towards the possible solution of the vexed problem.

To begin with, philosophy taught a person to have a comprehensive understanding of things and also help to develop a proper worldview. Ethics is a broad way of thinking about what constitutes a good life and how to have a good life. It addresses questions of right and wrong, making good decisions, and the character or attributes necessary to live a good life. Applied ethics address these issues with a special emphasis on how they can be carried out in a practical manner. Environmental ethics apply ethical thinking to the natural world and the relationship between humans and the earth. Some important subject matters of applied ethical environmental issues constitute the followings:

Climate Change

The high amounts of air pollution due to the development of several industries, and water pollution due to discarding of toxic waste in oceans and other waterbodies, and the high rate of deforestation, are also contributing towards a drastic climate change. This widespread misuse is causing global warming like never before. Erratic changes in weather, brutal blizzards and floods, and vicious heat waves, are now affecting lands where such phenomena were not so common.

Overpopulation

The rapid growth of population and the subsequent overpopulation is another among the many global environmental issues that has affected every nation. With the advancement in medicine and technology, life expectancy has increased, which is a boon in its own way, but has adversely affected the environment. Earth is now overpopulated, and because of the other problems that are affecting it, it is not going to be able to sustain this excess for very long. Also, though family planning measures have been strictly implemented in several countries, they are still not as effective to control the rapidly increasing population.

Pollution

Different kinds of pollution are having a horrific impact on the planet and also to human beings. Water pollution, air pollution, acid rain due to air pollution, land pollution, noise pollution, are all adversely affecting the environment and people. Some countries are so polluted that children are born with birth defects, such as mutations of different body parts, while several others develop such defects later in life, due to their exposure to different types of pollution.

Land Degradation: Due to mass migration to urban life because of searching better employment and opportunities has had a deep impact on the land that we live on. For one, to accommodate the rising urban population, a lot of deforestation has taken place. This not only affects the climate, but also destroys the natural habitat of other life forms, leading to the increasing number of extinct animals and endangered animals, and thereby disturbing the natural cycle of the environment. Agricultural practices such as intensive farming, overgrazing, and use of harsh pesticides, render several agricultural lands useless. Furthermore, soil erosion contributes to land degradation and its subsequent effects on humankind.

Resource Depletion

Due to overpopulation, and the relaxed manner in which different natural resources are utilized, there is a serious lack of resources that can be used by us human beings now. We are experiencing the phenomenon of rising fuel prices due to their constantly decreasing amounts. Several countries face huge water problems where some houses get water only for an hour a day, and where the ability to provide water to people depends on the erratic rains that elude those who solely depend on it as a source of water. Electricity is another serious problem in certain countries that is not available to everyone. Due to the continuous depletion of all these natural resources, experts have predicted that survival on planet Earth is only going to get further challenging and difficult. The least we can do is try to adopt some energy saving methods so that it is efficiently utilized, evenly distributed and made available to everyone.

Loss of Biodiversity

Earth comprises several life forms that together contribute to the biological diversity that exists on the planet. Because of the aforementioned environmental problems, we are experiencing degeneration of biodiversity. Biodiversity is important because all life species on this planet play a crucial role in its sustenance. Moreover, healthy biodiversity ensures its own sustenance, and allows for the development of further species, which in turn is likely to enhance the overall quality of life of the planet.

This was just some of the current environmental issues that are plaguing life on this planet. The list of issues that affect the environment is never-ending, with every action contributing to different environmental problems. The least we can do is understand these problems, and try to make an effort on our part to reduce the suffering of mankind and nature. If everyone of us tries to make a difference, we are likely to have a positive overall outcome, leading to a better, healthier life for all living species on this planet.

Moral reasoning is not a substitute for science, but it provides a powerful complement to scientific knowledge about the earth. Science does not teach us to care. Scientific knowledge does not, by itself, provide reasons for environmental protection. Science and economics provide data, information, and knowledge. Environmental ethics turns to this information and asks: how then, should we live? Why should we care? Environmental ethics builds on scientific understanding by bringing human values, moral principles and improved decision makings into conversation with science. Environmental ethics is necessarily inter-disciplinary, meaning it draws on other fields of academic inquiry; it cannot stand by itself. Often, the simple question, "What is the right thing for us to do?" can open up fresh perspectives on environmental problems. Thinking ethically about the environment has the potential to help someone to contribute to creating environmental solutions.

In the most general sense, environmental ethics invites us to consider three key propositions:

1. Does the Earth and its creatures are worthy of our ethical concern;
2. Does the Earth and its creatures have moral value merely because they exist, not only because they meet human needs;
3. Drawing from the idea of ecosystem human beings should consider "wholes" that include other forms of life and the environment.

There are many different principles on which to draw in moral reasoning about specific environmental problems. But let us limit ourselves to three basic pairs of principles: justice and sustainability; sufficiency and compassion; solidarity and participation. It will demonstrate how environmental concerns challenge us to extend these principles to include the well-being of the natural world and our human duties to it. It concludes with a description of three general types of arguments that can be used in moral reasoning about the environment.

The three classic ethical principles of justice, sufficiency and solidarity can be traced back to many different sources: Greek philosophy, religious teachings, and reflection on human experience. In the face of any decision involving environmental ethics, we should ask how each of these ethical principles—also known as ethical norms—can be applied to the situation at hand. Ethical principles are standards or benchmarks against which we can evaluate our actions. They are also signposts to orient us toward the difference between right and wrong, especially in conditions where there are multiple problems, and the interests of more than one party. Ethical principles are different from scientific principles in that they are generally not as hard and fast. They are less likely to give us one correct answer, but can be used to evaluate conflicting claims, a decision making process, or the outcome of a decision.

Justice and Sustainability

The classic formal principle of justice is that equals should be treated equally unless there is a sufficient reason to treat anyone unequally. It is clearly relevant in the field of ethics called environmental justice, but this principle cuts across many issues. Environmental justice is concerned with the inequitable access to environmental resources (clean food, air and water) and the injustice of greater pollution that often characterize lower-income communities—not wealthy suburbs. The notion of justice underlies concern about animal welfare. On the basis of what values are other animals considered different from the human animal and thus subject to consumption by humans? Recent advances in biology have shown that the differences between humans and other animals are much less than many of us might think. Does the equality of humans and animals as living creatures require far more humane treatment of animals? Or even the total non-use of animals? To apply justice to an environmental decision, we should ask:

1. Are all human beings involved in this situation being treated equally and, if not, why not?
2. Are all living creatures involved in this situation being treated equally and, if not, why not?

Sustainability extends justice into the future. Sustainability can be defined as meeting the needs of the present generation without compromising the ability of future generation to meet their own needs. We are consuming or degrading many resources (such as fossil fuel energy, topsoil and water) today faster than they can be naturally replenished, which means they will not be available to people in the future. The ethical principle of justice is at play because it underpins the need to equitably balance the needs of those alive today (the rich and poor) with future generations. Thus, environmental ethics takes the notion of fundamental fairness and stretches it to include those yet to be born. To apply the principle of sustainability to an environmental decision, we should ask:

1. What are the immediate and long-term effects of the problem before us?
2. Who—humans and otherwise—is affected today by the problem before us and who will likely be affected by this problem in the future?

Sufficiency and Compassion

The principle of sufficiency mandates that all forms of life are entitled to enough goods to live on and flourish. The principle also means no one should waste or hoard resources intended for the sufficiency of all. Upholding the norm of sufficiency makes demands upon individuals—to share, to live more simply, to think creatively—and on human communities: to ensure that everyone has access to the goods that they need to live a life of dignity. The ethical norm of sufficiency is closely tied to the notion of moral significance, which means that something is worthy of our ethical concern. This means that we include the needs of others in our consideration of what is important, or worthy of our concern. When we consider the needs of others, such as poor individuals in our society or poor countries in the world, we are asserting the moral principle of sufficiency. This principle helps us think about whom else we need to consider, to whom we have moral duties. It underlies the practice of empathy. This principle can conflict, at least in some people's minds, with the notion that the Earth does not have sufficient goods to meet everyone's needs. To apply the principle of sufficiency to an environmental decision, we should ask:

1. Will the decision permit all those involved, especially the poor, to have enough resources on which to live and flourish?
2. Is there any aspect of the decision that indicates the presence of waste or excess? Or a failure to be creative?

Compassion extends the notion of sufficiency to the Earth. Environmental ethics asserts that other animals, plants, and the elements (such as water, soil or air) are morally significant, and that humans have responsibilities to act so that their needs are met too. Some environmental ethicists, such as Deep Ecologist, assert that non-human forms of life have moral significance equivalent to humans. Most people, however, believe that other forms of life have some moral worth, but that humans are of greater moral significance. Even if you think animals are far more worthy of your concern than plants or elements, recognize that all animals depend, either directly or indirectly on plants for food, and that no creatures can live without sufficient clean water. To assert that any wild animal is worthy of our moral concern begins the process of learning about the interdependence of all creatures on the habitat and food resources provided by other creatures in an ecosystem. It is simply impossible to consider the well-being of one other creature in isolation from their environment. Ultimately, the future of humans is tied to the well-being of all other creatures. To apply the principle of compassion to an environmental decision, we should ask:

1. What duties do we have to the other creatures likely to be affected by our actions?

2. What does sufficiency mean for other creatures, especially those threatened with extinction?
3. What would it mean to extend the principle of compassion to non-human creatures?

Solidarity and Participation

The principle of solidarity invites us to consider how we relate to each other in community. It assumes that we recognize that we are a part of at least one family—our biological family, our local community, or our national community—but then challenges us to consider the full range of relationships with others. In a globalizing economy, we participate in a vast, international economic community, one in which goods and services are provided for us by those on the other side of the world. Solidarity requires us to consider this kind of extended community, and to act in such a way that reflects concern for the well-being of others. To apply the principle of solidarity to an environmental decision, we should ask:

1. Who are all the human stakeholders involved in this situation?
2. Who are all the natural stakeholders?
3. Is there a community of life involved?
4. Are there any stakeholders—human and non-human—who are especially vulnerable?

Participation extends the idea of solidarity to make it practical. The demands of solidarity point us to the principle of participation, so that those affected by an environmental decision can shape how it is made. Many environmental problems stem from decisions being made by private individuals or companies that have wide ranging implications. In some cases, in this country and others, governments make environmental decisions without fully securing the consent of the public. Often, those most affected are unaware of the decisions or the long-term effects on their health and the well-being of their environment. The ethical principle of participation requires us to recognize all of the parties—human and non-human—likely to be affected by a decision, and to recognize that all parties should have a say in how the decision is made. Genuine participation requires transparency, meaning that each individual has access to the same information that everyone else has. To apply the principle of participation to an environmental decision, we should ask:

1. Do all stakeholders in this decision actually have a say in how the decision is going to be made?
2. Are there any stakeholders who cannot represent themselves? Or who have little power? How will their interests be represented in the decision-making process?

Modes of Ethical Reasoning about the Environment

We now come to the "what" of environmental ethics, in other words, to the kinds of ethical reasoning that uses standards for environmental behaviour or decisions. If we reflect on how we already think, we can see several common modes of ethical reasoning. For the sake of simplicity and by using a sort of short-hand, let us consider these modes as three—moral reasoning about commands, consequences, and character. Whenever we consider an ethical problem, we usually find ourselves reasoning along one or more of these lines. And this is as much the case in environmental ethics as in any other kind of ethics.

Commands: We can use the notion of "commands" as a shorthand way for referring to those things that we ought to do, no matter what the consequences. This kind of reasoning is also associated with such ethical categories as commandments, laws, rights, and justice. In terms of environmental ethics, perhaps the classic command is one of the classic commands in all of ethics, "Do no harm." That is, our first general duty toward the environment is to do no harm. Moreover, we are reasoning in a command mode when, for instance, we think that animals have rights and, therefore, that justice requires that we not harm them; this is often the ethical conviction behind those who do not eat meat.

Consequences: The ethical notion of consequences is most

often associated with the philosophical school of utilitarianism. According to this mode of ethical reasoning, commands are not sufficient in themselves to tell us what we ought to do. Instead, we need to think carefully about the consequences of our actions. Thus we can determine the correct ethical action by choosing the one that will produce the greatest balance of good consequences over bad consequences. This kind of reasoning helpfully invites us to consider the totality of a situation and to identify its positive and negative aspects. More to the point, in this kind of reasoning, commands or laws or rights can be overridden if doing so will yield a greater balance of benefits over harms. This means, for instance, that something like the rights of animals can be overridden for the sake of some perceived human benefit. In consequential reasoning, it is often difficult to specify what qualifies as a "benefit" and a "harm" or, similarly, a "benefit" and a "cost," or "good" and "bad," etc. Frequently in environmental cases, costs and benefits are considered only in monetary terms. But while the assessment of such financial costs is an essential part of many ethical analyses, it cannot be the whole of such analyses. And it is important to try to name what else constitutes harm and benefits. One way of doing this might be to say, for instance, that harm is constituted by things like premature death, undue pain, or the violation of human economic or political rights. An environmental action that leads or very likely will lead to such harms would be ethically problematic. Working to protect the full diversity of life on Earth is an example of ethical action with a positive consequence.

Character: When we speak of "character," we are not doing so precisely in the way that we often hear the word: As referring to a role in a play or movie. Rather, we are referring more to the notion that "he or she has got good character" or to the notion that "he or she is a person of conscience." In the face of a situation of environmental ethics, we are asking: What does this particular action that may affect the environment mean for my character? Or, similarly, what kind of person am I becoming by engaging in these actions in relation to the environment? Am I becoming more just, more humble, more generous? This mode of ethical reasoning invites careful and honest self-reflection. It can also be a kind of reasoning used very well by a group. The fact is, we become what we do—whether what we do involve only other people or also involve the natural world.

References

Attfield, Robin, *The Ethics of Environmental Concern,* (Oxford: Basil Blackwell, 1983).

Barry, Brian, "Sustainability and Intergenerational Justice" in Dobson, Andrew (ed.), *Fairness and Futurity,* (Oxford: Oxford University Press, 1999): 93-117.

Blackstone, William T., "Ethics and Ecology" in Blackstone, William T. (ed.), *Philosophy and Environmental Crisis,* (Athens, University of Georgia Press, 1972): 16-42.

Bookchin, Murray and Foreman, Dave, *Defending the Earth,* (New York: Black Rose Books, 1991).

Callicott, James Baird, "Animal Liberation: A Triangular Affair", *Environmental Ethics,* 2 (1980): 311-328.

Callicott, James Baird, "The Conceptual Foundations of the Land Ethic", in Zimmerman, Michael E.; Callicott, J. Baird; Sessions, George; Warren, Karen J.; and Clark, John (eds.), *Environmental Philosophy: From Animal Rights to Radical Ecology,* (New Jersey: Prentice Hall, 2nd ed., 1998): 101-123.

Ehrlich, Paul, *The Population Bomb,* (New York: Ballantine Books, 1968).

Gewirth, Alan, "Human Rights and Future Generations" in Boylan, Michael (ed.), *Environmental Ethics,* (New Jersey: Prentice Hall, 2001): 207-211.

Golding, Mark, "Obligations to Future Generations", *Monist,* 56 (1972): 85-99.

Johnson, Lawrence E., *A Morally Deep World: An Essay on Moral Significance and Environmental Ethics,* (Cambridge: Cambridge University Press, 1993).

Naess, Arnc, "The Deep Ecological Movement Some Philosophical Aspects", *Philosophical Inquiry,* 8, (1986): 1-2.

Singer, Peter, *Practical Ethics,* (Cambridge: Cambridge University Press, 2nd ed., 1993).

Zimmerman, Michael E.; Callicott, J. Baird; Sessions, George; Warren, Karen J.; and Clark, John (eds.), *Environmental Philosophy: From Animal Rights to Radical Ecology,* (New Jersey: Prentice Hall, 2nd ed., 1998.

14

Environmental Philosophy

An Ethical Response to Nature

Wojanbeni Shitiri Yanthan

Environmental ethicists have for some years now been arguing for revisions with regard to man's relation with nature,[1] and as a step towards it, environmentalists have urged philosophers to look into the philosophical aspects of environmental issues.[2] But at this very juncture a rather inquisitive question that could be expected is, why philosophy and not any other discipline? For instance, disciplines such as politics and science seem capable of dealing with environmental issues but why philosophy? For example, environmental problems created due to alarming growth in the civilization of a nation could be looked into from a political perspective by enquiring about the privatisation of property, whether legal or not and those acts that are affecting the use of land could be dealt with. Science which is regarded as the first order of enquiry in the field of knowledge and which depends on observation and experimentation, can, for example, tackle the level of pollution in the atmosphere through the best possible ways, but what seems to make itself known here is that, they can, but only to a limited portion. Besides, the most important aspect of environmental issues remains untouched, and they are the numerous ethical questions that demands rational explanations. Philosophy can handle such issues as there is no other discipline that addresses them. Environmental issues have been explored in a philosophical sense only in recent times. The two terms 'environment' and 'philosophy' have been seen as separate issues.[3]

Louise points out that, ". . . . on the surface the question about whether an environmental issue is also a philosophical issue is not that apparent. However, when thinking more deeply about environmental issues, especially those in crisis, you can begin to see how closely they are both related". Louise further adds, "Once you begin to look at environmental issues and the nature of philosophy you can begin to argue that environmental issues could be philosophical issue."[4]

According to Eugere C. Hargrove, Aldo Leopold's *The Land Ethic* has also very clearly convinced many environmentalists that the foundation of environmental problems were philosophical.[5] Rusling also holds that, "environmental issues are essentially philosophical issues."[6]

But then neither question answers, what is the role of philosophy in solving environmental problems?[7] The answer is simple. Philosophy critically evaluates and seeks to give a systematic knowledge of life and the universe.[8] One of the main tasks of philosophy according to Sanyal is to, "Determine the correct relation between human life and the universe around us, and give a complete and synoptic view of the universe in harmony with the various aspects of human experience, intellectual, aesthetic, moral and religious."[9] Besides this, it also enquires into the nature, meaning, purpose, origin and destiny of human life. It is the interpretation of life, its values and meaning. It enables man, who is a rational being to critically reflect upon the meaning, purpose and value of life and the environment. Most importantly, philosophy is a rational reflection on life.[10]

Environmental problems call upon for a deep and critical *rational reflection* on man's relation towards nature. The problems being ethical in nature, it requires critical and ethical investigation, which philosophy deals with at close proximity. With the rise in numerous ethical dilemmas concerning environment, the need and importance for this branch of philosophy is even more felt. All of this makes it difficult to separate philosophy from environmental issues.[11] Therefore, it can be said that philosophy has a greater role to play in solving environmental problems.

One thing that cannot be denied is the fact that philosophy can contribute some valuable ideas to environmental issues.[12] In fact, there is a part in philosophy that is directed towards the environment. It is called **Environmental philosophy**.

According to Tad Beckman, "Environmental philosophy is a young field that brings together the traditional nurturing of wisdom with a specific interest in the environment. Part of environmental philosophy is, therefore, exploring what we know and justifiably believe about the environment. But, we have to be careful not to stop there. Environmental philosophy requires us to develop wisdom about the environment and that means, as above, discussing what is best for the environment, especially with respect to our own actions within the environment."[13]

Christopher Belshaw says environmental philosophy is a branch of philosophy that is concerned with the natural environment and humans' place within it.[14] Environmental philosophy includes environmental aesthetics, eco-feminism, environmental theology and environmental ethics.[15]

Environmental ethics is the part of environmental philosophy, which deals with the ethical relationship between human beings and the natural environment.[16] Stanford encyclopaedia of philosophy defines it as the discipline in philosophy that studies the moral relationship of human beings to, and also the value and moral status of, the environment and its non-human contents.[17] Others point out that Environmental ethics is properly but a sub-section of environmental philosophy, which includes environmental aesthetics, environmental theology, and indeed all the branches of philosophical investigations such as epistemology, metaphysics, philosophy of science, etc.

According to J. Baird Callicott, "Environmental ethics maybe understood to be but one among several new sorts of applied philosophies, the others of which also arose during the seventies. That is, it may be understood to be an application of well established conventional philosophical categories to emergent practical environmental problems."[18]

Kanti Lal Das holds that, "Environmental ethics is surely a new addition to the so-called traditional or humanistic ethics, as traditional ethics is predominantly humanistic in nature because here only human beings are considered to be the legitimate moral agents."[19] He holds that traditional ethics denies or ignores the value of nature. It pleas for moral dualism or ethical subjectivism, which is currently known as Anthropocentrism. The sole object of environmental ethics is contrary to traditional ethics. It tries to annihilate the view that only human beings are the legitimate moral agents and apart from humans no other sentient beings have the right. It moves towards the moral dignity of all biotic community.[20]

Environmental ethics in the academic field has grown over the years. It grew up in response to the work of scientist such as Rachel Louise Carson, Lynn White, Garrett Hardin, Aldo Leopold and events like Earth Day 1970.[21] All the above mentioned, have played a crucial role in creating awareness about the ethical problems relating to environment. For instance, Lynn Townsend White, Jr. (1907-1987) is best known for his ideas on the causes of modern environmental problems. Lynn White in a much-cited essay published in 1967 on the historical roots of the environmental crisis, argues that the main strands of Judeo-Christian thinking had encouraged the overexploitation of nature by maintaining the superiority of humans over all other forms of life on earth, and by depicting all of nature as created for the use of humans.[22] White's thesis is widely discussed in theology, history, and has been subject to some sociological testing as well and being continuously discussed by philosophers.[23] Garrett James Hardin (1915-2003) was a widely-known ecologist from Dallas, Texas. He brought to light the dangers of overpopulation and warned about the damage it would inflict on the environment.[24] The First Earth Day (1970) was organised to highlight the deep concern over the deterioration of the environment and the careless use of resources. According to Garylord Nelson, "that day left a permanent impact on the politics of America. It forcibly thrust the issue of environmental quality and resources conservation into the political dialogue of the Nation. That was the important objective and achievement of Earth Day."[25]

Over the years, the attitude towards nature has been strongly dominated by an anthropocentric outlook which considers the world only in terms of its utility. The value here is that of the use value or resource value and as such, Anthropocentricism may rightly be referred to as the instrumental value.[26] Anthropocentrism is believed to be found at the root of the Western Philosophy and Culture.[27] It is seen in the views of some western philosophers such as Aristotle, Descartes, Kant,[28] and twentieth century philosopher such as John Passmore. Aristotle, a Greek philosopher, is one of the two or three most influential philosophers, and one of the most important founding figures in the history of Western philosophy. During the fifth and sixth centuries B.C., Greek thought was for most part preoccupied with the mystery of the universe and man's place in it,[29] and Aristotle like the rest sought to provide a reasonable explanation, and he does so in his book *Politics.* He holds that man has a higher status in the society. Man alone of all the animals is furnished with the faculty of language.[30] He differentiates language from sounds. Mere sounds only serves to indicate pain or pleasure, and this is what animals possess, but language assists in delivering and, in his words, "declaring what is advantageous and what is the reverse, therefore language serves to declare what is just and what is unjust."[31] Further, he establishes a psychic hierarchy. He considers plants as having the 'vegetative' soul,[32] animals as having the 'sensitive' soul[33] and humans as having the 'rational' soul.[34] It is the highest in the hierarchy of the soul, and thus reaffirms his position of man as the dominant being. Aristotle is considered to be a supporter of Anthropocentrism based on what he wrote in his book *Politics.* He writes, "Plants exists for the sake of animals—domestic animals for his use and food, wild ones (or at any rate most of them) for food and other accessories of life, such as clothing and various tools."[35]

For Aristotle, nature is to be understood as an organic whole, and the things in it are meant to serve a purpose.[36] He believed that nature has made all things specifically for the sake of man, therefore, plants and animals were on earth for the instrumental use of man.[37] Benjamin Jowett in his translation on Aristotle's *Politics,* translates the above text as "we may infer that, after the birth of animals, plants exist for their sake, and that the other animals exist for the sake of man, the tame for use and food, the wild, if not all at least the greater part of them, for food, and for the provision of clothing and various instruments."[38]

Aristotle's view that nature exists for instrumental purpose is also seen in the works of Réné Descartes, a French philosopher and a great mathematician in the seventeenth century.[39] He was an admirer of Aristotle. He agreed with him that only humans have the 'rational' power. Human beings having the faculty of language are, therefore, higher than plants or lower animals. No plants and animal can enjoy rationality as they do not have the faculty of language.[40] Aristotle denied the 'rational' soul to animals, and so did Descartes. However, Descartes' view on animals is considered to be somewhat harsher than that of Aristotle. Aristotle considered animals as having the 'sensitive' soul, but Descartes holds that animals do not perceive, choose, nor feel. In fact, they are not conscious.

So the next question that follows is, what are they? Descartes calls them *automata*.[41] Descartes considers them as ever more ingenious mechanical toys, with which the leisured classes of the time used to amuse themselves; but of a superior sort. Animals are automata. They cannot reason or feel pain and are like *robots*.[42] Here it needs to be pointed out that Descartes did consider animals as living organic creatures. He did not deny life to animals,[43] but he denies all thought, by which he means consciousness, to animals. Thinking cannot be enjoyed by those who do not have rationality.[44] According to him, animals are "thoughtless brutes," *automata*, machines, that despite their appearance they are not aware of anything, they do not see nor hear, smell nor taste, they do not feel heat nor cold. In fact, Descartes goes on to state that they do not even experience hunger nor thirst. For him, animals are like clocks. Clocks can keep better time, but like clocks they are not conscious.[45] Further, animals were considered as incapable of suffering. It is believed that the conditions of animals reached their lowest point during the time of Descartes.[46]

Another eminent philosopher who holds an anthropocentric view is Immanuel Kant; a German philosopher from Kaliningrad, Russia. Kant's moral philosophy shared a human dominated view.[47] According to him, human beings should be treated with respect necessary for all human beings on the virtue of being a rational being. Kant holds that a human being must not be treated as a means to an end since he believes that every human should be treated as an end in himself. For instance, a utilitarian would be willing to sacrifice a man if it is important and necessary for saving the Earth or of the many, but Kant on the other hand would allow no such thing.[48] Human beings hold a higher status than other animals for Kant. The reason is that, sentience or the ability to feel pleasure and pain is not what made human special and different from other animals, but what differs and what made humans rank in higher status than other animal is the faculty of reason. He states, "Man really finds in himself a faculty by which he distinguishes himself from all other things, even from himself so far as he is affected by objects. This faculty is reason."[49] Further, Kant believed that non-human animals had no moral standing and our treatment of them is unimportant and insignificant. According to Kantian philosophy, "Genuine ethical behaviour must be driven entirely and exclusively by ethical principles derived from pure reason."[50]

So because non-human animals do not have the ability to rationalise, Kant concludes that they cannot behave in a moral way or qualify as a moral agent.[51] Immanuel Kant famously denied that animals have intrinsic moral significance. If it is wrong to treat animals in certain ways, he held, it is not because the animal is wronged but because some human being who takes an interest in the animal is wronged.[52]

In the twentieth century an Australian philosopher John Passmore is credited for having shaped public debate and for opening up domains of applied philosophy and the history of ideas to the wider world. He is well known for his book, *Man's Responsibility for Nature*. In his book, Passmore argued and pointed out that there is an urgent need to change our attitude to the environment, and that we cannot continue unconstrained exploitation of the biosphere. However, he argued from an anthropocentric perspective. For him, doing so does not demand for a new and revised ethical framework that seeks to attribute intrinsic value to nature like the non-anthropocentric view does, which to him is but a misguided mysticism or irrationalism, instead he retains the special status of human beings based on the scientific rational explanations.[53] John Passmore being a critic of deep ecology holds that nothing is gained by insisting that human beings share a moral community with the rest of nature.

Passmore argues, "Bacteria and human beings do not recognise mutual obligation, nor do they have common interests. In the only sense in which belonging to a community generates ethical obligation, they do not belong to the same community. To suggest, then, that animals, plants, landscapes have 'right to exist', is to create confusion. The idea of 'rights' is simply not applicable to what is non-human."[54] He asks, "Is it so obvious that a universe consisting of human beings and a cobra is better than a universe consisting of humans only? Should St. Patrick be condemned for driving the snakes out of Ireland? And if to drive them out of Ireland is worthy of praise, should it not be equally praiseworthy to drive them out of the world?"[55] Tom Duddy explains Passmore view by stating that, for Passmore, "The core concepts of morality, such as the concepts of right, do not apply to something called Nature. Animals and plants, both individually or collectively, do not recognise mutual obligations and, therefore, do not participate in the moral community. The claim that it is intrinsically wrong to cut down trees, or clear a wilderness, or even destroy a species of animal or plant, is 'merely ridiculous'. It is ridiculous because it introduces a concept of morality which is barely intelligible to us, as if new moralities are the kinds of things that can be devised at will."[56]

John Passmore made it clear that although there is a need to change our attitude to the environment, there is no need for a change in the ethical framework wherein moral status is extended to the non-human world.

However, such considerations do not satisfy the demands of those who hold the view that the non-human world must be valued because they all possess intrinsic value and not instrumental value. This attitude towards nature is known as Non-Anthropocentrism. Non-Anthropocentrism unlike Anthropocentric approach gives serious attention to the moral status of non-human animals and inanimate objects. According to non-anthropocentrists, many of the early perspectives on environment being human-centred or anthropocentric in nature,[57] it cannot accommodate within its sphere other non-human forms of life and, therefore, over the years attempts have been made to shift from the traditional human-centric attitude to nature-centred approach. The traditional definition of ethics reveals such an anthropocentric attitude that M.N. Mitra states, "Ethics is traditionally defined as a normative science of human conduct where the word 'conduct' is taken to refer to the collection of voluntary actions. This definition implies that ethics basically deals with human beings and how they relate to other human beings. Its objective is to look after the interest of the members of the human species, their mutual growth and welfare. The traditional concept implies that our moral universe consists only of human beings. Man has moral responsibility towards fellow beings; he has no moral responsibility towards others. Thus, killing a human individual falls within the moral preview, but killing an animal or felling a tree is not, unless it affects the interest of human beings."[58]

It is exactly this attitude to non-human life forms, considering them fit for a moral preview if only it affects the interest of the human beings, that non-anthropocentrists fights for. Non-human life forms need to be considered worthy of a moral preview even without their instrumental contributions. They need to be accounted for the intrinsic value that each one of them possesses. Non-Anthropocentrists argue that Anthropocentrism cannot be the foundation of environmental ethics.[59] Jeremy Bentham, Albert Schweitzer, Aldo Leopold, Rachel Louise Carson, founder of deep ecology Arne Naess, Tom Regan, Peter Singer, are some who support this view.

Jeremy Bentham is widely recognised as one of the earliest proponents of animal rights.[60] Unlike philosophers such as Aristotle, Descartes and Kant who held the view that there can be no moral considerations to other non-human beings due to the lack of rationality, Bentham believed that rationality cannot be the ground for allocating morality to animals. His view on animal rights can be seen in his book *Introduction to the Principles of Morals and Legislation.*[61] He argued that the ability to suffer and not the ability to reason must be what it should be based upon. According to him, if reason alone were the criterion by which we judge who ought to have rights, human infants and adults with certain forms of disability might fall short too. And they would also have to be treated as though they were things.[62] He wrote in 1789, just as slaves were being freed by the French, but were still held captive in the British dominions, "The day has been, I grieve to say in many places it is not yet past, in which the greater part of the species, under the denomination of slaves, have been treated by the law exactly upon the same footing, as, in England for example, the inferior races of animals are still. The day may come when the rest of the animal creation may acquire those rights which never could have been withholden from them but by the hand of tyranny. The French have already discovered that the blackness of the skin is no reason a human being should be abandoned without redress to the caprice of a tormentor. It may one day come to be recognised that the number of the legs, the villosity of the skin, or the termination of the *os sacrum* are reasons equally insufficient for abandoning a sensitive being to the same fate. What else is it that should trace the insuperable line? Is it the faculty of reason or perhaps the faculty of discourse? But a full-grown horse or dog is beyond comparison a more rational, as well as a more conversable animal, than an infant of a day or a week or even a month old. But suppose the case were otherwise, what would it avail? The question is not, Can they reason? Nor can they talk? But, Can they suffer?"[63] Bentham holds that moral status should be given to animals on the ground that they suffer.

Albert Schweitzer, an activist for animal rights, also presents a Non-Anthropocentric approach. In 1915 he argued in his book *Reverence for Life* the ethical standard for killing. Schweitzer believed that we should take life only for necessary reasons and even then, it should be done with respect for what was killed.[64] Schweitzer defended a bio-centric ethics that locates inherent value in all living things. According to him, all life is "sacred" and "something possessing value in itself."[65] His approach when compared to Immanuel Kant's rational *a priori* approach holds a rather contrasting view. Schweitzer's work shows that his ethics is rooted in the experience of life as an empirical hypothesis, and as such, in this sense closely related to Friedrich Nietzsche and Arthur Schopenhauer. Schweitzer was influenced by Arthur Schopenhauer's voluntarist metaphysics according to which ultimate reality is *will.* "Behind all phenomena" there is will-to-live, and each organism constitutes part of that will—a will both to survive and to develop according to its natural tendencies.[66] However, unlike Schopenhauer, Schweitzer though his religious convictions were highly unorthodox, yet he was deeply religious. They hovered somewhere near pantheism but were closer to biotheism—the view that God is manifested in and constituted by all life.[67] According to him, "The Essence of Being, the Absolute, the Spirit of the Universe, and all similar expressions denote nothing actual. The only reality is the Being which manifests itself in phenomena."[68] He writes, "I am a will-to-live, with desire for self-preservation, self-perfection, pleasure, happiness, and avoiding pain. All other organisms have these same desires, feelings and aspirations. as in my own will-to-live there is a longing for pleasure, with dread of annihilation and wider life and for pain; so is it also in the will-to-live all around me."[69]

Therefore, since I value my life I must (in consistency) value all other life, "for I shall know that it longs for fullness and development as deeply as I do myself."[70]

Martin maintained that, "Schweitzer's outlook has had a "cumulative impact in moving us toward a sense of oneness with nature of a sort aptly conveyed in the phrase '*reverence for life*'—reverence for life as a whole, as well as for particular organisms."[71]

Non-Anthropocentrism has extended itself not only to the welfare of the animals alone but also to that of the land, water, ecosystem, etc. This is seen in the works of Aldo Leopold who stresses on the intrinsic value of land. His book, *A Sand County Almanac,* (1949),[72] is one among the most outstanding works directed towards the natural world. Further, Leopold's essay titled "The Land Ethic," published in *A Sand County Almanac,* (1966), is now considered as an important text of American environmental ethics for his important revolutionary ideas were revealed in this very chapter. Carrie Wilson states that it is here that, "Leopold displayed concern for the intrinsic value of non-human life and also that of life communities or ecosystems. His view of life value exceeded that of plants and animals to include waters and soils as well. He also introduced the idea of "biotic right".[73] In which all life sharing the earth had an equal right to live and sustain life regardless of their presence or absence of economic advantage to us. Though Leopold was not the first to suggest the idea of ethical extension, he is still thought of as the most important mind of holistic and bio-centric ideas.[74] He argues that "we have a well-articulated human-to-human ethic; what we need is a comparable human-to-land ethic."[75] He writes, "land is to be loved and respected"[76] an act that can only be possible with an extension of moral status. He calls upon for the need of re-evaluating man's relationship to the land that is being inhabited and to act in accordance with a "land ethic" that "enlarges the boundaries of the community to include soils, waters, plants, and animals, or collectively: the land".[77] For Leopold, the land and the biotic community were beings with an intrinsic right to exist. His book very clearly points out that ethics and rights need to be extended to the land, as according to him, doing so necessarily "changes the role of *Homo sapiens* from conqueror of the land-community to plain member and citizen of it."[78] Huey-li-Li states that "Leopold acknowledges the intrinsic values of nature in the theorizing of environmental ethics."[79]

Another Non-Anthropocentric approach to non-human life forms is seen in the works of Rachel Louise Carson, an American marine biologist and conservationist who wrote books that are today being enormously credited for advancing the global environmental movement.[80] She has been called the founder of the U.S. environmental movement.[81] In the late 1950s, Carson turned her attention to conservation and the environmental problems caused by synthetic *pesticides.* This followed the publishing of an important work *Silent Spring* (1962), which effectively brought environmental concerns to the American public. This book focused on the problem of pesticide and other chemical pollution.[82] Rachel Carson is considered to be an important environmental thinker.[83] She gave importance to the evaluative or ethical premises, and this is reflected in her work *Silent Spring* which is filled with ethical statements and arguments that were short yet emphatic. Carson attempts to point out the necessity of the moral considerability of non-human beings.[84] According to her, creatures both wild and domesticated are innocent of any harm to man and, therefore, do not deserve the cruelty mankind inflicts on them. Inflicting unnecessary suffering and causing unnecessary loss of non-human life are morally wrong. In fact their existence is responsible for a pleasant living, and further adds that such acts of cruelty only diminishes one as a human being. Carson certainly extends moral considerability to the animals' part and moral responsibility on our part. She further argues that a true civilization is not that which seeks to dominate or destroy the non-human world, but it is that which seeks to protect and understand it.[85] Carson's ethics were Non-Anthropocentric as she recognised the moral considerability of non-human beings. She recognised the flaws of Anthropocentrism and thus made attempts to transcend anthropocentrism which is seen in her earliest book, *Under the Sea-Wind and those that followed later.*

Carson was followed by Arne Næss, a highly influential Norwegian philosopher whose ideas about ecology and humans' relationship with the environment have informed and enriched many of today's green activists and movements.[86] He is considered to be the first to have made the distinction between Shallow and Deep Ecologists. He defined Shallow Ecologists as anyone whose concerns are confined to his fellow humans and to a narrow selection of non-human life, mainly those that serve human purposes, besides Shallow Ecology, he believed, meant thinking that big ecological problems could be resolved within an industrial, capitalist society, whereas deep meant asking deeper questions and understanding that society itself has caused the Earth-threatening ecological crisis. For him, what we need is an attitude of 'respect for nature' which will not be centred on human interest alone. His platform of Deep Ecology involves the following formulations.

The flourishing of non-human life on earth has as much intrinsic value as the flourishing of human life.[87]

The value of non-human species is independent of the usefulness these may have for narrow human purposes.[88]

The richness and diversity of the earth's life-forms are

valuable in themselves and contribute in any case to the flourishing of all life forms on Earth.[89]

Humans have no right to reduce this richness and diversity except in so far as it is necessary to satisfy vital needs.[90]

His deep ecology entered the mainstream green movement in the 1980s and was later elaborated by George Sessions in Deep Ecology for the Twenty-first Century (1995). Næss taught that ecology should not be concerned with man's place in nature but with every part of nature on an equal basis, because the natural order has intrinsic value that transcends human values. He urged the green movement to "not only protect the planet for the sake of humans, but also, for the sake of the planet itself, to keep ecosystems healthy for their own sake."[91] Næss hoped for this movement to widen compassion towards non-humans; however he made it clear that it did not imply diminishing compassion towards humans. Stephan Harding, a close friend of Næss argued that Næss accepted that "since we are humans, we have to put humans first," but at the same time he was against violence. According to him, "We don't say that every living being has the same value as a human, but that it has an intrinsic value which is not quantifiable. It is not equal or unequal. It has a right to live and blossom. He states, "I may kill a mosquito if it is on the face of my baby, but I will never say I have a higher right to life than a mosquito."[92]

Tom Regan, an American philosopher who contributed largely in animal rights theory, also presents a Non-Anthropocentric outlook on animals. He is universally recognised as the intellectual leader of the animal rights movement.[93] Among many of his works that he has focused on the philosophy of animal rights he is best known for his book, *The Case for Animal Rights*.[94] It has significantly influenced the modern animal liberation movement. It is here Regan argues that non-human animals bear moral rights. Regan argues that rationality cannot be the condition for extending moral rights to humans and non-humans. He made an argument against the Kantian stance of animal morality, as Kant holds that animals do not deserve moral status as they are not rational beings. Regan argues that moral consideration should not be based on our ability to reason. While Regan supports that reason is a great and positive feature, he challenged that reason alone cannot account for making a life valuable or morally worthy. For him, one common attribute that each of us has is a *life* and that is what matters to us. It is the crucial attribute to both humans and non-humans. In Regan's terminology, we each experience being the "subject-of-a-life." If this is the true basis for ascribing inherent value to individuals, to be consistent we must ascribe inherent value, and hence moral rights, to all subjects-of-a-life, whether human or non-human. The basic right that all who possess inherent value have, he argues, is the right never to be treated merely as a means to the ends of others.[95] And never to be treated as a means, that one has the right to be treated with respect, and which further includes the right not to be harmed. According to Regan, "there would be more harm in the death of a normal, healthy dog than there would be in the death of a person who was irreversibly comatose, as the dog would have more opportunities for satisfaction than the irreversibly comatose human."[96]

Peter Albert David Singer, a philosopher of the twentieth century wrote a book titled *Animal Liberation* in 1975[97] that greatly influenced the field of animal ethics. Through this book, Singer argues and presents the utilitarian idea that "the greatest good of the greatest number" is the only measure of good or ethical behaviour. He holds that there is no reason not to apply this to other animals. His most comprehensive work in ethics is his *Practical Ethics* in 1979.[98] Singer upholds the view that there needs to be "a sound moral basis for relations with those outside our own species—the non-human animals".[99] This according to him can be possible only when we accept the principle of equality, in which rests the principle of equal consideration of interests. For Singer, as equality is usually accepted as embracing and extending to all human beings, it only implies that all humans are equal, which is to say again that no one person's interest, or no groups, must take precedence over those of other person's or groups simple because they are that person or a member of that group.[100] The sense of equality is summed up in Singer's principle of equal consideration of interests as, "The principle of equal consideration of interests acts like a pair of scales, weighing interests impartially. True scales favour where the interest is stronger or where several interests combine to outweigh a smaller number of similar interests; but they take into account of whose interests they are weighing."[101]

This shows Singer's utilitarian approach. The principle of equality implies that concern for others ought not to depend on what they are like or what abilities they possess. According to him, the fact that other animals are less intelligent does not entitle one to exploit them or disregard their interests. This principle provides for a sound moral basis for relations, and this according to him cannot be limited only to humans. It needs to be extended. He argues that extending the principle of equality beyond our own species is simple, and that is to understand the nature of principle of equal considerations of interests.[102] In his 1975 book *Animal Liberation*, Singer presents his agenda. He points out the mistreatments imposed on animals by the human race and argues that although human beings have a long history of mistreating animals, there is no moral justification for such behaviour. He considers causing unnecessary suffering is morally wrong. According to him, the fact (in so far as it is a fact) that non-human animals lack human intellect and moral understanding is irrelevant here; it is no more right to make a dog suffer than it is to do the same to a human imbecile or new-born baby. An entity should matter to us if it has the capacity of mattering to itself. However, if it is unable to do so, then, as Peter Singer says, "Nothing that we can do to it could possibly make any difference to its welfare. [and consequently,] there is nothing to be taken into account."[103] Singer tackles the ethical issues of non-human animals from a utilitarian perspective.

With the destruction on environment surfacing even more distinctly and attracting some serious attention on itself, most of the research literature is on this modern problem. Facts about species-extinction are interwoven with facts about global warming, the effects of acid rain, the pollution of water, air, soil, etc. In this regard one may ask the questions; Who then is responsible for this "environmental destruction", "global warming?" Why are such matters being debated as serious issues? What is the root cause of all this? Do we human beings have greater role to play in maintaining better, sustainable and healthier environment as moral agents? Do we have any ethical obligations to the natural world? Some of the major ethical dilemmas that have been debated over the past few decades are: Is the motivation to do good based on selfish interest alone or are we to include the interest of all the living and even the non-living? Do we need to rethink in a completely new way about nature, even to the extent of granting rights to all non-human beings such as animals, plants and to nature generally? Is this justifiable? Do other species have an intrinsic right? Or for that matter, going down to the very root of this by asking: Should there in fact, even be an *ethical* response to environmental crisis at all? That each individual should make an effort to perceive the need of responding to this with the conscience each one of us have. Are we to take into consideration the way we act on our natural environment? And if we did, then do we need to go a step further and think about what our objective will be or should be? Will it be directed to nature itself or on ourselves or both?

Environmental philosophy as an ethical response to nature, analyses what conceptual resources it can offer[104] to the ever growing ethical issues of environment.

Notes

1. Robin Attfield and Andrew Belsey, (1994), *Philosophy and the Natural Environment*, Cambridge University Press, p. 1.
2. "Environmental Ethics", Retrieved on May 7, 2011 from en.wikipedia.org/wiki/Environmental_Ethics.
3. Louise Rusling, "The Role of Philosophy in Environmental Debates", Retrieved on May 13, 2011 from http://www.helium.com/items/462446-the-role-of-philosophy-in-environmental-debates.
4. *Ibid.*
5. Madhabendra Nath Mitra, (2003), *Truth and Value*, New Bharatiya Book Corporation, Delhi, India, p. 406.
6. Louise Rusling, "The Role of Philosophy in Environmental Debates", Retrieved on May 13, 2011 from http://www.helium.com/items/462446-the-role-of-philosophy-in-environmental-debates.
7. Madhabendra Nath Mitra, (2003), *Truth and Value*, New Bharatiya Book Corporation, Delhi, India, p. 406.

8. Jagadiswar Sanyal, (1991), *Guide to General Philosophy*, Sribhumi Publishing Company, 79, Mahatma Gandhi Road, Kolkata, p. 3.
9. *Ibid.*
10. *Ibid.*
11. *Ibid.*, p. 17.
12. *Ibid.*
13. Tad Beckman, "What is Environmental Philosophy", Retrieved on May 10, 2011 from http://www2.hmc.edu/¬tbeckman/essays/position.htm.
14. Christopher Belshaw, "Environmental philosophy", Retrieved on May 10, 2011 from www.2knows.com/index.php?q=Environmental_Philosophy.
15. "Environmental Philosophy", Retrieved on May 10, 2011 from http://dictionary.sensagent.com/Environment_Philosophy/en-en/
16. Doris Schroeder and Ruth Chadwick (ed.), (2002), *Applied Ethics: Critical Concepts in Philosophy*, Routledge, Taylor and Francis Group, New York, p. 25.
17. "Environmental Ethics", Retrieved on May 20, 2011 from http://plato.stanford.edu/entries/ethics-environment/
18. J. Baird Callicott, (October 1984), "Non-Anthropocentrism value theory and Environmental Ethics", *American Philosophical Quarterly*, Vol. 21, number 4, p. 299.
19. Kanti Lal Das, (July-October 2006), "The Metaphysical Basis of Environmental Ethics: A Spinozistic Approach", *Indian Philosophical Quarterly*, Vol, XXXIII, No. 3-4, p. 265.
20. *Ibid.*
21. "Environmental Ethics", Retrieved on June 2007 from en.wikipedia.org/wiki/Environmental_Ethics.
22. Lynn White, (1967). "The Historical Roots of Our Ecological Crisis", *Science*, 55:1203-1207; reprinted in Schmidtz and Willott 2002.
23. Elspeth Whitney, (1993), "Lynn White, Ecotheology, and History" *Environmental Ethics*, 15: 151-169, and R. Attfield (2001), "Christianity", Chapter 7 in D. Jamieson (ed.), *A Companion to Environmental Philosophy*, Blackwell Publishers, Oxford.
24. Garett Hardin, Retrieved on May 7, 2011 from http://en.wikipedia.org/wiki/Garett_Hardin
25. Garylord Nelson, "Earth Day '70: What it meant", Retrieved on May 7, 2011 from http://epa,gov/history/topics/earthday/02.htm.
26. Doris Schroeder and Ruth Chadwick (ed.), (2002), *Applied Ethics: Critical Concepts in Philosophy*, Routledge, Taylor and Francis Group, New York, p. 25.

27. Madhabendra Nath Mitra, (2003), "Reflections on Environmental Ethics" in Raghunath Ghosh's Truth and Value, (Essays in honour of Dr. Pabitrakumar Roy) New Bharatiya Book Corporation, Delhi, India, p. 408.
28. *Ibid.*, p. 409.
29. Michael P. T. Leahy, (1994), *Against Liberation, Putting Animals in Perspective*, Routledge, London and New York, p. 76.
30. *Ibid.*
31. *Ibid.*, p. 76.
32. *Ibid.*, p. 78.
33. *Ibid.*, p. 79.
34. *Ibid.*, p. 81.
35. Madhabendra Nath Mitra, (2003), "Reflections on Environmental Ethics" in Raghunath Ghosh's Truth and Value, (Essays in honour of Dr. Pabitrakumar Roy) New Bharatiya Book Corporation, Delhi, India, p. 408.
36. Michael P.T. Leahy, (1994), *Against Liberation, Putting Animals in Perspective*, Routledge, London and New York, p. 77.
37. Lawrence E. Johnson, (1991), *A Morally Deep World, An Essay on Moral Significance and Environmental Ethics*, Cambridge University Press, p. 14.
38. Benjamin Jowett, "350 BC, Politics by Aristotle", Retrieved on May 25, 2011 from http://jim.com/arispol.htm
39. D. J O'Connor, (1964), *A Critical History of Western Philosophy*, The Free Press of Glencoe, New York, p. 171.
40. Michael P.T. Leahy, (1994), *Against Liberation, Putting Animals in Perspective*, Routledge, London and New York, p. 78.
41. *Ibid.*, p. 75.
42. Lawrence E. Johnson, (1991), *A Morally Deep World, An Essay on Moral Significance and Environmental Ethics*, Cambridge University Press, p. 24.
43. Michael P.T. Leahy, (1994), *Against Liberation, Putting Animals in Perspective*, Routledge, London and New York, p. 89.
44. *Ibid.*, p. 78.
45. Tom Regan, (1983), *The Case for Animal Rights*, University of California Press, Berkeley. Los Angeles, p. 3.
46. Michael P.T. Leahy, (1994), *Against Liberation, Putting Animals in Perspective*, Routledge, London and New York, p. 75.
47. *Ibid.*, p. 75.
48. Robert Johnson, "Kant", Retrieved on May 31, 2011 from http://www.mightystudents.com/essay/kant.essay.37640.

49. D.J. O'Connor, (1964), *A Critical History of Western Philosophy*, The Free Press of Glencoe, New York, p. 309.
50. Carrie Wilson, "The Role of Philosophy in Environmental Debates", Retrieved on May 13, 2011 from http://www.helium.com/items/1436902-ethics-environmental.
51. *Ibid.*
52. "Animal Ethics", Retrieved on May 31, 2011 from http://animalethics.blogspot.com/2005/01/conservation-and-animals-rights-im.html
53. "John Passmore", Wikipedia, Retrieved on June 1, 2011 from http://en/wikipedia.org/wiki/John_Passmore
54. John Passmore, (1980), *Man's Responsibility for Nature*, 2nd ed., Duckworth, London, p. 116.
55. *Ibid.*, p. 118.
56. Tom Duddy, (1997), "Ethics and the Environment", Retrieved on June 20, 2007 from http://www.ul.ie/¬philos/vol1/paper4.html
57. Carrie Wilson, "The Role of Philosophy in Environmental Debates," Retrieved on May 13, 2011 from http://www.helium.com/items/1436902-ethics-environmental.
58. Madhabendra Nath Mitra, (2003), "Reflections on Environmental Ethics" in RaghunathGhosh'sTruth and Value, (Essays in honour of Dr. Pabitrakumar Roy) New Bharatiya Book Corporation, Delhi, India, p. 409.
59. *Ibid.*, p. 410.
60. "Jeremy Bentham", Wikipedia, Retrieved on June 8, 2011 from http://en.wikipedia.org/wiki.Bentham.
61. "Jeremy Bentham", Wikipedia, Retrieved on June 8, 2011 from http://en.wikipedia.org/wiki/Sentient.
62. Jonathan Benthall, (April 2007) "Animal Liberation and Rights", Anthropology Today, Vol. 23, issue 2, p. 1.
63. Lawrence E. Johnson, (1991), *A Morally Deep World, An Essay on Moral Significance and Environmental Ethics*, Cambridge University Press, p. 43.
64. Carrie Wilson, "The Role of Philosophy in Environmental Debates", Retrieved on May 13, 2011 from http://www.helium.com/items/1436902-ethics-environmental.
65. Albert Schweitzer, (1987), *The Philosophy of Civilization*, Prometheus Books, Buffalo, p. 57.
66. *Ibid.*
67. Reginald H. Fuller, (trans.), (1969), *Reverence for Life*, Harper & Row, New York, p. 115.

68. Albert Schweitzer, (1987), *The Philosophy of Civilization*, Prometheus Books, Buffalo, p. 304.
69. *Ibid.*, p. 309.
70. Albert Schweitzer, (1936), "The Ethics of Reverence of Life", In Christendom, Vol. 1, p. 230.
71. Mike W. Martin, (1993), "Rethinking Reverence for Life", Between the Species, Vol. 9, pp. 204-213.
72. Aldo Leopold, (1949), *A Sand County Almanac*, Oxford University Press, New York.
73. Carrie Wilson, "The Role of Philosophy in Environmental Debates," Retrieved on May 13, 2011 from http://www.helium.com/items/1436902-ethics-environmental.
74. *Ibid.*
75. Aldo Leopold, (1949), *A Sand County Almanac and Sketches Here and There*, New York, Oxford University Press, p. 203
76. *Ibid.*, foreword viii-ix.
77. *Ibid.*, p. 239.
78. Aldo Leopold, (1966), *A Sand County Almanac*, New York, Oxford University Press, p. 240.
79. Huey-li Li, "On the nature of Environmental Education," University of Akron, Retrieved on June 7, 2011 from http://www.ed.uiuc.edu/EPS/PES-yearbook/96_docs/li.html.
80. "Rachel Carson", Wikipedia, Retrieved on May 7, 2011 from en.wikipedia.org/wiki/Rachel_Carson
81. Philip Cafaro, (2008), "Rachel Carson's Environmental Ethics," Encyclopaedia of Earth, Retrieved on June 7, 2011 from http://www.eoearth.org/article/Rachel_carson's_environment_ethics
82. *Ibid.*
83. *Ibid.*
84. *Ibid.*
85. *Ibid.*
86. Arne Naess: "Philosopher who invented 'Deep Ecology'," Retrieved on June 8, 2011 from http://www.independent.co.uk
87. Arne Næss, (1989), *Ecology, Community, and Lifestyle*, Cambridge: Cambridge University Press, p. 29.
88. *Ibid.*
89. *Ibid.*
90. *Ibid.*
91. *Ibid.*
92. Arne Naess: "Philosopher who invented 'Deep Ecology'", Retrieved on June 8, 2011 from http://www.independent.co.uk.

93. Arne Naess: "Philosopher who invented 'Deep Ecology'", Retrieved on June 8, 2011 from http://www.independent.co.uk
94. Tom Regan, (1983), *The Case for Animal Rights*, University of California Press, Los Angeles.
95. "Tom Regan", Wikipedia, Retrieved on June 10, 2011 from http://en.wikipedia.org/wiki/Tom_Regan.
96. Tom Regan, (1983), *The Case for Animal Rights*, University of California Press, Berkeley, p. xxxiii.
97. Peter Singer, (1975), *Animal Liberation, A New Ethics for our Treatment of Animals*, New York Review/Random House, New York.
98. Peter Singer, (1979), *Practical Ethics*, Cambridge University Press. London
99. *Ibid.*, p. 48.
100. Michael P.T. Leahy, (1994), *Against Liberation, Putting Animals in Perspective*, Routledge, London and New York, p. 15.
101. Peter Singer, (1979), *Practical Ethics*, Cambridge University Press. London, p. 19.
102. *Ibid.*, p. 49.
103. Peter Singer, (1975), *Animal Liberation, A New Ethics for Our Treatment of Animals*, New York Review/Random House, New York, p. 8.
104. Doris Schroeder and Ruth Chadwick (ed.), (2002), *Applied Ethics: Critical Concepts in Philosophy*, Routledge, Taylor and Francis Group, New York, p. 25.

References

Attfield, Robin and Belsey, Andrew, (1994), *Philosophy and the Natural Environment*, Cambridge University Press.

Benthall, Jonathan, (April 2007) "Animal Liberation and Rights", Anthropology Today, Vol. 23, Issue 2.

Callicott, J. Baird, (1987), "The Conceptual Foundations of the Land Ethic," in *Companion to A Sand County Almanac: Interpretive and Critical Essays*, The University of Wisconsin Press.

Das, Kanti Lal, (July-October, 2006), "The Metaphysical Basis of Environmental Ethics: A Spinozistic Approach", *Indian Philosophical Quarterly*, Vol. 33 (No. 3-4).

Fuller, Reginald H., (trans.), (1969), *Reverence for Life*, Harper & Row, New York.

J O'Connor, D., (1964), *A Critical History of Western Philosophy*, The Free Press of Glencoe, New York.

Johnson, Lawrence E., (1991), *A Morally Deep World, An Essay on Moral Significance and Environmental Ethics*, Cambridge University Press.

Leahy, Michael P.T., (1994), *Against Liberation, Putting Animals in Perspective*, Routledge, London and New York.

Leopold, Aldo, (1949), *A Sand County Almanac and Sketches Here and There,* New York, Oxford University Press.

_______. (1949), *A Sand County Almanac*, New York, Oxford University Press.

_______. (1966), *A Sand County Almanac,* New York, Oxford University Press.

Martin, Mike W., (1993), "Rethinking Reverence for Life", Between the Species, Vol. 9.

Mitra, Madhabendra Nath, (2003), *Truth and Value*, New Bharatiya Book Corporation, Delhi, India.

Næss, Arne, (1989), *Ecology, Community, and Lifestyle*, Cambridge University Press, Cambridge.

Passmore, John, (1980), *Man's Responsibility for Nature*, 2nd ed., Duckworth, London.

Regan, Tom, (1983), *The Case for Animal Rights*, University of California Press, Berkeley. Los Angeles.

Sanyal, Jagadiswar, (1991), *Guide to General Philosophy*, Sribhumi Publishing Company, 79, Mahatma Gandhi Road, Kolkata.

Schroeder, Doris and Chadwick, Ruth, (ed.), (2002), *Applied Ethics: Critical Concepts in Philosophy*, Routledge, Taylor and Francis Group, New York.

Schweitzer, Albert, (1987), *The Philosophy of Civilization*, Prometheus Books, Buffalo.

Singer, Peter, (1975), Animal Liberation, *A New Ethics for our Treatment of Animals*, New York Review/Random House, New York.

_______. (1979), *Practical Ethics*, Cambridge University Press, Cambridge, New York.

Whitney, Elspeth, (1993), "Lynn White, Ecotheology, and History." *Environmental Ethics* 15: 151-169, and R. Attfield (2001), "Christianity", Chapter 7 in D. Jamieson (ed.), *A Companion to Environmental Philosophy*, Blackwell Publishers, Oxford.

Schweitzer, Albert, (1936), "The Ethics of Reverence of Life", In Christendom, Vol. 1.

White, Lynn, (1967). "The Historical Roots of Our Ecological Crisis", *Science*, 55:1203-1207; reprinted in Schmidtz and Willott 2002.

http://animalethics.blogspot.com/2005/01/conservation-and-animals-rights-im.html
http://dictionary.sensagent.com/Environment_Philosophy/en-en/
http://en.wikipedia.org/wiki.Bentham
http://en.wikipedia.org/wiki/Environmental_Ethics
http://en.wikipedia.org/wiki/Garett_Hardin
http://en.wikipedia.org/wiki/Rachel_Carson
http://en.wikipedia.org/wiki/Sentient
http://en.wikipedia.org/wiki/Tom_Regan
http://en/wikipedia.org/wiki/John_Passmore
http://epa,gov/history/topics/earthday/02.htm
http://jim.com/arispol.htm
http://plato.stanford.edu/entries/ethics-environmental/-environmental
http://www.2knows.com/index.php?q=Environmental_Philosophy
http://www.ed.uiuc.edu/EPS/PES-yearbook/96_docs/li.html
http://www.eoearth.org/article/Rachel_carson's_environment_ethics
http://www.helium.com/items/1436902-ethics-environmental
http://www.helium.com/items/462446-the-role-of-philosophy-in-environmental-debates
http://www.independent.co.uk
http://www.mightystudents.com/essay/kant.essay.37640
http://www.ul.ie/¬philos/vol1/paper4.html
http://www2.hmc.edu/¬tbeckman/essays/position.htm

Index